A Feminist Companion to
the Deutero-Pauline Epistles

A Feminist Companion to

the Deutero-Pauline Epistles

edited by

Amy-Jill Levine

with Marianne Blickenstaff

THE
PILGRIM
PRESS
Cleveland

Published in the USA and Canada (only) by
The Pilgrim Press
700 Prospect Avenue East, Cleveland, Ohio 44115-1100 USA
pilgrimpress.com

Copyright © 2003 The Continuum International Publishing Group, Inc.

Published by The Continuum International Publishing Group, Inc.
The Tower Building, 11 York Road, London SE1 7NX
15 East 26th Street, Suite 1703, New York, NY 10010

www.continuumbooks.com

The Pilgrim Press edition published 2003. All rights reserved

British Library Cataloguing-in-Publication Data
A catalogue record for this book is available from the British Library

Library of Congress Cataloging-in-Publication Data
A catalogue record for this book is available from the Library of Congress

Printed on acid-free paper in Great Britain

ISBN 0-8264-6335-5 (hardback)
       0-8264-6336-3 (paperback)

USA and Canada only
ISBN 0-8298-1609-7

CONTENTS

PREFACE

A Feminist Companion to the Deutero-Pauline Epistles represents the sixth volume in a new series with excellent precedent. These volumes on the texts and history of Christian origins adopt the model established by Athalya Brenner, editor of the enormously successful Feminist Companion to the Bible series. This sister series to FCB marks an important new dimension in Sheffield Academic Press's list of titles in the areas of feminist hermeneutics and theology, and its contents underline the extent to which feminist critique is established as a core discipline of biblical, historical and theological research.

The new series, like FCB, contains contributions by new as well as established scholars; it presents both previously published work (primarily from sources either out of print or difficult to find) and new essays. In some cases, scholars have been invited to revisit their earlier work to examine the extent to which their arguments and approaches have changed; in others, they have sought to apply their earlier insights to new texts.

We wish to thank Marianne Blickenstaff for her numerous organizational contributions as well as her discerning insights. We also wish to thank the Carpenter Program in Religion, Gender, and Sexuality at Vanderbilt Divinity School for financial and technical support.

It is our hope that this series will quickly establish itself as a standard work of references for scholars, students and others interested in the New Testament and Christian origins.

Amy-Jill Levine, Vanderbilt Divinity School
Philip R. Davies, Sheffield Academic Press

ACKNOWLEDGMENTS

The publishers are grateful to the following for permission to reproduce copyright material:

- The Society of Biblical Literature for portions of 'The Widows' Tale: A Fresh Look at 1 Tim. 5.3-16', by Jouette Bassler, from the *Journal of Biblical Literature* 103, and for portions of 'The Transformative Potential of Ephesians in a Situation of Transition', by Elna Mouton, from *Semeia* 78;
- *Studies in Religion/Sciences Religieuses* for 'Early Christian Women Married to Unbelievers', by Margaret MacDonald, from *Studies in Religion/Sciences Religieuses* 19.2;
- Güterloher Verlagshaus for 'Der Brief an die Gemeinde in Kolossä und die Erfindung der "Haustafel"', by Angela Standhartinger, from *Kompendium Feministische Bibelauslegung*; and
- Intervarsity Press for '1 Timothy 2.9-15 and the Place of Women in the Church's Ministry', by David M. Scholer, from *Women, Authority and the Bible*.

ABBREVIATIONS

AB	Anchor Bible
ABD	David Noel Freedman (ed.), *The Anchor Bible Dictionary* (New York: Doubleday, 1992)
ANRW	Hildegard Temporini and Wolfgang Haase (eds.), *Aufstieg und Niedergang der römischen Welt: Geschichte und Kultur Roms im Spiegel der neueren Forschung* (Berlin: W. de Gruyter, 1972–)
ANTC	Abingdon New Testament Commentaries
ATR	*Anglican Theological Review*
BAGD	Walter Bauer, William F. Arndt, F. William Gingrich and Frederick W. Danker, *A Greek–English Lexicon of the New Testament and Other Early Christian Literature* (Chicago: University of Chicago Press, 2nd edn, 1958)
BibLeb	*Bibel und Leben*
BJS	Brown Judaic Studies
BNTC	Black's New Testament Commentaries
BTB	*Biblical Theology Bulletin*
BWANT	Beiträge zur Wissenschaft vom Alten und Neuen Testament
CBQ	*Catholic Biblical Quarterly*
CH	*Church History*
CIL	*Corpus inscriptionum latinarum*
EBib	Etudes bibliques
EKKNT	Evangelisch-Katholischer Kommentar zum Neuen Testament
EvT	*Evangelische Theologie*
HDR	Harvard Dissertations in Religion
HR	*History of Religions*
HTKNT	Herders theologischer Kommentar zum Neuen Testament
HTR	*Harvard Theological Review*
HTS	Harvard Theological Studies
HUT	Hermeneutische Untersuchungen zur Theologie
IDB	George Arthur Buttrick (ed.), *The Interpreter's Dictionary of the Bible* (4 vols.; Nashville: Abingdon Press, 1962)
Int	*Interpretation*
JAAR	*Journal of the American Academy of Religion*
JAC	*Jahrbuch für Antike und Christentum*

JBL	*Journal of Biblical Literature*
JETS	*Journal of the Evangelical Theological Society*
JFSR	*Journal of Feminist Studies in Religion*
JHS	*Journal of Hellenic Studies*
JRelS	*Journal of Religious Studies*
JSNT	*Journal for the Study of the New Testament*
JSNTSup	*Journal for the Study of the New Testament*, Supplement Series
JTS	*Journal of Theological Studies*
JTSA	*Journal of Theology for South Africa*
LCC	Library of Christian Classics
LCL	Loeb Classical Library
LSJ	H.G. Liddell, Robert Scott and H. Stuart Jones, *Greek–English Lexicon* (Oxford: Clarendon Press, 9th edn, 1968)
NCBC	New Century Bible Commentary
Neot	*Neotestamentica*
NIGTC	New International Greek Testament Commentary
NIV	New International Version
NovT	*Novum Testamentum*
NovTGr[26]	Eberhard Nestle and Kurt Aland *et al.* (eds.), *Novum Testamentum Graece* (Stuttgart: Deutsche Bibelgesellschaft, 26th edn, 1979)
NovTGr[27]	Eberhard Nestle, Barbara Aland and Kurt Aland, *Novum Testamentum Graece* (Stuttgart: Deutsche Bibelgesellschaft, 27th edn, 1993)
NovTSup	*Novum Testamentum*, Supplements
NRSV	New Revised Standard Version
NTD	Das Neue Testament Deutsch
NTS	*New Testament Studies*
OBT	Overtures to Biblical Theology
OTP	James Charlesworth (ed.), *Old Testament Pseudepigrapha*
RB	*Revue biblique*
RNT	Regensburger Neues Testament
RSR	*Recherches de science religieuse*
SBL	Society of Biblical Literature
SBLDS	SBL Dissertation Series
SBLMS	SBL Monograph Series
SBLSP	SBL Seminar Papers
SBM	Stuttgarter biblische Monographien
SIG	*Sylloge Inscriptionum Graecarum*
ST	*Studia theologica*
TDNT	Gerhard Kittel and Gerhard Friedrich (eds.), *Theological Dictionary of the New Testament* (trans. Geoffrey W. Bromiley; 10 vols.; Grand Rapids: Eerdmans, 1964–)
TF	Theologische Forschung (monograph series)

TSF	*Theological Students Fellowship*
UBSGNT	United Bible Societies' *Greek New Testament* (London: United Bible Societies, 3rd edn, 1971)
USQR	*Union Seminary Quarterly Review*
WBC	Word Biblical Commentary
WUNT	Wissenschaftliche Untersuchungen zum Neuen Testament

Jouette M. Bassler, Perkins School of Theology, Southern Methodist University, Dallas, TX, USA

Mary Ann Beavis, Department of Religious Studies and Anthropology, St Thomas More College, University of Saskatchewan, Saskatoon, Saskatchewan, Canada

Margaret Y. MacDonald, St Francis Xavier University, Antigonish, Nova Scotia, Canada

Virginia Ramey Mollenkott, Professor of English Emeritus, William Paterson University, Wayne, NJ, USA

Elna Mouton, Faculty of Theology, University of Stellenbosch, Stellenbosch, South Africa

Lilian Portefaix, Uppsala University, Uppsala, Sweden

David M. Scholer, Fuller Theological Seminary, Pasadena, CA, USA

Angela Standhartinger, Philipps-Universität Marburg, Marburg, Germany

Bonnie Thurston, Wheeling, WV, USA

INTRODUCTION

Amy-Jill Levine

Whether regarded as written by Paul or as pseudonymous productions by the apostle's theological heirs, the later Pauline texts offer the New Testament's most problematic treatments of women's roles and household systems. Should one claim that First Corinthian's injunction that women 'be silent in the churches' is a case-specific commandment addressed to one particular circumstance, such as an abuse of spiritual gifts, First Timothy insists that women's silence is the proper result of Eve's original disobedience. Should one rely on the potential for equality often located in Gal. 3.28, the household code in Colossians begins the canon's formal relegation of women along with slaves and children to the ranks of the disempowered, and Ephesians promotes the authority of husband over wife on the model of the authority of the Christ over his Church. Should the Church be hailed as the extended home wherein widows are supported and their contributions to their fellow Christians recognized, the Pastorals rather limit both their funding and their authority. The epistles thus appear to support one stereotype of the late-first and early-second century New Testament Church: unfaithful to its charismatic origins, sunk in the mire of Roman patriarchy, capitulating to the status quo, and lacking any women who claim personal or institutional authority.

Such stereotypes work because they present enough detail to make them seem cogent. Yet it is precisely such stereotypes that feminist interpretations disrupt. The discussions of power, gender and class offered by the later Pauline letters are much more complicated than these narrow classifications suggest. While some interpreters find the texts even more pernicious than the typical view espouses, others find — through attention to linguistic nuance, study of contemporaneous groups, archaeological investigation, pan-Mediterranean anthropology, tradition history — alternatives that allow them to celebrate parts of these highly contested documents. As with all Scripture, liberating and constraining elements can be located within the Pauline corpus. The essays in this collection, appropriately, find both.

Margaret MacDonald begins this volume with her study of 'early Christian women married to unbelievers'. The title itself shatters one common image of family organization in antiquity: the wife did not always participate in the same system of either practice or belief as did her husband, although it was the case that she was expected to follow her husband's religion. We find more examples of Christian women married to 'non-believers' (the better term would be 'believers in other gods') than of Christian men married to non-Christian Jews, Samaritans or gentiles. Both Paul's own letters (e.g. 1 Cor. 1.16; 7.12-16) and the Acts of the Apostles (16.32-33; 18.8) attest to this situation. But as eschatology waned and the Church needed to establish itself as a long-term institution, the lives of such women became increasingly difficult.

To affiliate with the Church represented more than simply a shift in one's belief system. A Christian woman married to a gentile non-believer lived in a hostile environment: her husband would expect her to eat the foods he ate and served to his guests, including food sacrificed to idols; she was to wear the fashion of the time, regardless of her sense of modesty; her husband would expect her to subscribe to his own cultic and political values and to inculcate them in her children. Obedience to his concerns marked not only her marital fidelity (the last thing the pagan husband wanted to hear was his wife's commitment to a celibate life dedicated to the Christ) but also her role in protecting the honor of the household. Although Roman women had a greater presence in the public sphere than did their earlier Athenian counterparts, their increasingly visible activities had a greater possibility of impacting their husbands' social standing and their household's reputation.

Consequently, the Christian woman's loyalty would necessarily have been divided: to (the honor of) her husband and her family on the one hand, and to her Lord and her Church on the other. Making this situation worse: Church leaders recognized how dangerous her position was, not only to herself, but also to all her Christian brothers and sisters. The Christian wife could be accused of disloyalty manifested in religious practice, sexual activity, financial support of her religion; her affiliation could even prompt charges of immorality and sedition. Church documentation attests to the divorce of Christian women by their pagan husbands, and Clement of Rome compares such women to martyrs.

'To appreciate the search for equilibrium' undertaken by such women requires, as MacDonald admits, 'an exercise in historical imagination'. Our texts at best yield only hints, for they represent the injunctions of male ecclesiastical leaders, not of the women in the pagan household. Nor can we gain access to the extent to which these women accepted the advice of their Christian advisors. Likely those separated from pagan husbands were supported by the Christian community, but even in such cases, as MacDonald notes and the several essays following on the Pastorals confirm, 'the divorced wives of unbelievers would be subject to new pressures from a society whose legislation included penalties for celibacy and reward for fecundity'. Within this society, the communities represented by the later Pauline epistles had to accommodate religious orientation to political expedience, and the results were not always either harmonious or of direct benefit to women.

Christian women who were either divorced by their non-Christian husbands or who separated from them in the hopes of living within the new family of faith did not necessarily find an easier life. Mary Ann Beavis poignantly illustrates the economic as well as psychologically debilitating circumstances enjoined upon many women—especially single women—who dedicate their life to the Church. Beavis opens her essay with a case study of 'Miriam', a college-educated, divorced mother of a disabled child. Miriam receives insufficient support either financially or emotionally from the institutional Church for which she works professionally, but her employment status precludes her from receiving the government benefits she and her disabled child require. Although Miriam models Paul's example by working 'night and day' (1 Thess. 2.9), she is condemned rather than praised: socially and economically, she is seen as a failure, even by family and fellow Church members. Worse, others attribute her increasingly desperate economic situation to her own indolence: surely if she worked harder, she'd have more money. Governmental bureaucracy, ecclesiastical indifference, and social stereotype thus trap the woman Church worker.

Miriam's counterparts, those under-appreciated, under-funded, and worrisome single women who sought their own roles in the Church, populate the later Pauline epistles. Beavis engages the connection through 2 Thess. 3.6-15, 'Paul's excoriation of the ἀτάκτως ('idle, disorderly') who refuse to follow the tradition of self-support. Although these ἀτάκτοι are usually understood simply as slothful, lazy sponges who rely on Church support, Beavis cogently argues for a narrower referent, for elsewhere in the Pauline corpus the subject of material support refers only to *ministers*. Paul insisted that whereas a laborer (minister) is worthy of his wages, his own practice was one of self-support. (Then again, Paul did not have children.)

The Pastorals express similar concern about financially supporting Church functionaries. Both 1 Thessalonians and First Timothy warn against ἀτάκτοι and 'busybodies' who 'wander about', both recommend 'good works', and both limit the congregation's responsibilities toward those who claim 'support by virtue of their service as ministers and leaders'. Perhaps then, Beavis proposes, the Thessalonian 'idlers' — those ministers who felt themselves entitled to support — may have included women.

Within the Pastorals, support by the community had a gendered component. According to 1 Timothy, widows receive assistance only if they are old, poor, and without family and then only if they pray 'night and day' (5.5); in contrast, all the πρεσβύτεροι (elders) are deserving of their wages (5.18) and are 'worthy of double honor' (5.17). The contributions of the true widows to the Church are thus devalued, their economic position precarious, their single status unwelcome. They are burdens on the community rather than treasured assets and role models. They are, in effect, Miriam's foresisters and, as Beavis concludes, they 'stand in prophetic judgment over the "elders" and "priests" who so confidently arrogate a "double portion" to themselves'.

Confident arrogation of another sort prompts Virginia Ramey Mollenkott's Evangelical-liberationist critique of feminist scholarship. Drawing upon her own experiences as well as the testimonies of other Evangelical women, Mollenkott finds sinister not only the traditional reading of Ephesians 5 that relegates women to subservient status and so is used to keep women in abusive relationships, but also the complicity of feminist scholars in perpetuating this reading rather than seeking emancipatory elements within the passage. Many Evangelical women lack the option of simply dismissing a text as antithetical to a more pristine (but just as self-selected) gospel; they will not defy what they believe to be a divinely inspired text. If the only interpretation they have of Eph. 5.23, that the 'husband is the head of the wife, even as Christ is the head of the Church', is one that promotes a 'just battering' (comparable to 'just war') system within which the husband has the right to 'discipline' his wife, then they are condemned either to apostasy or to submitting graciously: to beatings, to unwanted sexual contact, to abuse of their children. A feminist reading, Mollenkott contends, requires other options.

Beginning with Elisabeth Schüssler Fiorenza's thesis, Mollenkott agrees that Christianity abolished 'social-political stratifications of religion, class, slavery, and patriarchal marriage' by 'making everyone "equal in Christ"', and that (here not citing Schüssler Fiorenza explicitly) 'Jesus of Nazareth developed around himself a discipleship of equals'. They depart, however, at Schüssler Fiorenza's negative evaluation of Ephesians' analogy between Christ and the husband, the Church and the bride. For Schüssler Fiorenza, this paradigm locates the Church-bride as dependent and subordinate and so reinscribes inequality. Mollenkott, instead, lifts up the subjection of each Christian to the other, regardless of gender (Eph. 5.21) and so highlights the text's insistence on mutuality rather than hierarchy. Next, she argues that the analogy of the Christ to the husband is limited to the loving Christ who participates in self-sacrifice (5.25), and this limitation consequently requires the husband to yield any patriarchal privilege. Women, she claims, were not offered this model because they lacked such privileges; the text's lack of explicit mutuality, specifically of the call to husbands to submit to their wives and masters to their slaves, she attributes to the 'political dangers of Christian egalitarianism'. Finally, she points to the connotation of 'head' in Eph. 5.23 ('For the husband is the head of the wife just as Christ is the head of the Church, the body of which Christ is the savior') as 'source' rather than 'moral and intellectual authority', and certainly not as 'ruler' or 'governor'.

Responding to E. Elizabeth Johnson's critique that Ephesians' divine standard sets an impossible model, Mollenkott insists that ideals can be positive goals. Eph. 5.21-33 creates an ideal for Christian marriage, just as the Ten Commandments or the Golden Rule establish ideals for human behavior. Nor is Mollenkott convinced by Johnson's argument that Ephesians gives men a 'self-serving motivation' for loving their wives. Instead, she finds self-love and body-love necessary mandates in a world wracked by self-hatred. Anticipating Angela Standhartinger's essay on Colossians, she finds in that epistle a specific example of such self-giving love, namely, the report that Paul's death was for the sake of Christ's body, the Church (Col. 1.24).

The authors with whom Mollenkott is in dialogue—Schüssler Fiorenza, Johnson, as well as Susan Thistlethwaite, Mary McClintock-Fulkerson, and others—all share with her the goal of emancipating the oppressed. But Mollenkott laments her fellow feminists' failures, at least in the case of Ephesians, to recognize the biblical-prophetic insights she sees through her experiences in and commitment to Evangelical perspectives.

Elna Mouton, like Mollenkott, combines exegetical expertise with personal insight in locating Ephesians' presentation of sacrificial love. Reading within the contexts of South Africa's deep social divisions, its need for moral agency informed by Scripture, and her location as a 'white South African woman from within the Reformed tradition', Mouton develops an emancipatory reading of Christ's power (1.22) in relation to wifely 'submission' (5.22). Mouton highlights the reoccurrence of the term ὑποτάσσω, usually defined as 'to subject' or 'to bring under control'; in the middle form (cf. 5.24), it means 'take the subordinate role' in a relationship. Consequently, Mouton argues that Ephesians modifies the connotation of imposed loyalty to one of willing reverence, not only between Christ and the Church, but also among Church members. Thus, like Mollenkott, she finds a positive message. Yet she also recognizes how the language of sonship, head, one new man, wifely submission, and obedient slaves lends itself to readings that obscure the Church's vision of mutuality.

Anthropological categories of liminality, rites of passage and *communitas* inform Mouton's approach as she locates Ephesians' implied readers within the transition between an exclusivistic, cult-oriented identity to one defined by a single household. In her reconstruction, the originally gentile readers negotiate the transition away from the separation of Jew and gentile to a unity, and away from a focus on covenant, law, circumcision and temple to unity with Christ; thereby, they participate in a cyclical movement of reinterpretation and renewal. As the readers are continuously reoriented to the Christ, they are precluded from attitudes of complacency and from retaining a closed ethical system.

In this understanding of Ephesians, election, covenant, law and temple (the article repeats the list) all present 'dividing walls' that need to be reinterpreted. Yet the negative valence both epistle and article give these categories precludes any chance that either text or scholar will combat, along with the intractable problems of sexism, classism and ethnocentrism, the sin of anti-Judaism/anti-Semitism. Mouton mentions those who were 'looked down upon by the Jews' and 'excluded from Israel' (cf. 2.11-19); omitted is any comment on converting to Judaism. And while some Jews did hold to an extremely exclusive soteriology, others subscribed to the model of the Noachide commandments, wherein 'righteous gentiles' were also, to use Pauline terms, in a right relationship with God. Mouton celebrates the point that Ephesians does not 'bind us in a rigid legalistic way' (the phrase cannot avoid a law/grace dichotomy and so again negatively stereotypes Judaism). In like manner, she speaks of how, 'in showing compassion to women, children...Jesus subverts the established values of power in the moral world of first century Palestine', and thus implicitly categorizes Judaism as a tradition lacking in compassion for women and children. What is unity and integration from one perspective is erasure to another.

Ironically, Mouton's own reading of Ephesians provides the corrective to such impressions. She correctly acknowledges that the epistle not only celebrates the new creation in Christ, it also recognizes cultural limitations and the need for continual struggle. As long as the reader remains in a liminal position, there is opportunity for yet another shift away from the comfortable. The shift away from sexism and subordination within marriage is the same shift that leads readers away from anti-Judaism. We are moved by the epistle, Mouton argues, to 'grow beyond all limited and stereotypical views of humanity'; her 'hermeneutic of liminality' in which persons adopt the past history of others provides an excellent mechanism to accomplish such corrective healing.

Colossians, written in the names of both Paul and Timothy and addressed not simply to the Church at Colossae but to everyone everywhere, contributes its own legacy of oppression, as Angela Standhartinger observes. Colossians' earliest New Testament version of the household code (3.18–4.1) again adduces language of submission: of women to men, children to fathers, and slaves to lords. Here too appear analogies for the relationship of Christ to the Church, but with an imperial rather than domestic ground, for the epistle's ecclesiology depicts the relationship between Christ and the Church according to the relationship between the emperor and his body, the Empire. And again, as Standhartinger reveals in her rigorously historical study, the text undercuts its own hierarchical presentation.

Liberatory movements in the epistle are numerous. For example, Standhartinger notes that in Epaphras, the 'very dear fellow slave', the author—whom she calls 'Pauline' and codes as female—has created a double, one also a servant (διάκονος) of God and trustworthy deputy. The model of leadership is collective, and even the slave is a 'fellow citizen' (4.12). If the list of those to be greeted is an embellishment of the names recorded in Philemon (including mention of Onesimus, who is here not described as a slave), then 'Pauline' had added a woman, Nympha (4.15). Concerning the hymn of 1.15-20, Standhartinger remarks not only that the 'he' being celebrated is not explicitly identified, but also that if the masculine pronouns are replaced with feminine forms, the passage reveals itself to be a Wisdom hymn. Col. 3.11 evokes Gal. 3.28's formula for the renewed human being, and in this rendition not only religious and social differences but also ethnic ones are abrogated. Given such alternatives to social norms, the household code stands out as anomalous. Indeed, the code seems so general and so misplaced that some commentators even propose it to be a gloss. After investigating numerous Roman legal codes, Standhartinger concludes that while the text is original to the document, its odd placement and content provide clues to its more socially subversive function.

'Pauline' adapts her message to the political situation. Rome viewed the home as the nucleus of the state; proper imperial order depended upon proper domestic order, as numerous economic works indicate. A minority group, a *religious* minority group, could not afford to be seen as promulgating an ethos contrary to prevailing norms. For this reason, perhaps, Col. 3.11 eliminates 'male and female' from its recapitulation of Gal. 3.28. The unity within the Church mirrors the unity within the Empire, represented by men alone; the household code thereby attests the Church's loyalty. Nevertheless, insiders are prompted to read the code 'against the grain'. Focusing on the keyword ἰσότητα (equality) (4.1), Standhartinger finds a call that undermines slavery: masters are to show their slaves what is 'equality'. In the community idealized by Colossians, class differentiation is abolished.

Ephesians and Colossians along with 1 Cor. 14.33b-36 continue to trouble many who seek the full enfranchisement of women within Church and society, but 1 Timothy remains, as David M. Scholer frankly states, 'the clearest and strongest' biblical text cited by those who would limit women's preaching, teaching and authority, particularly within Evangelical circles. Appropriately refusing to discard the Pastorals as 'not from Paul'—regardless of authorship, if they appear in the canon, then, as Mollenkott also insists, they must be addressed as Scripture— Scholer seeks an understanding that comports with both historical investigation and Evangelical interest. The resulting essay reveals a wealth of perspectives often overlooked, dismissed or deliberately ignored by the more secular feminist biblical interpreter.

Beginning with exegetical considerations, Scholer demonstrates how several Evangelical writers focus only on 1 Tim. 2.11-12 or 11-14 and ignore verse 15; they thereby show, in Scholer's words, 'an irresponsible and symptomatic neglect of reading texts in their contexts'. Finding v. 15 the climax of the unit, Scholer then notes how numerous interpreters once again skew the data. For example, regarding the NIV's more socially palatable translation of 15a, 'But women will be kept safe through childbirth', Scholer avers that in the Pauline context, 'salvation' language refers not to physical health but to soteriology. Similarly, he uncovers the flimsy attempts to make Eve the subject of 'will be saved'. The verse means what it grammatically says: that women 'find their place among the saved' providing that they conform to the culture's maternal and domestic gender roles. Given this interpretation, Scholer then contextualizes all of 2.11-15 in terms of Greco-Roman notions of propriety.

As Standhartinger argues with respect to Colossians, so Scholer argues with respect to the Pastorals: the epistles show particular concern with the Church's reputation. The concern was exacerbated by the author's opponents, who apparently forbade marriage (1 Tim. 4.3) and encouraged women to meet together (1 Tim. 5.13-15 and cf. Titus 2.3-5). Warnings against this heresy provide the Pastorals' domestic agenda, and therefore, Scholer claims, 1 Tim. 2.8-15 should be seen not as the purpose of the epistle but as a component of its *ad hoc* advice contained in an occasional letter.

Regarding the term αὐθεντεῖν, usually translated 'to have authority over' (2.12), Scholer remarks first on its rarity and second on its connotations of 'domineer' or 'usurp authority'. He concludes that 1 Tim. 2.12 does not signal the type of (proper) authority or leadership discussed throughout the Pauline corpus. Rather, the injunctions in 2.11-12 refer to women involved in heretical teachings who have abused proper exercise of authority. The point is not that women did not and cannot exercise authority in the Church; they obviously did, as Scholer demonstrates by demolishing Evangelical arguments to the contrary.

Exegetical precision likewise marks the essay's discussion of 1 Tim. 2.13-14. Scholer indicates the false logic involved in the claim that 'any injunction followed by a scriptural allusion is absolute', notes that Paul throughout his letters uses Genesis 2–3 selectively, and shows how most Evangelicals read some texts (e.g. 1 Cor. 11.3-16) that appeal to Genesis 2 as historically limited. For Scholer, then, the appeal to Eve's deception is again not a timeless prescript but part of the specific argument against false teachings. Moreover, he directly vanquishes any reading claiming that women are 'by nature' more open to deception than men are or that Adam's deliberate sin (i.e. the giving up of paradise and immortality out of loyalty to his fallen spouse) marks men as more capable of religious leadership.

Scholer ends with several hermeneutical considerations that would be at home in many a feminist text. These include the effects of privileging one text over another (e.g. 1 Tim. 2.11-12 over Gal. 3.28), the dangers of equivocation (e.g. if women cannot teach or have authority, why do those holding such claims allow women missionaries or Bible study leaders? Why do they read theological books written by women or allow women positions on seminary faculties?), and, as he puts it, 'the cultural conditioning of the text and its interpreter' with specific attention to sexism and misogyny. The essay ends with detailed argument against the 'ill informed' who label any attempt fully to enfranchise women within the Church as influenced by secular feminism or in opposition to biblical authority. Admitting that all biblical interpreters have an agenda that surpasses simply a commitment to biblical teaching and authority, Scholer recognizes the genuine fidelity of those who seek to limit women's roles in the Church even as he insists that his own fidelity and that of the numerous men and women he cites who do seek a broader role be equally recognized.

Jouette Bassler, whose work on the Pastorals Scholer cites, confirms the occasional nature of 1 Timothy by turning to 5.3-16 and tracing the role of widows in the developing church. Penetrating behind the 'demeaning stereotype, obfuscating rhetoric, and confused syntax' of the epistle, Bassler reconstructs the author's view of how things ought to be even as she speculates on how things were.

Bassler begins with the observation that Gal. 3.28 may not be the emancipatory statement many (including, for this collection, Mollenkott and Standhartinger) believe it to be, but rather an erasure of sexual differentiation in favor of a masculine norm and its attendant performance in celibacy. Yet celibacy itself could promote women's autonomy as well as authority. Women who chose this lifestyle, especially younger women, were not however automatically freed from social control. The cultural norm was marriage, and despite the Roman esteem for the *univira*, the once-married woman, young widows as well as divorced women were expected to marry. Like Ephesians and Colossians, the Pastorals in Bassler's view respond to the societal anomaly of female independence by promoting traditional hierarchical family values and admonishing women to submissive domesticity.

For the Pastorals, the problem of the widows—as autonomous celibate women—emerges with stark complexity. Even the details themselves pose questions concerning the relationship between 'true' widows (5.3-8, 16) and 'enrolled widows' (5.9-15). Whereas the first set of verses emphasizes solitude and material need, the second set offers standards of age, lifestyle and deeds. Bassler resolves the cleavage by suggesting that the author has united two categories of widows with the intent of limiting the Church's responsibility to these single women.

The precipitating problem, Bassler cogently argues, was not economically based; injunctions against ostentatious dress (1 Tim. 2.9), interest in slaves (1 Tim. 6.1-2) and instructions to the rich (1 Tim. 6.9-10; 17–19) indicate a relatively prosperous community. Instead, the problem was likely a broadening definition of the term 'widow' (χήρα). The term could connote not just women whose husbands had died, but women living without husbands (e.g. because of divorce, separation, life-long celibacy). As Bassler puts it, 'sexual abstinence, not bereavement, was the determinative factor'. Most likely, it was celibacy that attracted these women, given celibacy's links to autonomy and authority. For the author of 1 Timothy, these widows are idle and gadabouts, gossips and busybodies (5.13). Otherwise put, they are free from domestic responsibilities and, in particular, free to say what they believe. Likely they spoke without the authority of the (male) Church leaders on topics these leaders disapproved. Worse still, they appear to have promoted the celibate lifestyle taught by the author's opponents (5.15).

To combat this freedom, the author first seeks to limit the number of women in the circle to 'real' (i.e. bereaved) widows without economic or familial support. Second, the author seeks to form a group that will support the socially normative gender roles in the same way that numerous religious cults, such as those of Fortuna and Isis and even Dionysius, did. By limiting the circle to elderly women and by insisting that the widows display both domestic virtues (including child rearing) and Christian piety, the author turns a potentially autonomous group into an advocacy movement for cultural values. Whether motivated by public opinion, internal theological debate, or a distrust of women's authority, 1 Timothy's author sought to limit women's authority. Whether the effort was immediately successful is yet another question.

Echoing the concern for external reputation sounded in several of the essays in this volume and remarking as well upon the broader definition of the term 'widow' (χήρα), Lilian Portefaix looks specifically to Roman rule rather than to the more frequently adduced problem of internal theological debate to determine how women's position in the Pastorals is best understood. Specifically, she sets the Pastorals within the political climate of Augustan family values, the later empire's fear of slave revolts and foreign cults, and the actualized persecution attested in the letters of Ignatius. Concerning women, Augustus as well as Plutarch anticipates the Pastorals in his promoting of childbearing, his condemnation of busybodies and his decrying of ostentatious jewelry and clothing. Pliny's description of the ideal wife could have been easily embraced by the Church, as could the eulogy for Turia that appears on her tombstone.

This literary evidence does not, however, indicate an Empire-wide acceptance of 'family values'. Rather, ordinances to marry, restrictions on inheriting by the unwed, and rewards for child production met widespread opposition from the time of Augustus through the reign of Justinian. Portefaix cites, for example, Tacitus's *Annales*, which indicate the failure of Augustus's attempt to advance marriage and larger families. Given this setting, the Pastorals' promotion of family values should be recognized as in part a reaction to Roman law and custom. To sponsor celibacy would suggest unpatriotic views, and on a more utilitarian level, women would have faced financial loss by refusing marriage and childbearing. At the same time, the Pastorals sought to limit the number of women entering the widows' circle because of such factors as divorce by pagan husbands, their possible prosecution for adultery or prostitution (cf. 2 Tim. 3.6-7), and the inability of some to afford a dowry. Although as Bassler argues, the Church may have been well off, increasing numbers of single women insisting on support may have strained finances, interpersonal relations, or both.

The final essay in this volume, Bonnie Thurston's study of widows, complements the essays by Bassler and Portefaix by analyzing its subject in light of both the male-defined official roles described in 1 Tim. 3.1-7, 8-13, and 5.17-19 and the various textual and inscriptional evidence for widows in financially secure leadership positions. Thurston argues, based on the context of the Pastorals, the terms τίμα ('honor') and καταλεγέσθω ('to enroll'), and the suggestion that enrolled widows took a vow or pledge, that the Pastorals establish 'orders' for select women comparable to the roles of elders, deacons and bishops. The descriptions for each category of widows then respond to the social needs of the Christian gathering: promoting social acceptability, avoiding heresy, and maintaining Church order.

The formalizing of women's roles reveals a clear double standard. As Thurston demonstrates, of all the offices, 'only the widows are limited with regard to support, finances, and sexual continence'. Further, notes Thurston, as the Church continued to adapt to the conservative status quo, applicants for the widows' order increased. Yet the very limitation of widows' roles suggests an initial freedom, documented in fictionalized form by several Apocryphal Acts, that conjoined sexual continence, teaching activity and substantial social autonomy.

Thurston's essay concludes by marking how the Church, ironically and paradoxically, both promoted and prohibited women's authority. By structuring itself on the model of the household and by encouraging the development of the 'house Church' supported by independent, wealthy women, the system promoted women's leadership. Yet the very nature of the οἶκος ('household') dictated gender-determined responsibilities, such as care for children and the elderly, food and clothing production, overseeing of slaves, and other distaff matters that limited women's participation. The increasing prominence of celibacy attracted many women (and men) to the Church, but the freedom from domestic responsibilities as well as religious authority that celibacy granted women made them a threat to the household structure of the Church and thus to the institution's safety within the wider imperial setting. Women who entered the widows' orders may have done so to escape society's promotion of marriage, yet the Pastorals reinscribe domesticity as the entry requirement. Finally, by attempting to reduce the number of enrolled widows and so maintain internal order, external reputation and proper theology, the Pastorals and their promoters may well have prompted many women to seek alternative theological and ecclesial homes. This final supposition receives support, as Thurston comments, by the renewed efforts the Great Church made in the third and fourth centuries to restrain its 'widows'. Beavis's depictions of today's 'Church widows' who do not conform to society's 'family values' demonstrate that the problem has yet to be resolved.

The charismatic leadership and eschatological enthusiasm that marked the earliest years of the Pauline churches gradually yielded to a formalized institution pressured to accommodate prevailing social expectations. A surface reading of the canonical documents presents one side of this historical picture. Both in antiquity and throughout the history of the Church, messages of liberation have been located both in the texts themselves and in the groups generated in rivalry with or response to them. Whether the traditionally problematic sections, such as Col. 3.18–4.1; Eph. 5.21-33; 1 Tim. 2.9-15, the Pastorals' various comments on women, or even 2 Thess. 3.10 are to be deemed social capitulations, protective measures, or even advancements given the broader society will remain debated by feminist and non-feminist interpreters alike. So too, whether readers should regard these texts in light of an 'egalitarian' community promoted by Jesus and Paul (cf. Mollenkott and Standhartinger) or find throughout the texts nuggets of egalitarianism despite lack of evidence for its actual practice (let alone conceptualization) will remain debated.

Although achieving no consensus, feminist interpretation has nevertheless advanced scholarly discussion of the later Pauline texts. The inclusion of Evangelical voices disrupts the stereotypes of confessional unanimity on the question of women's roles and in exegetical interpretation. The interest in women's place within the broader social context fractures the apologetic tendencies to see the Church as somehow more 'progressive' than its Jewish and pagan neighbors. Attention to how women today both interpret and are interpreted by the text insists that commentators recognize that we do more than arid, objectivist history when we approach canonical materials. The thoroughness that brings discussions of slavery as well as class and ethnic division into the study of gender roles reveals systemic issues and so keeps the feminist agenda from being narrowly focused on the abstract category 'woman'. Mindfulness of how the materials that occupy the canonical compositions appear both in 'heretical' and 'orthodox' works forestalls the tendency to limit the study of gender, sexuality, authority and theology to the pages declared 'sacred'. Finally, the debates even within this volume attest to the richness and the health of the feminist enterprise. Methods and conclusions will (necessarily and appropriately) differ, but as they do, we all draw nearer to achieving such goals as recognition of the ignored, recovery of the unnoticed, enfranchisement of previously silenced, and liberationist insight for all readers.

EARLY CHRISTIAN WOMEN MARRIED TO UNBELIEVERS[*]

Margaret Y. MacDonald

In his study of private life in late antiquity Peter Brown has spoken insightfully about the challenge of Christian fidelity:

> Much of the history of the early Christian churches is the history of an urgent search for equilibrium among those whose ideal of single-hearted loyalty to each other and to Christ was constantly eroded by the objective complexity of their own position in Mediterranean society.[1]

This paper considers one aspect of the position of early church members in Mediterranean society which must have greatly tested their loyalty to each other and to Christ. Some married members of the church found themselves daily in the awkward, even dangerous, situation of eating with, sleeping with and caring for the children of unbelievers. How difficult it must have been for those who entered church communities without their spouses to avoid the condition of 'double-mindedness' mentioned by Hermas when he addresses the threat to solidarity that accompanies preoccupation with business ventures and contacts with pagan friends.[2] Despite the accounts of heroic determination in literature, one wonders how many of those who were married to unbelievers were a source of frustration for church leaders who saw in their behavior the instability of a wave of the sea that is driven and tossed by the wind (Jas. 1.6-8).

Although references to the problem of marriage to unbelievers are not numerous, beginning with 1 Corinthians they are found consistently throughout the first four centuries of Christian literature. In keeping with his tendency to speak of the respective obligations of males and females throughout 1 Corinthians 7, Paul makes parallel references to

[*]   Originally published in *Studies in Religion/Sciences Religieuses* 19.2 (1990), pp. 221-34. Reprinted by permission.
    1.   P. Brown, 'Late Antiquity', in P. Veyne (ed.), *A History of Private Life: From Pagan Rome to Byzantium* (Cambridge, MA: Belknap Press/Harvard University Press, 1987), pp. 235-311 (259).
    2.   Brown, 'Late Antiquity', p. 259. See Hermas, *Mandates* 9–10; *Similitudes* 8.8.

men and women who are married to unbelievers (1 Cor. 7.12-16). Yet later evidence strongly suggests that the problem involved mainly the mixed marriages of pagan husbands to Christian wives.[3] That it was less likely for a Christian householder to be married to a pagan woman should come as no surprise given the social arrangements of Greco-Roman society.[4] Accounts of entry into the church of a certain believer and his household (e.g. Acts 16.32-33; 18.8; 1 Cor. 1.16) point to the tendency for the wife to share her husband's Christian allegiance.

In order to appreciate the search for equilibrium undertaken by the women of the early church who were involved in mixed marriages we must engage in an exercise of socio-historical imagination. By themselves the texts provide us with only a partial view — often more about the writer than the audience exhorted or the lives described. Being fully aware that only tentative conclusions are possible we need to revive the women who were comforted, challenged, but perhaps also burdened, by the advice they received. For example, we need to consider how Paul's prevailing advice that a believing partner should not simply divorce an unbelieving partner (1 Cor. 7.12-13; cf. Justin, *Second Apology* 2) would have been received by its mainly female recipients.[5] Obviously this means focusing upon a variety of sources that can tell us about such matters as marriage, divorce and attitudes to the religious activities of women in Greco-Roman society.

As will become clear in what follows, when the historical material relevant to the situation of women involved in mixed marriages is assembled, norms associated with the household repeatedly emerge. While one cannot simply assume cultural identity over time, comparison of this ancient material with the contemporary work of anthropologists on Mediterranean society is suggestive for the present study.[6]

3.   See later in this section discussion of *Constitutions of the Holy Apostles*; of Jerome, section 2; of the *Apocryphal Acts*, section 3; of Clement of Rome, Tertullian and Justin, section 5. See also R.L. Fox, *Pagans and Christians* (Harmondsworth: Penguin Books, 1986), pp. 310-11.

4.   See below, section 4, 'Public Opinion on the Religious Activities of Women'.

5.   I am indebted to L. Portefaix for her approach in *Sisters Rejoice: Paul's Letter to the Philippians and Luke–Acts as Received by First-Century Philippian Women* (Stockholm: Almqvist & Wiksell, 1988).

6.   On employing insights from the social sciences in the study of early Christianity see M.Y. MacDonald, *The Pauline Churches* (Cambridge: Cambridge University Press, 1988), pp. 9-28. On the use of anthropological studies of Mediterranean societies for understanding the ancient world see D. Cohen, 'Seclusion, Separation, and the Status of Women in Classical Athens', *Greece and Rome* 36 (1989), pp. 3-15 (3-5).

1. *The Cultural Ideal of Women 'at Home'*

It is generally recognized that in traditional Mediterranean society men are associated with the outside or public sphere (commerce, politics, the marketplace, cafés, fields, the place of assembly, etc.) and women are associated with the inside or private sphere (the home). Moreover, this dichotomy is related to the preservation of honor in Mediterranean society. In his study of women in classical Athens, D. Cohen has succinctly expressed the consensus of several anthropologists:

> The house is the domain of secrecy, of intimate life, and honor requires that its sanctity be protected. Any violation of the house is an attack on the honor of its men and the chastity of women, even if the intruder be only a thief. The separation of women from men and the man's public sphere within this protected domain is the chief means by which sexual purity is both guarded and demonstrated to the community.[7]

The ancient historian might argue that the anthropological conclusions seem far more applicable to the wife of classical Athens than to the Roman wife. The Roman woman was certainly more publicly visible, had greater freedom of movement, and exerted more influence (often subtly but effectively) in the world of politics.[8] But it is important not to assume that emergence from behind the walls of a house means the absence of separation of the men's public/outside sphere from women's private/inside sphere. Commenting on the emancipation of Roman women, Jane F. Gardner has warned that highly visible activities were frequently more formal than real, offices were honorific and political influence to further the careers of men 'exercised on a personal basis, on private occasions in private houses'.[9]

Even those exceptional women who urged their way into the public domain, perhaps as donors and protectors of cultic associations or as upwardly mobile businesswomen, were subject to cultural ideals which reminded them of their primary responsibility to the household. During the late first century CE the historian Tacitus looked back to the 'good old days' when household responsibilities were taken seriously in the Roman family and wives were neither idle nor indifferent:

> In the good old days, every man's son, born in wedlock, was brought up not in the chamber of some hireling nurse, but in his mother's lap, and at

---

7.   Cohen, 'Seclusion', p. 6.

8.   See G. Clark, *Women in the Ancient World* (New Surveys in the Classics, 21; Oxford: Oxford University Press, 1989), pp. 17-20.

9.   J.F. Gardner, *Women in Roman Law and Society* (London: Croom Helm, 1986), pp. 264-65.

her knee. And that mother could have no higher praise than that she managed the house and gave herself to her children.[10]

Earlier in the same century Philo expressed an ideal of rigid separation between the male sphere of public life and the female sphere of household management in relation to the Jewish women of Alexandria:

> Market-places and council-halls and law-courts and gatherings and meetings where a large number of people are assembled, and open-air life with full scope for discussion and action—all these are suitable to men both in war and peace. The women are best suited to the indoor life which never strays from the house, within which the middle door is taken by the maidens as their boundary, and the outer door by those who have reached full womanhood.[11]

Philo's comments call to mind Plutarch's advice on marriage to a young friend and his wife at the beginning of the second century CE: the model wife is one who is most conspicuous when she is with her husband but stays carefully hidden indoors when he is away (apparently simultaneously protecting her sexual purity from, and announcing it to, the world outside).[12] Against a background of growing unease about the stability of the family the cultural ideal of division between the female/domestic and male/public realms was proclaimed in the days of the Empire.[13]

Beginning with the New Testament we also find evidence of this ideal in early Christian literature. Composed by Paul or by a later interpolator 1 Cor. 14.33-35 calls for women to ask questions to their husbands at home; they are not to speak in the public arena of the ἐκκλησία (cf. 1 Tim. 2.9-15). John Chrysostom quoted this passage when he addressed the problem of Christian women of fourth-century Antioch partaking of Jewish festivals and attending synagogue. Husbands were exhorted to be very careful to keep their wives at home.[14] 'Keep your hands busy with spinning and stay at home' was the advice that Tertullian had given over a century earlier to women when he discussed the importance of modest apparel.[15] Like wives, widows were to devote themselves to the indoor life. Both the Pastoral Epistles (1 Tim. 5.13-15) and the third-

10. Tacitus, *Dialogue* 28.4-5 (trans. E.S. Forster and E.H. Heffner; LCL).

11. See Philo, *Spec. Leg.* 3.169-75; excerpt from R.S. Kraemer (ed.), *Maenads, Martyrs, Matrons, Monastics: A Sourcebook on Women's Religions in the Greco-Roman World* (Philadelphia: Fortress Press, 1988), pp. 29-30.

12. See Plutarch, *Moralia* 138A-146A.

13. For more evidence of this dichotomy see J.P. Hallett, *Fathers and Daughters in Roman Society* (Princeton, NJ: Princeton University Press, 1984), pp. 7-8, 29-30 n. 46.

14. John Chrysostom, *Against Judaizing Christians* 2.3-6; 4.3.

15. Tertullian, *On the Apparel of Women* 13; excerpt from R.J. Deferrari (ed.), *The Fathers of the Church* (New York: Fathers of the Church, 1959).

century *Didascalia Apostolorum* tell of the problems caused by widows who are gadabouts.[16]

There are several indications in early Christian literature, however, that the ideal of female seclusion did not always correspond to reality. As with the study of women in ancient society generally it is often difficult to understand the relationship between cultural ideals and social practice, and hence to judge the extent of emancipation.[17] Despite the difficulty of reconciling their activities with 1 Cor. 11.2-16 and 14.33-36 it is evident that female fellow workers assisted Paul in public ministry. For example, Euodia and Syntyche are described as struggling in the cause of the gospel with Paul (Phil. 4.2-3). Of course to call the ministry of these two women 'public' is somewhat misleading for much of it may have taken place 'in house'. Paul's letters provide several indications that the ἐκκλη-σία gathered in houses (Rom. 16.5; 1 Cor. 16.19; Phlm. 2) and, as indicated above, households seem to have provided an important arena for conversion. The fact that so much significant activity took place in the sphere traditionally associated with them must have increased the possibility of involvement by women (see Acts 16.14-15, 40).

Women seem to have lost some of their capacity for leadership and teaching in later centuries but the deaconesses and widows may well have made an important contribution to the expansion of the church. From the fourth-century *Constitutions of the Holy Apostles* we hear of the special ministry that the deaconess has to women who are part of unbelieving households: 'For sometimes thou canst not send a Deacon, who is man, to the women in certain houses, on account of the unbelievers. Thou shalt therefore send a woman, a Deaconess, on account of the imaginations of the bad.'[18] One gains the impression that rumors of sexual promiscuity were hovering over the association of believing men and the daughters and wives of unbelievers. Facing the possibility of scandal it seemed far more prudent to send a deaconess whose entry into the house would be more likely to go unnoticed. But we know that some Christian women were indeed noticed by pagan observers. In the first systematic attack on Christianity Celsus accused Christians of seeking out children and women ignorant as themselves. Although visible enough to have been observed by him the evangelizing efforts of Christians were generally performed in private in women's quarters or in

---

16. See R.H. Connolly (ed.), *The Didascalia Apostolorum* (Oxford: Clarendon Press, 1929), pp. 133-34.

17. See Cohen, 'Seclusion', pp. 6-7.

18. *Constitution of the Holy Apostles* 3.15; excerpt from Kraemer (ed.), *Maenads*, p. 239. Cf. Connolly (ed.), *Didascalia*, pp. 146-48.

shops where women may reasonably have worked. According to Celsus potential converts 'must leave their fathers and their instructors, and go with the women and their playfellows to the women's apartments, or to the leather shop, or to the fuller's shop, that they may attain to perfection'.[19]

2. *The Evangelizing Potential of Household Relationships*

Even when Church Fathers seemed to have forgotten the freedoms of first-century Christian women it was impossible to deny that at times women did make very good evangelists. When Jerome advised Laeta on how to rear a virgin Christian daughter at the beginning of the fifth century he expressed his hope that the child's example might win her grandfather—a man of highest distinction but one who still walked in darkness: 'When she sees her grandfather, she must leap upon his breast, put her arms round his neck, and, whether he likes it or not, sing Alleluia in his ears.'[20] Jerome began his letter by quoting Paul's treatment of marriage to unbelievers (1 Cor. 7.12-16). The fact that he began his quotation at 1 Cor. 7.13 with the case of a woman with an unbelieving husband (omitting the previous reference to a man with an unbelieving wife, 7.12) suggests that this is the situation with which he was familiar. To illustrate the wisdom of the apostle's counsel he pointed out that Laeta herself was the offspring of a Christian husband. Like the author of 1 Peter, Jerome believed that household relationships could announce the good news. Writing at the time when the survival of the church was far less certain the author of 1 Peter declared his conviction that women who were married to unbelievers might win their husbands by their reverent and chaste behavior, but without a word (1 Pet. 3.1-2).

The hope that mixed marriages will yield new church members is also expressed by Paul in 1 Cor. 7.12-16. His response to the issue culminates in a question which applies equally to both partners: How do you know whether you will save your husband/wife (1 Cor. 7.16)?[21] In the process

---

19.   Origen, *Contra Celsum* 3.55; excerpt from S. Benko, 'Pagan Criticism of Christianity During the First Two Centuries A.D.', *ANRW*, 23.2, pp. 1055-1118 (1104-1105). For other examples of women being noticed by pagans see B.B. Thurston, *The Widows: A Women's Ministry in the Early Church* (Minneapolis: Fortress Press, 1989), pp. 73-75. On women and work see S.B. Pomeroy, *Goddesses, Whores, Wives and Slaves: Women in Classical Antiquity* (New York: Schocken Books, 1975), pp. 198-200.

20.   *Letter 107*, Jerome to Laeta; excerpt from Kraemer (ed.), *Maenads*, p. 130.

21.   On the missionary intent of this question see O.L. Yarbrough, *Not Like the Gentiles: Marriage Rules in the Letters of Paul* (Atlanta: Scholars Press, 1985), pp. 111-12.

of his discussion the Apostle may have provided us with a faint glimpse of the success that contributes to his determination to preserve mixed marriages. Perhaps in response to ascetic Corinthians who see divorce as an escape from the immoral influence of an unbelieving spouse, Paul argues for the rightness of mixed marriage by appealing to the status of the children. He expects that the Corinthians will be convinced of the sanctifying nature of marriage between believers and unbelievers on the basis of the fact that the children of such marriages are not unclean, but holy.[22] Paul seems to presume here that the holiness of the children will be clearly visible to the Corinthians. Surely such visibility would not be possible unless the children were mainly believers. 1 Cor. 7.16 makes clear that Paul does not mean to imply that unbelieving spouses are members of the community *ipso facto*, but the example of the holy/believing children confirms the general holiness of the union and holds out the possibility of the future acceptance of the gospel by the spouse.

Traditionally responsible for the religious education of children, women in Greco-Roman society were in a natural position to preach the gospel to them.[23] As the example of Laeta illustrates, even in mixed marriages such missionary work took place. The special opportunity to evangelize could be disrupted fatally, however, if the unbelieving husband desired to separate: 'After divorce, the father retained *potestas* (control), and with it the right to keep the children with him.'[24] The thought of losing a child to a pagan father and stepmother must have inspired some mothers to keep their religious affiliations carefully hidden from unbelieving husbands.

Although they were given no official title women involved in mixed marriage must have identified with less secluded church members who were engaged in the evangelization process. Conscious of its position in the society at large and of household relations as missionary beacons the church urged these women to remain as obedient wives in the home, essentially to meet the demands of the household ideals (see 1 Pet. 3.1-6). Yet the call that they were to remain in the household meant that the wives of mixed marriages were continuously to weigh compromise and conviction against each other.

---

22. Yarbrough, *Not Like the Gentiles*, pp. 111-12. On the Jewish background of Paul's thought see M. Newton, *The Concept of Purity at Qumran and in the Letters of Paul* (Cambridge: Cambridge University Press, 1985), pp. 105-106; 145 n. 31.

23. See Portefaix, *Sisters Rejoice*, pp. 33-42, 193-94.

24. Gardner, *Women*, p. 146. She notes that from the time of Antoninus Pius appeal could be made to a magistrate so that a child might continue to live with its mother, but the father's *potestas* remained otherwise untouched.

3. *Religious Sensibilities and Life among Pagans*

Since membership in the church was marked with a profound sense of separation from the wicked world, anxiety must frequently have resulted from adherence to Paul's advice that mixed marriages should be preserved if possible.[25] Departing from Paul's wisdom on the matter the *Apocryphal Acts* (late second and/or third century) contain legends of women who understood their Christian conversions as precluding sexual union with unbelievers. While they may not describe actual historical persons they likely provide information about conversion patterns in certain Christian circles of relatively high social status.[26] *The Acts of Peter*, for example, contains the story of Xanthippe who was inspired by Peter to separate from her husband. Albinus was horrified that his wife 'would not even sleep in the same bed with him, was raging like a wild beast and wished to do away with Peter'.[27] Although referring to the dissolution of an engagement rather than a marriage, the *Acts of Paul and Thecla* convey vividly the offence that asceticism could hurl at Greco-Roman society especially when it directly affected the lives of those who were unsympathetic. Thecla's mother cries: 'Burn the lawless one! Burn her that is no bride in the midst of the theatre, that all the women who have been taught by this man (Paul) may be afraid!'[28] Separation from the pagan world for the women in these legends means conflict with the cultural ideal of wife, mother and mistress of a household.

An interest in the relationship between separation from the pagan world and marriage is also revealed by *Joseph and Aseneth*, a Greco-Roman Jewish romance written at some point between the first century BCE and the second century CE.[29] The words of Joseph to the as yet unconverted Aseneth might well express the sentiments of scrupulous early church members who were anxious to remove themselves from associations that yoked them intimately with the outside world:

> It is not fitting for a man who worships God, who will bless with his mouth the living God and eat blessed bread of life and drink a blessed cup of immortality and anoint himself with blessed ointment of incorruptibility to kiss a strange woman who will bless with her mouth dead and dumb idols and eat from their table bread of strangulation and drink from their

25. On the sense of separation see MacDonald, *Pauline Churches*, pp. 32-39.

26. See R.S. Kraemer, 'The Conversion of Women to Ascetic Forms of Christianity', *Signs* 6.2 (1980), pp. 298-307 (298-99).

27. *Acts of Peter* 34; excerpt from E. Hennecke, *New Testament Apocrypha* (2 vols.; Philadelphia: Westminster Press, 1963–65).

28. *Acts of Paul and Thecla* 3.20; excerpt from Hennecke, *Apocrypha*.

29. See Kraemer (ed.), *Maenads*, p. 408.

libation a cup of insidiousness and anoint herself with ointment of destruction.[30]

The link between abhorrence of food sacrificed to idols and repulsion at the thought of physical intimacy with a woman who participates in such meals would not surprise an anthropologist. In her study on women, food and social boundaries in rural Greece, Jill Dubisch states:

> Concern with what comes and goes in the body, with things that move from inside to out and those that go from outside to in, parallels the concern with what goes inside and outside the house and reflects the larger preoccupation with the boundaries of the family and their protection. Through bodily orifices pollution can occur.[31]

A variety of New Testament texts connect the desecration of sexual immorality with eating food sacrificed to idols (e.g. 1 Cor. 10.8; Rev. 2.14, 20).[32] While mixed marriage was generally accepted by the church as non-polluting, the rigorist Corinthians whom Paul seems to be addressing in 1 Cor. 7.12-16 and the heroines of the *Apocryphal Acts* suggest that some members were not completely convinced. With respect to idolatrous food Paul's moderately lenient advice (1 Cor. 8.10) gave way to the conviction that complete avoidance was a sign of orthodoxy.[33] Concern about both of these issues was related to a preoccupation with the boundaries of the social group. For the Christian woman married to the unbeliever whom Justin described, the risks of participating in a wicked world were frighteningly revealed in the acts of eating with and sleeping with her husband (in Justin, *Second Apology* 2).

4. *Public Opinion on Religious Activities of Women*

To add to the pressures of eating with and sleeping with unbelievers, the wives of mixed marriages came under the watchful eyes of a society

---

30. *Joseph and Aseneth* 8.5; excerpt from *OTP*. Cf. 2 Cor. 6.14–7.1. Although commonly regarded as an interpolation, 2 Cor. 6.14–7.1 would lead one to question whether remaining married to an unbeliever was appropriate; see W. Meeks, *The First Urban Christians* (New Haven: Yale University Press, 1983), p. 227 n. 113, for relevant bibliography.

31. J. Dubisch, 'Culture Enters through the Kitchen: Women, Food, and Social Boundaries in Rural Greece', in *idem, Gender and Power in Rural Greece* (Princeton, NJ: Princeton University Press, 1986), pp. 195-214 (210). See also the work of M. Douglas, *Purity and Danger* (London: Routledge & Kegan Paul, 1966), and *idem, Natural Symbols* (London: Barry & Rockliff, 1970).

32. See C.K. Barrett, 'Things Sacrificed to Idols', *NTS* 11 (1964–65), pp. 138-53 (138-41).

33. Barrett, 'Things Sacrificed', pp. 138-53.

where women were considered especially susceptible to bizarre religious impulses that could break through the boundaries of the household. Plutarch insists that a wife must share her husband's gods and must 'shut the front door tight upon all queer rituals and outlandish superstitions. For with no god do stealthy and secret rites performed by a woman find any favor.'[34] From the early fourth century CE comes (pseudo-)Lucian's description of wives who 'leave the house immediately and visit every god that plagues married men, though the wretched husbands do not even know the very names of some of these'. The return home is characterized by 'long baths, and by heavens, sumptuous meals accompanied by much coyness towards the men'.[35] In addition to being accused of neglect of household duties (including the duties of intimacy with one's husband) wives were criticized for spending household funds on expensive initiations into mystery religions.[36] Intrusion within the house and roaming of women were considered to be far more than annoying; they were an assault on the social order of the family which separated the female/private sphere from the male/public sphere.[37]

In the wide perspective of the state the most serious accusation that could be leveled at an unauthorized cult with respect to women was that it produced sedition and immorality.[38] From the second century comes a speech, probably authored by Marcus Cornelius Fronto, in which Christians are accused of the most grotesque debauchery:

> from the lowest dregs the more unskilled, and women, credulous and, by the facility of their sex, yielding, establish a herd of a profane conspiracy, which is leagued together by nightly meetings, and solemn fasts, and inhuman meats—not by any sacred rite, but by that which requires expiation—a people skulking and shunning the light, silent in public, but garrulous in corners.[39]

The popular charge about the immoral behavior of Christians may also be reflected in the following excerpt from Apuleius's *Metamorphoses*. The speaker here has been transformed into an ass and sold to a baker. He

---

34. Plutarch, *Moralia* 140D (trans. F.C. Babbit; LCL).

35. Lucian, *Amores* 52 (trans. M.D. MacLeod; LCL). See Portefaix, *Sisters Rejoice*, p. 54.

36. See Strabo 297; cited in Portefaix, *Sisters Rejoice*, p. 55; see pp. 53-55.

37. See Juliet du Boulay, *Portrait of a Greek Mountain Village* (Oxford: Clarendon Press, 1974), p. 133.

38. See discussion of the cult of Dionysus, the Isis cult and Judaism in D.L. Balch, *Let Wives Be Submissive: The Domestic Code in 1 Peter* (SBLMS, 26; Chico, CA: Scholars Press, 1983), pp. 65-80.

39. This source was used by the Christian Minucius Felix in his book *Octavius*; see excerpt of *Octavius* 8–9 in Benko, 'Pagan Criticism', pp. 1082-83.

finds himself in an opportune position to observe what otherwise might have remained between husband and wife:

> his wife was the wickedest of all women and he suffered extreme miseries to his bed and his house so that I myself, by Hercules, often in secret felt pity for him. There was not one single vice which that woman lacked, but all crimes flowed together into her heart like into a filthy latrine; cruel, perverse, man-crazy, drunken, stubborn, obstinate, avaricious in petty theft, wasteful in sumptuous expenses, an enemy to faith, and chastity, she also despised the gods and instead of a certain religion she claimed to worship a god whom she called 'only'. In his honor she practiced empty rights and ceremonies and she deceived all men and her miserable husband, drinking unmixed wine early in the morning and giving up her body to continual whoring.[40]

While this description might fit a woman who was a Jewish proselyte it may also express a typical pagan observer's opinion of the Christian wife of mixed marriage. Celsus would certainly not have been surprised to hear of the baker's unhappy lot. When he attacked Christians at the end of the second century he described them as secretive lurers of women and children, disruptive and destructive enemies of the society.[41]

The early Christians lived in a world that believed women to be inclined towards religious fanaticism and which accused unauthorized cults of leading women of behaving immorally and of threatening the stability of society as a whole. In such a world, we would expect that the pagan family members and neighbors of the wives of mixed marriage would be sensitive to even the subtlest signs of illicit behavior. A lack of interest in relations with one's husband or in family matters generally, scruples about food and even a sudden preference for plainer, more modest clothing would cause people to ask questions. While exhorting church women on the importance of avoiding luxurious apparel Tertullian records the objection made by some of these women that the Christian name should not be blasphemed on account of a demeaning change in their former style of dress (*On the Apparel of Women* 11). More seriously, frequent absences from one's own home coupled with the mysterious visits of strangers (especially male strangers) would result in an eruption of rumors about a woman's adulterous behavior. The remarks of anthropologist Juliet du Boulay about female reputation in Greek village life seem equally applicable to ancient society:

> absence from the home or irregularities in customary activities which cannot be minutely and indisputably accounted for in society, will almost

---

40. Apuleius, *Metamorphoses* 9.14; excerpt from Benko, 'Pagan Criticism', p. 1090.
41. Origen, *Contra Celsum* 3.55.

inevitably be taken as evidence of surreptitious liaisons…since, according to the conception of feminine nature, a woman's shame is the seat of her virtue, lack of virtue in aspects of life completely unrelated to sexuality may, if occasion arises, be referred back to a woman's basic moral nature.[42]

The pagan husband whose Christian wife fell under suspicion would have good reason to feel ashamed since the visible sexual purity of his wife was an important means of demonstrating his honor to the community.[43]

5. *The Consequences of Public Visibility*

As early as the New Testament era we find evidence that Christian communities are being burdened by slanderous rumors (1 Pet. 2.12; 3.15-16; 1 Tim. 3.6-7; 5.14).[44] Far from being a minor aggravation, gossip can be an important conveyor of public opinion; ridicule can function to endorse the community's values of prestige and failure.[45] Paul Veyne's remarks about the power of public opinion in the Roman Empire remind us of the suffering that could be caused by rumors:

> Those who braved public opinion faced ridicule. Insulting songs (*carmen famosum*) were quietly circulated, and pamphlets (*libelli*) passed from hand to hand, heaping obscene insults and sarcasm upon the deviant in order to demonstrate that public opinion was stronger than any man.[46]

At the beginning of the second century Christians were apparently bearing the brunt of ridiculing literature. When the Emperor Trajan replied to Pliny the Younger's letter concerning the Christians of Pontus-Bythinia, he instructed Pliny to disregard anonymous pamphlets accusing Christians, for they would set a very bad precedent and were not in keeping with the civilization of that age.[47]

---

42.   Du Boulay, *Portrait*, pp. 130-31.

43.   See J. Pitt-Rivers, 'Honour and Social Status', in J.G. Peristany (ed.), *Honour and Shame: The Values of a Mediterranean Society* (London: Wiedenfeld and Nicolson, 1965), pp. 19-77 (46-47). This is illustrated by the fact that in the Roman Empire harsh laws punished married women for adultery but husbands incurred no legal punishment. See P. Brown, *The Body and Society: Women and Sexual Renunciation in Early Christianity* (New York: Columbia University Press; London: Faber & Faber, 1988), p. 23.

44.   See MacDonald, *Pauline Churches*, pp. 108-109, 167-70.

45.   See J.K. Campbell, *Honour, Family and Patronage* (Oxford: Clarendon Press, 1967), p. 315; see pp. 190-91, 306-15.

46.   P. Veyne, 'The Roman Empire', in *idem* (ed.), *Writing History: Essay on Epistemology* (trans. M. Moore-Rinvolucri; Middletown, CT: Wesleyan University Press, 1984), pp. 5-234 (172).

47.   Pliny, *Epistles* 10.97; cf. 10.96.

Much mystery surrounds the question of how the Christian wives of unbelievers became publicly visible. But early Christian literature makes it clear that they did come to the fore and suffered greatly because of it. Although Paul does not speak about suffering explicitly, his argument that mixed marriages should continue unless unbelievers will not consent to live with believers leads to the obvious conclusion that some were not consenting, and hence probably treating believers with hostility (1 Cor. 7.12-16). At the end of the first century Clement of Rome appears to have connected the suffering of believing women who were divorced by pagan husbands with the indignities suffered by women before martyrdom (*1 Clem.* 6.2-3). About a century later Tertullian commented on the irony of the cruel treatment of Christians which follows a reformation of character. While a pagan husband should be rejoicing in the now chaste behavior of his wife, instead he casts her out of his house (Tertullian, *Apology* 3).

A detailed description of the difficulties experienced by a Christian wife of an unbelieving man is found in Justin's *Second Apology*. Having entered the church, the woman did not try to win her husband 'without a word' but actively began evangelizing him. The kind of household strife which the author of 1 Peter seemed intent on preventing (1 Pet. 3.1-6) was precisely the result.[48] Advised by friends to persevere in the hope that her husband might have a change of heart she suppressed her initial inclination to separate from him. But eventually her husband's indulgence in immoral behavior became too much for her and she divorced him (see Hermas, *Mandates* 4.1.5-9). In 'sharing his table and his bed' she risked becoming a partaker 'in his wickedness and impieties'.[49] The woman's suffering did not end with separation from her husband for the enraged spouse brought charges against her, perhaps hoping to retain at least part of her dowry.[50] While her appeal to the emperor (Antoninus Pius) was successful her teacher became the object of her husband's attack and was imprisoned for his Christian affiliations.

The remarks of Clement, Tertullian and Justin demonstrate the vulnerable position of believing women married to unbelieving men. It is worth considering the options available to women with respect to divorce in Greco-Roman society. Paul's exhortation on mixed marriage presupposes that the initiation of divorce was a possibility for both sexes. Moreover,

---

48. On discord in households shared by believers and unbelievers see *Recognitions of Clement* 2.29.

49. Justin, *Second Apology* 2; excerpt from A. Roberts and J. Donaldson (eds.), *Ante-Nicene Fathers* (10 vols.; Peabody, MA: Hendrickson, 1994), I, pp. 188-89.

50. See discussion of the case in R.M. Grant, *Greek Apologists of the Second Century* (Philadelphia: Westminster Press, 1988), pp. 69-73.

Justin tells of a Christian women who divorced her pagan husband. This is consistent with Roman law but women often had little control over the course of events in a world where divorce could mean political advantage or new hope for an heir. The historian Sarah Pomeroy has concluded: 'Beginning in the late Republic, a few women are notorious for independently divorcing their husbands, but, for the most part, these arrangements were in the hands of men.'[51] The difficulties facing a believing woman in her attempt to secure a divorce from a non-believing husband would surely be complicated by membership in a strange new religious group. For example, such membership might very well count against her in a plea to win necessary support from her own family.[52]

Social status would undoubtedly be related to the ability of wives of mixed marriage both to initiate divorce and to survive after divorce. For example, a freedwoman who was married to her patron was not able to divorce him without his consent.[53] It is likely that women who had little or no dowry for support found themselves divorced, isolated and penniless for the sake of the gospel.[54] Although often the only recourse open to women in such dire straits would be prostitution, church women who were thrown out of the house could at least turn to fellow believers for support.[55] Yet if they remained unmarried, the divorced wives of unbelievers would be subject to new pressures from a society whose legislation included penalties for celibacy and reward for fecundity.[56]

6. Conclusion

In order to appreciate the search for equilibrium undertaken by the believing wives of mixed marriage we must seek to understand the values of the Mediterranean society that embraced them. Despite the extent of their involvement in the church, early Christian women did not escape the paradoxes experienced by other women in Greco-Roman

---

51. Pomeroy, *Goddesses*, p. 158; see pp. 150-63; Gardner, *Women*, p. 260.

52. See S.B. Pomeroy, 'The Relationship of the Married Woman to Her Blood Relatives in Rome', *Ancient Society* 7 (1976), pp. 215-27.

53. Gardner, *Women*, pp. 82-83, 86-87. On freedpersons in early Christianity see Meeks, *First Urban Christians*, pp. 20-23, 51-73.

54. See Portefaix, *Sisters Rejoice*, p. 28.

55. On the church maintaining groups of women, see Portefaix, *Sisters Rejoice*, pp. 181-82.

56. Augustan legislation penalized unmarried women (20–50 years of age) including widows who had not remarried within two years and divorcées who had not remarried within eighteen months. For details of the scope and impact of these laws see Gardner, *Women*, pp. 20, 77-80.

society who showed signs of emancipation but who abided by codes that limited their public activities and interpreted their excesses of visibility as impropriety. The wives of mixed marriage, in particular, had the least opportunity to break through the normal expectations of female roles in rendering some service to the church. More restricted in their movements and subject to greater suspicion, these women were encouraged to act as discreet evangelists within their own homes. Yet in remaining faithful to their husbands and in exhibiting the kind of model wifely behavior that would have won them approval even outside of the ἐκκλη-σία they were subject to anxiety that came from touching the parameters of the pagan world and from awareness of the suffering that their discovery might bring.

'IF ANYONE WILL NOT WORK, LET THEM NOT EAT':
2 THESSALONIANS 3.10 AND THE SOCIAL SUPPORT OF WOMEN

Mary Ann Beavis

Case Study: Miriam

Miriam, a well-educated American single mother with a school-aged, disabled child finds herself in a series of low-paid jobs for which she is overqualified, with few or no employment benefits. As a graduate student, Miriam worked part-time as a campus chaplain, so many of her jobs are church-related. Unfortunately, often this means that her jobs are low-paying and insecure. After several years of struggling to keep financially afloat, with the help of credit cards, loans, extra part-time work, and minimal child-support payments from her estranged husband, she is dismissed from her job at a denominational school due to a disagreement with the principal, relegated to public housing and forced to collect social security. When she finds part-time work in a neighborhood church, she is told by a government official that the difference between her earnings and her unemployment benefits will be deducted immediately, although her first paycheck will not arrive for six weeks. Miriam's effort to earn her living by taking part-time work leaves her with far less cash than she requires to meet the basic necessities of life, and less money than she would have received had she relied on social security alone. When Miriam tells the government employee on the other end of the phone that she and her daughter cannot live on seven dollars a week for the next six weeks, she is told that the government simply doesn't care about her personal situation; she is earning money, and so her benefits must be cut immediately. In the meantime, Miriam simply must make do, by relying on family, friends and her own dwindling resources.

Although Miriam has family living nearby, she finds that as her economic status declines, she gets less and less sympathy and support from her parents, sisters and brothers. With each setback, Miriam receives more criticism and blame for her situation. Nor does she receive much support or encouragement from her church. Emotionally exhausted and unable to cope with the disapproval of family and community, Miriam becomes depressed, irritable, and confused. Why is she penalized for trying to work and earn money? Why does her family regard her as a failure, despite her persistent and exhausting efforts to support herself and her child with minimal resources? What will be the next rung on her descent down the economic ladder? Even with her commitment to work and middle-class values, she is barely able to buy groceries—will the next step be the food bank, the soup kitchen, the homeless shelter?

Miriam's mainstay is her strong Christian faith, and even that is sorely challenged in the face of constant and escalating reversals. What would Miriam make of 2 Thess. 3.6-13, the biblical prescription that the 'idle' should be required to work for their bread, rather than relying on support from others? Miriam is more than willing to work; in fact, she follows the Apostle's example by working 'night and day' (2 Thess. 3.8), both as a mother and in her paid jobs. Nonetheless, Miriam still has to struggle to put food on the table, and no doubt will for the indefinite future.

A part of Miriam's problem is that she does not fit into any of the approved social roles for women. She has not been a 'success' as a wife, and her husband's loss of interest in marriage and family life is blamed on her. Although she has a graduate degree, Miriam has never been able to earn enough money to count as a 'success' professionally. Miriam's inability to live up to approved standards of womanly achievement has branded her in the eyes of society, and even of her family, as a problem— as someone who does not really 'want' to look after herself and her child. She is even criticized for being a mother—surely a child is a 'luxury' for someone whose life has been as 'unstable' as Miriam's.

Case Study: Dorcas

Acts 9.36-43 tells the story of a 'female disciple' (μαθήτρια) from Joppa named Dorcas, known for her 'good works and mercy' (ἔργων ἀγαθῶν καὶ ἐλεημοσυνῶν) who died after a short illness. She is mourned by a group of widows (χῆραι), for whom Dorcas had made clothing, presumably to provide them with financial support. Possibly the other women also made garments, which they sold to sustain themselves as an economically self-sufficient community in service to God (cf. v. 39).[1] Whatever the economic arrangements, the fact that Dorcas's material contribution to the community of widows—her 'good handiwork'[2]—was significant is

---

1.   Lesly Massey, *Women in the New Testament: An Analysis of Scripture in the Light of New Testament Era Culture* (Jefferson, NC: McFarland & Co., 1989), p. 65.

2.   Although the phrase ἔργων ἀγαθῶν (v. 36) is usually interpreted in the sense

indicated by the general consternation that follows her death, so much so that the Apostle Peter is summoned by the Joppan disciples to address the situation. After Peter raises Dorcas from the dead in the presence of 'the holy ones and widows', word of the miracle spreads throughout the town, and many conversions ensue (v. 42). This story testifies to a group of Christian widows living together in Palestine, recognized by the disciples, being supported by their own labor. It may be the most ancient testimony to the existence of an emerging 'order' of Christian widows that existed for several centuries in the early church before being absorbed into the stream of monasticism.[3]

Although there is no evidence that Paul ever met Dorcas, he might have approved of her labor as conforming to his model of 'working day and night' in order to support her own and the widows' ministry.[4] This value is expressed most forcefully in 2 Thessalonians, a Pauline letter whose authorship is disputed, but which certainly embodies what has since become a classic expression of the 'Protestant work ethic' of 'if any one will not work, let them not eat' (2 Thess. 3.10). Whether the epistle was written by Paul or a disciple of Paul, the author of 2 Thessalonians would have seen Dorcas as a fine example of paying one's own way (2 Thess. 3.8), of earning one's living 'in quietness' by one's own work, and of never being weary in 'well doing' (καλοποιοῦντες) (3.13). Dorcas's industry and charitable works are rewarded; she is raised from the dead by Peter (Acts 9.40-41). The income earned by Dorcas relieves the larger community of 'saints' and 'disciples' (vv. 38, 41) from having to provide for the widows (cf. Acts 6.1-6), which may explain the consternation and dismay of both widows and disciples at her sudden death (Acts 9.38-39). Without Dorcas, the widows fear that they will have less access to resources, and the other members of the community worry that the widows will become a financial burden.[5] While Dorcas provides a positive model of a woman who is well able to support herself and 'those less fortunate', once she is gone, the widows are again in danger of slipping into the pitiable and dependent state expected of them. Like Miriam,

of 'charitable works', when applied to women's work, it could refer to the traditional female occupation of weaving and other handiworks (LSJ). On the role of spinning, weaving, and clothing manufacture in women's economic history, see Elizabeth Wayland Barber, *Women's Work: The First 20,000 Years* (New York: W.W. Norton, 1994).

3. See Bonnie Thurston, *The Widows: A Women's Ministry in the Early Church* (Minneapolis: Fortress Press, 1989), pp. 28-85.

4. Ronald F. Hock, *The Social Context of Paul's Ministry: Apostleship and Tentmaking* (Philadelphia: Fortress Press, 1980).

5. Cf. Thurston, *The Widows*, pp. 28-29.

their status is precarious, despite their membership in the Christian community.

2 Thessalonians 3.10: Working and Eating

Max Weber's classic *The Protestant Ethic and the Rise of Capitalism* contains an extensive discussion of the role of 2 Thess. 3.10 in making constant individual work in one's professional calling, self-sufficiency and amassing wealth unquestioned social values.[6] As Weber puts it:

> labour came to be considered in itself the end of life, ordained as such by God. St. Paul's 'He who will not work shall not eat' holds unconditionally for everyone. Unwillingness to work is symptomatic of the lack of grace.[7]

Through the vector of Calvinism and Puritanism, the slogan 'if any one will not work, let them not eat' has become a foundational principle in some formulations of Christian economics, especially in the United States. For example, a recent article in the evangelical *Journal of Biblical Integration in Business* cites this verse as illustrative of one of three principles underlying 'biblical views of work', that 'God hates laziness'.[8] An introductory textbook on Christian ethics cites 2 Thess. 3.10 as teaching that 'Even the belief that the end of the world was imminent was no justification for the cessation of labor'.[9]

This catchphrase, which has played such an important role in Western social and economic history, occurs in an exhortation appended to 2 Thessalonians (3.6-15), in which the writer addresses the issue of persons within the community who are ἀτάκτως (which means both 'idle' and 'disorderly'; the ambiguity is probably intentional) — people who do not follow the 'tradition' (παράδοσις) handed on to them by the Apostle, referring to Paul's practice of supporting himself by his own labor, so as not to 'burden' the community financially.

Commentators generally assume that the ἀτάκτοι were simply unemployed and indolent members of the church who were financially dependent on wealthier 'brothers and sisters' (ἀδελφοί).[10] However, when

6.   Max Weber, *The Protestant Ethic and the Spirit of Capitalism* (New York: Charles Scribner's Sons, 1958), pp. 155-83.

7.   Weber, *The Protestant Ethic*, p. 159.

8.   Lisa Klein Surdyk, 'Making Connections: Integrating Christianity and Economics', *Journal of Biblical Integration in Business* (1995–96) (http://www.cedarville.edu/dept/ba/jbib/index2.htm).

9.   Roger H. Crook, *An Introduction to Christian Ethics* (Upper Saddle River, NJ: Prentice–Hall, 3rd edn, 1999), p. 240.

10.   E.g., E. Elizabeth Johnson, '2 Thessalonians', in Carol A. Newsom and Sharon

material support is at issue elsewhere in the Pauline corpus, it is invariably in the context of community support of Christian *ministers*. For example, in 1 Thess. 2.9, Paul reminds the Thessalonians that while he was with them, he and his missionary colleagues (Silvanus and Timothy, 1 Thess. 1.1) had worked 'night and day' so as not to burden the church financially, even while they were proclaiming the 'gospel of God', dealing with each member of the church 'like a father with his children' (1 Thess. 2.11). In 2 Cor. 11.7-11 Paul reminds the Corinthians that he had not 'burdened' them financially but had preached the gospel 'as a free gift' (δωρεάν), and promises that on his next visit, he will do likewise (12.14-15). In this case, however, Paul admits that he had accepted support from ἀδελφοί from Macedonia (2 Cor. 11.9), which suggests that in Corinth, Paul did not practice his trade of tentmaking and was not altogether averse to accepting material support from his converts. In fact, Paul vociferously insists on his right as an apostle to receive payment for his services, although, again, in the case of the Corinthian church, he has proclaimed the good news 'free of charge' (ἀδάπανον) (1 Cor. 9.3-18).

Which functionaries within the church should be supported financially is explicitly at issue in the deutero-Pauline 1 Timothy with respect to the widows of the community. As Linda Maloney notes, there is 'astonishingly widespread' evidence for the existence of an order of widows in the early church.[11] In 1 Tim. 5.3-16, the author specifies that the order of widows within the community be limited to elderly women, who had only been married once, with no other means of support. All others claiming the status of widow — women under 60, never-married women, widows who had more than one husband, and women with relatives who could help them — should not be officially recognized, and should not receive financial help from the church. Widows who are 'gossips and busybodies' — perhaps referring to widows who visit other women's houses and engage in teaching — are especially worrisome to the author (v. 13; cf. 4.7). Only those widows who meet the stringent

H. Ringe (eds.), *The Women's Bible Commentary* (London: SPCK; Louisville, KY: Westminster/John Knox Press, 1992), pp. 351-52 (352); Arland J. Hultgren and Roger Aus, *I–II Timothy, Titus, II Thessalonians* (Minneapolis: Augsburg, 1984), p. 217; Charles A. Wanamaker, *Commentary on 1 and 2 Thessalonians* (NIGTC; Grand Rapids: Eerdmans; Exeter: Paternoster Press, 1990), pp. 285-90. Here, I follow Wanamaker's practice of translating ἀδελφοί in the Thessalonian letters inclusively.

11. Linda Maloney, 'The Pastoral Epistles', in Elisabeth Schüssler Fiorenza (ed.), *Searching the Scriptures: A Feminist Commentary* (2 vols.; New York: Crossroad, 1994), II, p. 371; see also Dennis Ronald MacDonald, *The Legend and the Apostle: The Battle for Paul in Story and Canon* (Philadelphia: Westminster Press, 1983), pp. 73-77; Thurston, *The Widows*.

requirements laid down by the author, and who limit their activities to offering 'supplications and prayers night and day' (5.5), should receive assistance (ἐπαρκέσις) from the community (5.16). The implication is that even the recognized widows should be supported not because of the value of their service to the church, but because they are advanced in years, needy, and utterly alone. The denigration of the widows' role is highlighted by contrast with 1 Tim. 5.17-22, where male elders (πρεσβύ-τεροι), who 'rule' (προεστῶτες, v. 17) are 'thought worthy of double honor' (διπλῆς τιμῆς ἀξιούσθωσαν), especially in their roles of preaching and teaching. Unlike the widows, elders are to be rewarded generously and ungrudgingly for their labor (v. 18). Charges against elders are only to be brought by 'two or three witnesses' (v. 19); compare this with the litany of anonymous accusations leveled at the widows in vv. 6, 11-13. There is no appeal to Paul's practice of self-support; elders are simply pronounced deserving of their wages (1 Tim. 5.18). The hypothesis that the deutero-Pauline author of the epistle belonged to the order of πρεσ-βύτεροι does not seem too far-fetched.

The rhetoric of 2 Thess. 3.6-15 and 1 Tim. 5.3-16 shows some fascinat-ing, yet elusive, similarities. First, there is the similarity of situations. 2 Thessalonians 3.6-15 warns against members of the community who are idle/disorderly, rather than gainfully employed; presumably they are being supported by others, as Paul, the Apostle, had the right to expect, but declined, preferring to earn his own living (v. 9). 1 Tim. 5.3-16 is concerned with a specific category of 'idle' person, the group of widows whom the author deems to be unworthy of community support. Besides the similarities in situation, the two passages tantalizingly echo one another in vocabulary. The persons referred to in 2 Thess. 3 are 'idle' or 'disorderly' (ἀτάκτως, vv. 3, 7, 11); similarly, the false widows of 1 Tim. 5.13 are 'idlers' (ἀργαί); the Thessalonian idlers 'wander about' (περιπατοῦντος), while the widows are described as 'gadding about (περιερχόμεναι) from house to house' (1 Tim. 5.13); both groups are made up of 'busybodies' (περιεργαζομένους, 2 Thess. 3.11; περίεργοι, 1 Tim. 5.13). The authors of both letters are concerned that the 'idlers' do appropriate work; the Thessalonian idlers should follow Paul's example and earn their own bread (2 Thess. 3.7-8, 12); 'true widows' should engage in prayer and supplication, and those who do not qualify as wid-ows should marry or ask their families for assistance (1 Tim. 5.5, 14-16). The authors of both epistles recommend 'good works' (καλοποιοῦντες, 2 Thess. 3.13; ἔργοις καλοῖς, παντὶ ἔργῳ ἀγαθῷ, 1 Tim. 5.10), which, for the 'true' widows, include 'women's work' such as bringing up children, washing the feet of the saints, and relieving the afflicted. The Thes-salonians are 'commanded and exhorted' to work 'quietly' (ἡσυχίας,

2 Thess. 3.12), implying that, from the author's perspective, some ἀδελ-φοί/ἀδελφαί are talking too much and about the wrong things; similarly, the young widows of 1 Tim. 5.13 are accused of 'saying what they should not' (λαλοῦσαι τὰ μὴ δέοντα; cf. 1 Tim. 2.12: ἀλλ᾽ εἶναι ἐν ἡσυχίᾳ).

One connection between 1 Timothy and 2 Thessalonians that can be made with some degree of assurance is that the ἀτάκτοι of 2 Thessalonians 3 are probably persons claiming *support by virtue of their service as ministers or leaders*, like the widows of 1 Tim 5.13. Possibly, the ἀτάκτοι claimed for themselves a social role analogous to the 'house philosopher', who lived in the house of a patron, and received support from him or her, to provide instruction to the patron's family and provide counsel (in this case, religious instruction and advice).[12] While the ἀτάκτοι, like the widows, regard their work for the church (or for the household to which they are attached) as a legitimate ministry worthy of support, their claim to the 'right' (ἐξουσία) of payment is not recognized by the author (1 Thess. 3.9). In this context, the exhortation to the ἀδελφοί in v. 13 not to grow weary in 'well-doing' (καλοποιοῦντες) may be an admonition to the 'idle/disorderly' among them to bear a double workload of Christian service *and* paid work, according to the example of the Apostle (vv. 7-9), or, more likely, simply to abandon their disapproved ministerial role. The nature of the ministry of the ἀτάκτοι, and whether there were women among their number, is uncertain, although the presence of females might well degrade the work further, in the eyes of the writer.[13] The fact that both the ἀτάκτοι and the widows are belittled as 'busybodies' (2 Thess. 3.11; 1 Tim. 5.13), and that the idle/disorderly among the Thessalonians and the women of 1 Tim. 2.11-12 are admonished to 'silence' is suggestive, but not definitive; the rhetoric of 2 Thessalonians may simply be a device to shame men who are acting 'like women'. Perhaps ἀτάκτοι are supporters of the doctrine alluded to in 2 Thess. 2.1-2, the teaching regarding the *parousia* of Jesus Christ, which the author so vociferously rejects as contrary to the true doctrine of Paul. Again, it is tempting to compare this group with the widows of 1 Tim. 5.13, 'gossiping' about what they should not. Like the author of 1 Timothy,

---

12. Hock, *Apostleship and Tentmaking*, pp. 53-54. House philosophers, like the ἀτάκτοι, were often criticized for relying on wealthy patrons for support. Hock deduces that the opponents of Paul in 2 Corinthians were Christian teachers attached to the households of rich Corinthians (Hock, *Apostleship and Tentmaking*, p. 65; cf. E.A. Judge, 'St. Paul and Classical Society', *JAC* 15 (1972), pp. 19-36.

13. On the patriarchal perspective of the author of 2 Thessalonians, see Mary Ann Beavis, '2 Thessalonians', in Schüssler Fiorenza (ed.), *Searching the Scriptures*, II, pp. 263-72.

the writer to the Thessalonians might characterize the teachings of the ἄτακτοι as 'old wives' tales' (γραώδεις μύθους, 1 Tim. 4.7).[14]

Epilogue: Miriam, Dorcas, the Widows, and 1 Thessalonians 3.10: A Typological Interpretation

This study began with two 'case studies', one the 'fictionalized' life story of Miriam, a single mother who cannot live up to the roles expected of her by society and church, and who is thus blamed for her inability to support herself and her child, and the New Testament story of Dorcas and the widows, a hard-working community of Christian women whose livelihood is threatened by the death of one of its members. In both cases, there is little social or ecclesial willingness to meet the economic needs of these women when they 'fall through the cracks' of their respective social safety nets of family, state, and church. Once these women have voluntarily or involuntarily departed from the roles expected of them (wife, widow, 'productive member of society'), they become ἄτακτοι in the eyes of society and church: they are idle, disorderly, parasitic — and easily dismissed.

Dorcas, the widows, and the ἄτακτοι can be interpreted as 'types' (τύποι) of contemporary women like Miriam, who do not 'fit' into accepted social molds. In two millennia since Dorcas and the widows, the patterns of thought laid down by the deutero-Pauline authors of 2 Thessalonians and 1 Timothy are still very much with us. Like the ἄτακτοι, and, later, the widows, Miriam's ministerial role in Christian institutions is tenuous, grudgingly financially supported, and radically questioned. Her genuine work for the church is undercompensated, and when she 'makes waves', she is dismissed for being 'incompetent' and 'insubordinate' — idle/disorderly. She is penalized for disagreeing with authority, rather than 'minding her own business' and being 'quiet'. Her 'disorderly' behavior (conscientious disagreement with the principal) is punished by dismissal: 'Take note of those who do not obey what we say in this letter; have nothing to do with them, so that they may be ashamed' (cf. 2 Thess. 3.14). Miriam is judged, by family, society, and church, by an exaggerated interpretation of the principle of 'if any one will not work, let them not eat', and made to feel 'ashamed'. Miriam, Dorcas, and the widows, the ἄτακται of society and church, stand in prophetic judgment over the 'elders' and 'priests' (πρεσβύτεροι) who so confidently arrogate a 'double portion' to themselves.

---

14.   On the role of 'old women' in transmitting mythic narratives, see MacDonald, *Legend and the Apostle*, pp. 13-15; on the role of women in early Christian storytelling, *Legend and the Apostle*, pp. 34-37.

EMANCIPATIVE ELEMENTS IN EPHESIANS 5.21-33:
WHY FEMINIST SCHOLARSHIP HAS (OFTEN) LEFT THEM UNMENTIONED, AND WHY THEY SHOULD BE EMPHASIZED[*]

Virginia Ramey Mollenkott

In the early 1980s when I served on the National Council of Churches' Inclusive Language Lectionary Committee, I was somewhat puzzled by the committee's reluctance to deal with Eph. 5.21-33. In *Women, Men, and the Bible,* first published in 1977, I had discussed the passage as a liberating one.[1] To my mind, the author of Ephesians was the first person ever to develop a theology of Christian marriage and therefore was important to any discussion of Christian male–female relationships. While I was aware of the horrific abuses of the text, I assumed that feminist scholars like those on the committee would be glad for the opportunity to provide a translation emphasizing the more egalitarian aspects of the passage. Eventually that did happen,[2] but the initial reluctance gave me much pause: What was it about Ephesians 5 that caused feminist scholars to view it with such unmitigated distaste?

To respond to that question, I must refer to my 44 years of teaching literature at the undergraduate and graduate levels. I was puzzled sometimes by the fact that discussions of a literary text would be more direct, fresh, and original in the undergraduate than in graduate classes. Then somewhere I read about an educational experiment in which students were presented with Robert Herrick's 'To the Virgins, to Make Much of Time', the famous seventeenth-century lyric beginning, 'Gather ye rosebuds while ye may'. The students were given the poem only — no author,

*   Thanks to Letha Dawson Scanzoni for her expert editing and word processing of this article.

1.   Virginia Ramey Mollenkott, *Women, Men, and the Bible* (New York: Crossroad, rev. edn, 1988), pp. 13-22.

2.   See Victor Roland Gold, *The New Testament and Psalms: An Inclusive Version* (New York: Oxford University Press, 1995), p. 299. Except in the quotations of other authors, it is this Oxford version that is used throughout my article. (For an even more inclusive translation, see Craig R. Smith [ed.], *The Inclusive New Testament* [Brentwood, MD: Priests for Equality, 1994], p. 336.)

no title, no context whatsoever. The graduate students immediately placed the lyric within the *carpe diem* tradition and had little else to say: the poem seemed to them graceful, secular or perhaps pagan, and somewhat obvious. The undergraduate students tended to notice a responsible concern with the proper use of time and a fatherly attitude toward those who were being addressed. A few of them even guessed (correctly) that the author was a priest. This experiment revealed what had been happening in some of my own classes: in the case of the graduate students, a little knowledge had interposed itself between the reader and a sensitive interaction with the tone, language choices, structures, and imagery employed in the text. Knowing less about literary traditions, the undergraduates made a more direct response to what was in front of them.

All of which brings me to the thesis of this article: Feminist Bible scholars have sometimes been complicit in the oppression of religious women by failing to lift up the emancipative elements in Eph. 5.21-33 and similar passages of Scripture. Why? I have no trouble understanding why traditionalists would emphasize a gender hierarchy in Ephesians 5, as Jerry Falwell did when he called the proposed Equal Rights Amendment 'a definite violation of holy Scripture' because it 'defies the mandate that "the husband is the head of the wife, even as Christ is the head of the church" (Eph. 5.23)'.[3] That is a political attempt to hold on to patriarchal privilege; and although I hate it, I understand the motives. More recently, the Promise Keepers have strongly urged men to 'take back the leadership of their families' and have refused to add an explicit commitment to gender equality, claiming that their seven promises inherently imply gender equality already.[4] (One wonders how 'taking back' male authority can possibly imply the equality of women and men. From whom are the men supposed to 'take back' leadership? The Southern Baptist Convention left no doubt in their June 1998 statement: 'A wife is to submit graciously to the servant leadership of her husband.'[5])

Feminist Scholars and Repressive Interpretations

But why would many *feminist* scholars agree with the most repressive possible interpretations of Ephesians 5? The answer, I believe, lies not in

3.   Jerry Falwell, *Listen, America!* (Garden City, NY: Doubleday, 1980), p. 151, quoted in Charlene Spretnak, 'The Christian Right's "Holy War" Against Feminism', in Charlene Spretnak (ed.), *The Politics of Women's Spirituality* (New York: Anchor Books, 1982), pp. 470-96 (472).

4.   Alice Evans, 'Common Ground in the Culture Wars?', *Oregon Quarterly* 77 (1998), p. 13.

5.   'Just the Facts', *Chicago Tribune*, Sunday 21 June 1998, sec. 13, p. 1.

their little knowledge but rather in their great knowledge of textual criticism, church history, and the history of biblical interpretation. They read Eph. 5.21-33 through the lens of the household codes that were part of the gradual accommodation of Christianity to patriarchal social norms. And since expectation breeds perception, many of them fail to acknowledge (perhaps even to see) the considerable power of the emancipative elements that nevertheless somehow found their way into the text.

That failure is particularly unfortunate because the interpretive history of Ephesians 5 is a bloody one, and the passage is still a matter of life and death to Christian women and children who face abuse in right-wing environments. I have neither space nor stomach to trace the devastating misogyny of church fathers and theologians through the centuries; that information is easily available.[6] But it does seem necessary to look at what our right-wing contemporaries have been doing with Eph. 5.21-33 and similar passages. Such an examination can help us grasp the extent of the damage that occurs when even feminist biblical scholars concede that such passages do indeed teach male primacy and female subordination.

Interpretations that Foster Wife Abuse and Low Self-Esteem in Women

According to the Reverend Marie Fortune, who directs the Center for the Prevention of Sexual and Domestic Violence in Seattle, abused women from conservative Christian churches have been given to understand on the basis of Eph. 5.21-33 that they must submit to their husband's abuse; that it is their wifely duty to have sex when and however their husband decrees; that the wife should not interfere when her husband beats their children; and that because the husband heads the household, wives dare not intervene even if they think the male is sexually abusing the children.[7] Mary Potter Engel has traced the antecedent of such views to Christian doctrine combined with European folk tales which taken together constitute a 'just battering' tradition that parallels the logic of the 'just war' tradition. According to that tradition, the husband has the authority to punish his wife when, in his judgment, punishment is

---

6. See, e.g., Rosemary Radford Ruether, *New Woman, New Earth: Sexist Ideologies and Women's Liberation* (New York: Seabury, 1993 [1975]); Beverly W. Harrison, *Making the Connections: Essays in Feminist Social Ethics* (Boston: Beacon Press, 1985); Elisabeth Schüssler Fiorenza, *Bread Not Stone: The Challenge of Feminist Biblical Interpretation* (Boston: Beacon Press, 1992); and Karen J. Torjeson, *When Women Were Priests: Women's Leadership in the Early Church and the Scandal of Their Subordination in the Rise of Christianity* (San Francisco: HarperSanFrancisco, 1993).

7. Marie Fortune, *Keeping the Faith: Questions and Answers for the Abused Woman* (San Francisco: Harper & Row, 1987), pp. 15, 17, 22, 26.

necessary to maintain his headship; but he is not supposed to beat his wife to death, nor is he to injure her in any permanent way.[8]

Given this 'just battering' theory, people who work with abusers should not be surprised to hear from them comments like those quoted in a State of New Jersey publication on domestic violence: 'All my life I was taught that a man is the head of the household. Who are you to tell me this is no longer true?' and 'The man is the head of the wife. I have the right to do what I have to do to keep things in order'.[9] But the fact is that it is husbands who provoke the violence 85 percent of the time, brutally assaulting their wives for such 'faults' as the crying of the baby, the dishes being unwashed, the dinner not to the husband's taste at the moment, or his or her wanting or not wanting to have sex.[10]

The church is profoundly complicit in perpetuating teachings that legitimate violence against women and children. The church's sins of *omission* are dual failures: to teach a liberating ethic of human equality, and to prepare seminarians and Bible students to deal humanely with domestic violence. James M. Nichols said, 'Of all the classes I had in family living, counseling, and the like, no one in Bible college had prepared me to help women with black eyes, broken ribs, and a concussion from her violent husband'.[11] Yet, as early as 1980, a study run by the United Methodists found that one in thirteen United Methodist wives had been physically abused by her husband, while one in four had been verbally abused by him.[12] One would have thought that the shock waves from such a study would have caused a massive curriculum revision in all denominational colleges and seminaries. Instead, the report was met with 'disbelief and an amazing capacity to rationalize the findings'.[13]

---

8.   Mary Potter Engel, *Revisioning the Past: Prospects in Historical Theology* (ed. Mary Potter Engel and W.E. Wyman, Jr.; Minneapolis: Fortress Press, 1992), pp. 51-75, as discussed by Susan Brooks Thistlethwaite, 'Violence Institutionalized', in Letty M. Russell and J. Shannon Clarkson (eds.), *Dictionary of Feminist Theologies* (Louisville, KY: Westminster/John Knox Press, 1996), pp. 307-309. See also Carol J. Adams and Marie Fortune, *Violence Against Women and Children: A Christian Theological Sourcebook* (New York: Continuum, 1995).

9.   Deborah J. Pope-Lance and Joan Chamberlain Engelsman, *Domestic Violence: A Guide for Clergy* (Trenton, NJ: New Jersey Department of Community Affairs, 1987).

10.   Murray Strauss, as cited in Pope-Lance and Engelsman, *Domestic Violence*, p. 8.

11.   As quoted in Pope-Lance and Engelsman, *Domestic Violence*, p. 33.

12.   Susan Brooks Thistlethwaite, 'Every Two Minutes: Battered Women and Feminist Interpretation', in Letty Russell (ed.), *Feminist Interpretations of the Bible* (Philadelphia: Westminster Press, 1985), pp. 96-107 (96).

13.   *Crisis: Women's Experience and the Church's Response: Final Report (1982)*, as quoted by Thistlethwaite, 'Every Two Minutes', p. 96.

But the church is also committing sins of *commission*, practicing irre-sponsible selectivity in the interpretation of Scripture. Although Eph. 5.21–6.9 and other 'household code' passages have in the past been used to justify slavery, no respectable modern denomination would suggest such a meaning today. Yet many churches continue to teach female subordination on the basis of the very same passages, or else manifest very little enthusiasm for an across-the-boards liberation not only of slaves from masters, but also children from abusive fathers and women from male dominators.

The Black church has been especially remiss in this regard, not because Black sexism is worse than White sexism, but because African Americans have *never* believed that slavery was consonant with Christianity, yet have continued to assume the subordination of women on the basis of the same passages that told slaves to be subject to their masters. Asks Womanist theologian Clarice Martin, 'How can black male preachers and theologians use a *liberated* hermeneutic while preaching and theologizing about slaves, but a *literalist* hermeneutic with reference to women?'[14] Similarly, Woman-ist Jacqueline Grant asks, 'How can a Black preacher preach in a way which *advocates* Paul's dictum concerning women while *ignoring* or *repu-diating* his dictum concerning slaves?'[15] They rightly suggest that:

> African American biblical interpreters must develop and adopt a liberation-ist biblical hermeneutic instead of a hierarchalist hermeneutic with regard to biblical narratives about women and women's 'place' in ecclesiastical arenas and hierarchies.[16]

If Paul is understood to have spoken within his own socio-historical context concerning slaves, the same must be true of women. And what is true for African Americans is no less true for biblical interpreters from other ethnicities: consistency is an interpretive virtue, especially when dealing with a sacred text that some people regard as the inerrant Word of God.

Writing out of her experience of studying the Bible with women who have been abused, Susan Thistlethwaite[17] explains that for those who care about violence committed against women and children in their own home, there is no substitute for learning and teaching a liberating inter-

---

14. Clarice Martin, 'The *Haustafeln* (Household Codes) in African American Bibli-cal Interpretation: "Free Slaves" and "'Subordinate Women"'', in Cain Hope Felder (ed.), *Stony the Road We Trod: African American Biblical Interpretation* (Minneapolis: Fortress Press, 1991), pp. 206-31 (226). Italics mine.

15. As quoted in Martin, 'The *Haustafeln*', p. 225.

16. Martin, 'The *Haustafeln*', p. 228.

17. Thistlethwaite, 'Every Two Minutes', p. 96.

pretation of Eph. 5.21-33 and similar texts. She points out that 'frequently, women with strong religious backgrounds have the most difficulty in accepting that the violence against them is wrong'.[18] She explains:

> Phone calls to [abused women's] shelters often begin with the phrase, 'I'm a Bible-believing Christian, but...' We begin to develop a feminist her-meneutic because the Bible is part of the fabric of the oppression of battered women... [T]hese women believe what they have been told the Bible says about their situations: that women are inferior in status before husband and God and deserving of a life of pain.[19]

Dr Thistlethwaite comments that 'some biblical material that appears not to address women, or even appears hostile to them, can be reworked to bring out liberating themes for abused women'. (The essential catalyst, she has found , is the insight that 'women are included in the category of the poor, the oppressed, and the outcast', with whom God identifies.[20]) Yet having said all that, Dr Thistlethwaite nevertheless interprets Eph. 5.21-33 as a patriarchal passage that sanctions the one-way submission of women to men and is therefore 'a primary legitimator of wife abuse'.[21] She therefore argues that:

> the metaphor of patriarchal marriage for divine–human relationships is not one of mutuality; it is an image of dominance and subordination in that cultural context. Likewise, tying marriage to the divine–human relationship clearly divinizes male superiority in the relationship.[22]

By drawing this conclusion, Dr Thistlethwaite leaves deeply religious abused women with no alternative other than to say that Ephesians 5 is wrong and must be defied if they are going to liberate themselves. But I well remember my own years as a fundamentalist wife in a dysfunctional marriage; I was not able to trust anyone who told me to flout Scripture, which I took to be the word-for-word-and-God-inspired rulebook for Christian living. Had Dr Thistlethwaite instead encouraged me to notice the limitations placed on the metaphor of husband-as-Christ (that the husband is compared to Christ *only in Christ's self-giving, self-humbling capacity*), I could have trusted her when she assured me that a domineer-ing and emotionally abusive husband had already violated Ephesians 5, so that it was proper for me to leave him.

Dr Thistlethwaite's important essay concerning abused women illus-trates the problem I am addressing: when even ardent feminist scholars

18. Thistlethwaite, 'Every Two Minutes', p. 99.
19. Thistlethwaite, 'Every Two Minutes', pp. 97, 99.
20. Thistlethwaite, 'Every Two Minutes', p. 102.
21. Thistlethwaite, 'Every Two Minutes', p. 105.
22. Thistlethwaite, 'Every Two Minutes', p. 107.

agree with the most right-wing preachers that an important sacred text really does teach female subordination, they help to trap women from the Religious Right in the assumption that God considers them inferior and deserving of lifelong suffering servanthood.

Perhaps the most influential interpretation of Eph. 5.21-33 by a feminist scholar has been Elisabeth Schüssler Fiorenza's in her groundbreaking book *In Memory of Her*.[23] A more recent feminist interpretation also has great potential influence because of its location in *The Women's Bible Commentary*.[24] I plan to interact with these two interpretations in an attempt to prove my thesis that feminist biblical scholars could help contemporary women and men by going beyond placing Eph. 5.21-33 and similar texts within their historical patriarchal context, taking pains also to lift up the liberating possibilities within the text.

Elisabeth Schüssler Fiorenza and Ephesians 5: A Critique

Elisabeth Schüssler Fiorenza discusses Eph. 5.21-33 in her chapter concerning 'Christian Mission and the Patriarchal Order of the Household'. She argues that we must take seriously the accusation of second-century pagan writers that Christianity destroys the household by attracting especially women, slaves, and young people.[25] This accusation, she says, was not unfounded: Christianity did indeed break Greco-Roman ancestral laws by abolishing social-political stratifications of religion, class, slavery, and patriarchal marriage and making everyone 'equal in Christ' (cf. Gal. 3.28).[26] Therefore, it was in order to become less threatening to established social norms—it was in order to survive—that the church gradually introduced the patriarchal social ethos to replace 'the genuine Christian vision of equality'.[27] Ephesians 5.21-33 is part of that adaptation, that process of patriarchalizing communities that had originally been liberationist.

---

23. Elisabeth Schüssler Fiorenza, *In Memory of Her: A Feminist Theological Reconstruction of Christian Origins* (New York: Crossroad, 1983). Although the overall effect of Schüssler Fiorenza's work is marvelously instructive and liberating, in *Sharing Her Word: Feminist Biblical Interpretation in Context* (Boston: Beacon Press, 1998) she still dismisses the 'household code texts' wholesale as 'kyriarchal injunctions to submission' (p. 119) that 'reformulated the ancient discourses of subordination in Christian terms' (p. 148).

24. Carol A. Newsom and Sharon H. Ringe (eds.), *The Women's Bible Commentary* (Louisville, KY: Westminster/John Knox Press, expanded edn, 1998).

25. Schüssler Fiorenza, *In Memory of Her*, p. 263.

26. Schüssler Fiorenza, *In Memory of Her*, p. 265.

27. Schüssler Fiorenza, *In Memory of Her*, p. 266.

Schüssler Fiorenza explains that the author of Ephesians depicts Christ as 'the head and source of peace for the church',[28] emphasizing unification of Jews and Gentiles within the Christian community. But whereas in Eph. 2.11-22 making peace involves mutual respect and supportiveness, in 5.21–6.9 wives, children, and slaves are told to subordinate themselves in a way that Jews are never told to do: 'While the author insists on the mutuality, unity, and equality of uncircumcised and circumcised here and now, he maintains such equality for slaves and freeborn only for the eschatological future.'[29] The same is true for Christian wives:

> The relationship between Christ and the church, expressed in the metaphors of head and body as well as of bridegroom and bride, becomes the paradigm for Christian marriage and vice versa. This theological paradigm reinforces the cultural-patriarchal pattern of subordination, insofar as the relationship between Christ and the church clearly is not a relationship between equals, since the church-bride is totally dependent and subject to her head or bridegroom.[30]

Had I still been bemired in my patriarchal marriage when I read those words, I would have felt all hope dissolving within me. If even a leading feminist scholar assures me that Ephesians 5 does indeed require of me an unequal subordination to my husband, then that must be God's will or it would never have been included in the inspired Word! According to Schüssler Fiorenza, Ephesians 5 teaches that within the Christian community as a whole, each Christian is to be submissive to every other Christian (5.21); but once marriage has taken place between any two Christians, the wife must submit to her husband in a way that he need not reciprocate. That is exactly what was taught in the conservative churches of my youth. For women from backgrounds like mine, it is demoralizing to find outstanding feminist scholars agreeing with hierarchalist theologians like George Knight III, who says that the basic exhortation of Ephesians 5 is that the wife is to be subordinate to the husband, who is *not* subordinate to her.[31]

As Susan Thistlethwaite explains, Roman Catholic women do not regard the text of Scripture as the primary religious authority in their lives and therefore have fewer qualms about entering into 'suspicion of

---

28. Schüssler Fiorenza, *In Memory of Her*, p. 267.
29. Schüssler Fiorenza, *In Memory of Her*, p. 268.
30. Schüssler Fiorenza, *In Memory of Her*, p. 269.
31. George Knight III, *The New Testament Teaching on the Role Relationship of Men and Women* (Grand Rapids: Baker Book House, 1977). For an accurate summary of both hierarchical and liberationist interpretations of the Bible, see Willard M. Swartley, *Slavery, Sabbath, War, and Women: Case Histories in Biblical Interpretations* (Scottsdale, PA: Herald Press, 1983).

the many texts we examined that seemed to legitimate violence against women'.[32] For such women, it is the church's teachings about women's roles, divorce, and contraception that have provided legitimation to the abuser. Perhaps that set of facts explains Roman Catholic scholar Schüssler Fiorenza's willingness to leave her interpretation of Ephesians 5 as the obvious patriarchal one. She has nothing driving her to search out the possibility that liberating angles might nevertheless be discovered within the text, placed there by the author either consciously (to subvert the patriarchy he at first seemed to be supporting) or else unconsciously (inspired, perhaps, by a well-nigh universal drive toward human wholeness and health).

An Alternative Interpretation of Ephesians 5

Whatever the case for Roman Catholics, the fact remains that for evangelical or fundamentalist Protestant women, a purely historical interpretation is devastating, even when accompanied by the disapproval of the feminist scholar who does the interpretation. Fundamentalist women are not free to say that whereas Jesus of Nazareth developed around himself a discipleship of equals, the authors of Ephesians and Colossians and 1 Peter and 1 Timothy were flatly wrong and can be explained away simply by noting the patriarchal circumstances under which they were operating. Having been taught that the entire canon is without error and God-inspired, such women cannot trust a person once she or he has swept aside any Scripture as erroneous. Perhaps after a period of building trust she could be persuaded to adopt as her interpretive norm Jesus' remarks about loving God and our neighbor as ourselves as the whole meaning on which all Scripture hangs (Mt. 22.36-40). After that, perhaps she could apply the 'hermeneutic of suspicion' to any passage that encourages unloving behavior, such as one-way male domination. But Marie Fortune is surely correct that anyone wishing to assist abused women should suggest liberating alternative interpretations of Scripture rather than initially issuing a direct challenge to the authority of the text.

The First Emancipative Element: Mutual Subjection
What then *are* the emancipating elements within Eph. 5.21-33? First, there is the fact that v. 21 calls for the mutual subjection of each Christian to every other Christian without regard to gender. This principle is intended to govern the interpretation of the whole passage. For that reason, v. 22 does not contain any verb, leaning on the verb in v. 21:

---

32. Thistlethwaite, 'Every Two Minutes', p. 104.

'Being subject to one another in [the] fear of Christ. The wives to their own husbands as to the Lord.'[33] To Schüssler Fiorenza, the statement that the wife is to be subject to the husband 'in everything' (5.24) wipes out any possibility that the mutuality of v. 21 is intended to govern the entire passage. But *how* is the wife to be subject 'in everything'? Only as the church is subject to Christ.

Schüssler Fiorenza's entire book *In Memory of Her* constitutes a major indictment of how the church has departed from the discipleship of equals that Jesus gathered around himself, yet the love of Christ has never been withdrawn from the church. As a member of the church which is Christ's body, never has anyone been coerced *by Christ* to make a personal decision that did not accord with the depths or core of the individual's being. Indeed, to consult one's deepest wisdom is precisely to submit oneself to the spirit of the Christ-Self within human being-ness. As an organization, the church is flawed and has developed coercive methods and inequitable structures; but to the degree it has done so, it has failed to submit to the egalitarian vision of the Christ.

So the analogy of wifely submission to husbandly headship 'in everything' is very much limited by what we know about the way Christ and the church are related to one another, in an utterly non-coercive voluntary pattern. Markus Barth pointed out in the Anchor Bible that to describe Christian subordination, Paul does not use the active mode, as he does to describe God's subjugating of the principalities and powers. Rather, for Christian submission Paul uses the passive mode in order to describe 'a voluntary attitude of giving in, cooperating, assuming respon-sibility, and carrying a burden'.[34]

Because Christ loves the church unfailingly, the church *ought* to be willingly subject to Christ 'in everything', although in fact it is not. And as Elizabeth Cady Stanton commented: 'If every man were as pure and self-sacrificing as Jesus is said to have been in his relations to the Church, respect, honor, and [even] obedience from the wife might be more easily rendered.'[35]

Schüssler Fiorenza concludes that the wife's instructions are 'summed up in the injunction [of v. 33] to fear or to respect her husband',[36] but she fails to contextualize that by reminding readers that women of New

33. *The Greek–English New Testament* (trans. A. Marshall; Washington, DC: Christi-anity Today, 1975), p. 973.

34. Markus Barth, *Ephesians* (AB, 34-34A; 2 vols.; Garden City, NY: Doubleday, 1974), II, pp. 709-10, as quoted in Swartley, *Slavery, Sabbath, War, and Women*, pp. 263-64.

35. Elizabeth Cady Stanton, *The Woman's Bible* (Seattle: Coalition Task Force on Women and Religion, 1974), p. 160.

36. Schüssler Fiorenza, *In Memory of Her*, p. 269.

Testament times had very little choice about who would *be* their husband. Men, who possessed the power of choice, are enjoined to love; but it would be unfair to tell a woman she must love a person whose partnership she perhaps had never wanted in the first place. It is impossible genuinely to love without respect, but it *is* possible to respect without the presence of love. Hence, the instructions to the husband are more far-reaching and demanding than those to the wife—especially when projected against a patriarchal social order, where wives were expected to be obedient, but husbands were not necessarily expected to be either respectful or loving.

Schüssler Fiorenza does admit:

> the patriarchal societal-code is theologically modified by the exhortation to the husband... Jesus' commandment 'to love your neighbor as yourself' (cf. Lev. 19.18) is applied to the marriage relationship of the husband. Moreover, the relationship of Christ to the church becomes the example for the husband. Christ's self-giving love for the church is to be the model for the love relationship of the husband with his wife. Patriarchal domination is thus radically questioned.[37]

She even allows that the author's intention might have been to transform the patriarchal pattern of the household code.[38] And this is precisely the approach that would set free women who previously thought the passage was teaching their inferiority to men.

But Schüssler Fiorenza undercuts her own liberating insight by asserting that in Ephesians 5, the christological modification of the husband's position is not strong enough theologically to *necessitate* transformation. So the fact is, she states, that 'Ephesians christologically cements the inferior position of the wife in the marriage relationship',[39] since 'the church-bride is totally dependent and subject to her head or bridegroom'.[40] What a disappointment for anyone eager for biblical permission to liberate herself!

Nevertheless, despite denials by various feminists and all hierarchalist interpreters, Eph. 5.21–6.9 *is* governed by the opener about subjection to one another out of reverence for the Christ. That the subjection is intended to be mutual is clarified by the phrase about 'reverence for Christ', which is then reinforced by the many references to Christ throughout the passage. The household code ends in 6.9 with the reminder that slave owners must treat their slaves 'in the same way' as the slaves are supposed to treat them, that is, as if they were the Christ (6.5-6, 9). That

37. Schüssler Fiorenza, *In Memory of Her*, p. 269.
38. Schüssler Fiorenza, *In Memory of Her*, p. 270.
39. Schüssler Fiorenza, *In Memory of Her*, p. 270.
40. Schüssler Fiorenza, *In Memory of Her*, p. 269.

principle, had it been obeyed, would have put an end to slavery among Christians within one generation. And had it been obeyed, the principle of mutual subjection would have ended male supremacy among Christians within one generation.

Because of Greco-Roman sensitivity to the political dangers of Christian egalitarianism, the Ephesians author could not jeopardize Christian survival by flatly saying 'as wives submit, so must husbands submit; as slaves submit, so must masters submit'. That would have challenged social norms so frontally that it would have called forth instant retaliation, probably in the form of persecution. But the principle of every relationship's ultimately being 'as unto Christ' brilliantly subverts patriarchal hierarchy and establishes equality.[41]

Jesus said to his followers:

> I do not call you slaves any longer, because those who are enslaved do not know what the one who enslaves them is doing; but I have called you *friends* because I have made known to you everything I have heard from my Father-Mother (Jn 15.15; italics mine).

Jesus established a discipleship of *equals*, as Schüssler Fiorenza so brilliantly proves; and he prayed that his disciples would learn that God loves each of them just as God loves him, and that his glory might be shared with them all (Jn 17.22-23). So for a man to relate to his wife as Christ relates to the church is to relate on an equal basis unheard of in patriarchy.

The Second Emancipative Element: The Husband's Self-Emptying
The second emancipative element in Eph. 5.21-22 is the precise limitation that is placed on the analogy of the husband to the Christ. Just as the wife is asked to submit only in the way the church submits to a Christ who lives within each of its members, so the husband/Christ comparison is limited only to a loving Christ in the experience of *kenosis*[42] or deliberate self-sacrifice: 'Husbands, love your wives, just as Christ loved the church and *gave up life for it'* (5.25; italics mine). The model for the Christian husband is Phil. 2.5-8: Christ's self-emptying of the privileges of divinity, voluntary servanthood, and obedience to God even to the point of death. What shockingly difficult news for a patriarchal male

---

41. See the chapters on 'The Christian Way of Relating' and 'The Patriarchal Way of Relating' in Mollenkott, *Women, Men, and the Bible.*

42. See Paula M. Cooey, 'Kenosis', in Russell and Clarkson (eds.), *Dictionary of Feminist Theologies,* for the ways feminist scholars have utilized the concept of *kenosis,* and for the Apostle Paul's insistence that Jesus' *kenosis* is a model for Christian behavior, especially the behavior of the 'strong' toward the 'weak' (p. 163).

accustomed to being waited on and getting his own way at all times! That he is expected to yield up his patriarchal advantages and humbly serve his wife's best interests just as Christ gave up everything in order to bring the church into being—no wonder this passage has rarely been fully implemented, and then only by a few of Christ's most dedicated disciples!

I remember getting a phone call years ago from Bill Gothard, who had developed the concept of women's being under male 'umbrellas of authority' and who filled auditoriums the size of Madison Square Garden, so popular were his seminars. Gothard told me he had recently read *Women, Men, and the Bible* and had a question for me: Since women were supposed to model for men the proper human relationship to God by being submissive to men, what would happen to the human race if everyone accepted my teachings about mutual servanthood? I responded by referring to Phil. 2.5: 'Why, Bill, in that case men as well as women would have to let that mind be in them which was also in Christ Jesus.' Gothard seemed never to have thought of such a possibility, but I believed then and I believe now that the concept of Christ's voluntary self-emptying of the privileges of divinity was precisely the model being offered to Christian husbands in Eph. 5.25. This model was not offered to women because they had no patriarchal privileges and power to surrender in the first place. Only the privileged male could 'love…even as Christ loved the church and gave himself up for it'. Only the male could Christianize the marital structure by stepping down to equality with his wife, as Christ stepped down to equality with human beings. Only the male in patriarchal society had sufficient status to honor his wife by raising her status to the point where he loved her as much as he loved himself. This is an exceedingly exacting standard.

Every analogy must be interpreted within the limits set by the person who creates the analogy; otherwise the meaning may become distorted. For instance, Jesus made an analogy between himself and a shepherd who knows and loves his sheep and would even lay down his life on their behalf (Jn 10.14-18). According to that analogy, we human beings are the sheep; and it is a fact that sheep are exceedingly stupid animals. But it would be wrong to use Jesus' analogy to lambaste human stupidity, because that is not at all in the loving spirit of the analogy. Similarly, to say that the comparison of the husband to Christ divinizes the patriarchal husband is to violate the precise parameters of the analogy. The husband is not compared to Christ in triumph and great glory as the judge of all the earth; the husband is compared only to the Christ who 'did not regard equality with God as something to be exploited, but emptied Christ's self, taking the form of a servant' (Phil. 2.6-7).

What is new in Ephesians 5 is not the dominant–submissive relation-ship of husband and wife, which was an established pattern in Greco-Roman society. What is new is the way both are instructed to relate to one another — as they relate to the Lord.[43] Obviously, there would be no wife-abuse in a home where the male took on Christlike servanthood. And no woman who knew that husband and wife are to be mutually supportive in reverence toward the Christ-nature within each of them would ever assume that she deserved to be abused during a life of one-way servanthood.

The Third Emancipative Element: The Interdependence of Head and Body
The third emancipative element in Eph. 5.21-33 is the concept of organic oneness between the husband as head and the wife as body: 'For the husband is the head of the wife just as Christ is the head of the church, the body of which Christ is the Savior' (v. 23). The Greek word for head, κεφαλή, refers to a human head, or to a point of origin such as the head of a stream, or to the chief support such as the head cornerstone of a building.

Hierarchalists have imagined that the headship of the Christian hus-band means that he is the decision maker who has the right to the final word. But in the Bible, the word 'head' is 'never connected with the intel-ligence. The ancient Hebrews were unaware of the function of the brain and, indeed, had no name for it; the intellectual powers were believed to be situated in the *heart*.'[44] Many passages indicate that the New Testa-ment authors also situated thought and decisions in the heart: Mt. 9.4, Mk 7.21, and the like. The heart was understood to be the seat of a human being's entire psychic life, including the emotions, the intellect, the volition, moral life, and the point of contact with God.[45] So if the author of Ephesians intended to say that the husband is the arbiter of the home's action plan, he would have written, 'The husband is the *heart* of the wife'. It is anachronistic to read into an ancient text a twentieth-century understanding of the cerebral cortex.

The body cannot live without the head, nor can the head survive with-out the body. If the results were not so devastating for human families and male–female intimacy, it would be amusing to notice how a patriarchal mindset can find hierarchy even in an image of utter mutual interdepen-dency. Interpreters such as Stephen Clark can see only the subordination

43.   Letha Dawson Scanzoni and Nancy Hardesty, *All We're Meant to Be* (Waco, TX: Word Books, 1974), pp. 98-100.

44.   R.C. Dentan, 'Head', *IDB*, II, p. 541.

45.   R.C. Dentan, 'Heart', *IDB*, II, p. 549.

of body to head, the wife to the husband: 'The two are supposed to function as one, and consequently the wife's life must be completely under the authority of the husband as head.'[46] Alas, Clark sounds like English Common Law, which defined husband and wife as one flesh, with that one flesh being *male* flesh.

It would appear that the concept of 'head' as moral and intellectual authority is a figment of the patriarchal imagination. The word κεφαλή is the only word used for 'head' in all the New Testament passages, whether they refer to a physical head or to a cornerstone or to a source. Yet in his famous concordance, Alexander Crudens says, without a shred of evidence, that Ephesians 5 uses 'head' in the sense of 'ruler, governor'. And in the *IDB* R.C. Dentan states:

> a characteristic biblical usage, apparently unknown to secular Greek, is that of the term 'head' as the leading member of a family (Exod. 6.14) or community (Deut. 33.3). Consequently it can be used to mean simply 'source of authority' as in depicting the superiority of man to woman in marriage (Eph. 5.23).[47]

Notice the astonishing lack of evidence and the failures of logic in the preceding quotation. If by Dentan's own admission 'head' does not mean 'leading family member' in secular Greek, and if the only biblical examples of such a meaning must be drawn from the Hebrew Scriptures, how can we know that the Greek of Ephesians 5 uses the word 'head' to mean 'leading family member'? Or that 'leading family member' is synonymous with 'source of authority'? Or that 'source of authority' is synonymous with 'superiority'? Only society's unquestioned patriarchal assumptions could have made Dentan's statement seem worthy of publication in a scholarly reference work.

Careful study of Eph. 5.21-33 would indicate that the word 'head' is being used chiefly in the sense of 'source'. Just as Christ is the source of the church because there could be no church before there was a savior, so the husband who empties himself of patriarchal privilege is the source of the Christian marital structure and, in that sense, the source of the Christian wife. If Christ were actually the head of the church as its leader, ruler, and governor, as patriarchalists insist, then surely the church could not be as fragmented, fractious, and unjust as it has been ever since its structure was adapted to Greco-Roman social norms. To interpret 'head' as 'leader' rather than 'source' is to blame the Christ for all the cruel faults

---

46. Stephen B. Clark, *Man and Woman in Christ: An Examination of the Roles of Men and Women in Light of Scripture and the Social Sciences* (Ann Arbor: Servant Books, 1980), p. 85.

47. Dentan, 'Head', p. 541.

of Christendom. Surely the burden of proof falls on those who insist on hierarchy where Jesus of Nazareth saw only a discipleship of equals!

Furthermore, although Eph. 5.23 depicts the human believer as the body of which Christ is the head, Eph. 5.30 also depicts Christ's own Self as the body of which believers are the members. How could the Ephesians author have emphasized organic interdependence more strongly than to compare marriage partners to head and body, and then to say that Christ's Self is *both* the head and the body?

Then again, as if to make assurance doubly sure, in Eph. 4.15 the author has urged the members of Christ's body to

> grow up in every way into the one who is the head — into Christ — from whom the whole body, joined and knit together by every ligament with which it is equipped, as each part is working properly promotes the body's growth in building itself up in love.

Lest anyone think the body/wife/church might be inferior to the head/husband/Christ, the members of the body are here enjoined to grow up into a complete identification with the head. In 4.15, just as in 5.23, *head* is used in the sense of 'source': it is from Christ the head/source that the whole body derives its organic unity, harmony, and mutual authority or mutual subjection.

If I were the author of Ephesians and could see the androcentric distortions of my head/body imagery, surely I would despair of trying to communicate with those who have no ears to hear. One batterer actually used the concept of being one flesh with his wife (5.31) and 'bone of my bones, flesh of my flesh' (Gen. 2.23) as justification for his violence against her, telling her when she complained of her injuries that 'your bones are my bones, just like it says in the Bible'.[48] Apparently the Ephesians author was blessedly unaware that certain experiences can cause people to hate and abuse their own bodies, for he claims that 'people never hate their own body, but nourish and tenderly care for it, just as Christ does for the church' (5.29). Unfortunately, victims of childhood abuse sometimes mutilate their own bodies, and certainly female socialization teaches girls to punish their bodies with diets (and possibly bulimia or anorexia) and uncomfortable shoes and clothing in order to meet standards of 'femininity'. Meanwhile male socialization teaches boys disdain for their own bodies by urging them to suffer (without crying) any amount of pain from sports injuries or during fitness training.

Despite this unawareness, though, the beauty of the author's intention is clear: a man is to love his partner's body as tenderly as the Christ/

---

48.   Quoted in Thistlethwaite, 'Every Two Minutes', p. 106.

head loves the church/body. Since Christ is the body as well as the head, by nourishing the church, Christ is nourishing Christ's own Self; as Christians we are all 'bone of Christ's bones, flesh of Christ's flesh'. Hence, 'husbands should love their wives as they do their own bodies' (5.28). To love one's partner is to love the Christ.

Another Unfortunate Example of Repressive Interpretation

It is painful to have to state that in *The Women's Bible Commentary*, E. Elizabeth Johnson retreats even farther than Schüssler Fiorenza from the emancipative elements in Eph. 5.21-33. Dr Johnson, who is Professor of New Testament at Columbia Theological Seminary, speaks of the 'rather unfortunate view of human marriage' in Ephesians 5 and charges the author with 'subordinating the interests of the women in the congregation to the interests of the church's public image'.[49] She emphasizes the problems she perceives in the text: First, although the Hebrew prophets use images of Israel as God's wife, the Ephesians author changes the metaphor into a description of reality, which makes the passage subject to enormous abuse. (For that matter, Womanist theologian Renita J. Weems has powerfully demonstrated that even the Hebrew marriage metaphors were conducive to real-life misogyny and abuse of women.[50])

Johnson argues that holding up a divine standard for human behavior creates an unavoidable contradiction when human beings cannot live up to the divine standard. However, it seems to me a positive thing to lift up an ideal toward which human beings can aspire. In the Ten Commandments, the Golden Rule, and most religious discourse, we habitually use a divine standard as a goal of human behavior. I would argue that creating an ideal for Christian marriage is the primary intention of Eph. 5.21-33, *not* the divinization of the husband and *not* the development of an impossible burden.

Second, Johnson argues that in Eph. 5.25 and 28, the analogy between Christ's love and husbandly love is illogical because 'husbands do not die for their wives as Christ died for the church, and Christ did not love his own body, as husbands are urged to do, but rather gave himself up for the church'.[51] Here Johnson's own logic has failed. Husbands *are* being asked to die for their wives metaphorically, by giving up the

---

49. E. Elizabeth Johnson, 'Ephesians', in Newsom and Ringe (eds.), *The Women's Bible Commentary*, expanded edn, pp. 428-32.

50. Renita J. Weems, *Battered Love: Marriage, Sex, and Violence in the Hebrew Prophets* (Minneapolis: Fortress Press, 1995).

51. Johnson, 'Ephesians', p. 431.

special privileges of male superiority. And Jesus' self-giving death for the church had nothing to do with lack of love toward his own body. Rather, Jesus was willing to lay down his physical body in order to create, nourish, and tenderly care for his larger cosmic body, the church, all the millions of sisters and brothers who share with Jesus the womb of God Herself (Acts 17.24-29). Because the incipient church/wife-in-patriarchy could do nothing until her identity was established, the activity of Eph. 5.25-27 is all on the part of the Christ/husband. The church/wife-in-patriarchy is passive and acted upon until such time as the structure of the marriage has been rendered Christian (that is, non-patriarchal, egalitarian, and mutual).

Third, Johnson charges that 'men are given an alarmingly self-serving motivation to love their wives' in Eph. 5.28. One wonders whether Johnson would similarly accuse Jesus (and Moses before him) for saying we should love our neighbors as we love ourselves (Mt. 22.36-40 and Lev. 19.18). It is not 'self-serving' to love our own bodies and our own selves; what is 'alarming' is that a feminist book would describe self-love and body-love as a 'self-serving motivation'. Most of the alarming brutalities in our culture arise from self-hatred, not from genuine self-love. For instance:

> Studies have found that the male spouse abuser has a poor self-image, feels he is less than he ought to be and feels he does not live up to society's ideal of masculinity. A man takes out his feelings of inadequacy and frustration on his wife because he feels he can, because he feels he can't tell off his boss, and because he feels that other men would respond to his aggression in kind.[52]

What abusers need is precisely to learn to love themselves so that they can learn to love others, including their wives.

Fourth, Johnson says:

> the parallel between Christ's being head of the church and a husband's being head of his wife is disrupted in the very same sentence, when Christ is identified as the 'savior' of the body, ...a role human husbands can scarcely assume on their wives' behalf.[53]

Johnson is apparently unable to move comfortably between metaphoric and literal levels. Here her collapse into literalism blinds her to the point being made in Eph. 5.23 and following: in the context of a patriarchal society, the husband has the opportunity to 'save' his wife from bondage

---

52.   Pope-Lance and Engelsman, *Domestic Violence*, p. 7.
53.   Johnson, 'Ephesians', p. 431.

and Christianize their marriage by imitating the self-giving of Jesus the Christ.

Fifth, Johnson accuses the Ephesians author of faulty logic for calling marriage a 'mystery', a word used elsewhere (Eph. 3.4) to refer to the inclusion of Gentiles within the church. For her, the analogy cannot work because 'in Ephesians the Jew/Gentile distinction is obliterated', whereas in marriage 'the distinction...regarding [gender] roles is strictly maintained'. She denies that the generic exhortation to mutuality (5.21) governs the ensuing passage and insists that 'the comparison of the unity of the church to the unity of a human marriage is yet another image that collapses under the weight of social inequality'. Although equality between Jew and Gentile received the author's blessing, 'any parallel equality between men and women remains a religious vision rather than a mark of everyday life in the home'.[54]

If by 'religious vision' Johnson means a promise of human equality in the sky bye and bye, then she is making a valid point, for Scriptures such as Gal. 3.28 and Eph. 5.21 are often said to refer to some future and ethereal justice, or perhaps to a metaphysical equality that makes absolutely no difference to human behavior here and now. But Johnson's generalization about 'religious vision' seems rather to demean all expression of social ideals grounded in concepts of the sacred. If biblical scholars think so little of religious vision, what can we expect from society in general?

Finally, Johnson assumes that instead of attempting to subvert hierarchical understandings of marriage, the Ephesians author actually teaches that hierarchy is inherent in the created order and necessary to the harmony of the universe. She claims that Eph. 5.31 quotes Gen. 2.24 in order to ground 'the [patriarchal] institution of marriage not in social order but in creation'. And she says that the concern of Ephesians is that the church must 'faithfully mirror the [hierarchical] creation and that the household [must] mirror the [hierarchical] church. The result for women is thus a retreat from the initial freedom promised them in Paul's preaching and a reassertion of conventional patriarchal morality.'[55]

The only liberating word for an oppressed woman reading Johnson's commentary is that one fleeting reference to early Christianity's promise of human freedom from race, class, and gender inequities. There is a flat denial that the call for mutual subjection is intended to govern the entire discussion of Christian marriage. There is no recognition that the husband is compared to the Christ only in Christ's self-emptying of superior

54. Johnson, 'Ephesians', p. 431.
55. Johnson, 'Ephesians', p. 431.

status, taking on voluntary servanthood. There is no recognition that the word 'head' is used not in the sense of 'boss' but in the sense of 'source'; nor is there any mention of the facts that Christ is identified with the body as well as the head, that the church/body is urged to grow up into the Christ/head, that the human head and body are mutually interdependent, and therefore that the Christian marital structure is depicted as an organic union of mutual subjection and inter-supportiveness. No misogynist could have trashed conservative religious women's hope for liberating insights more thoroughly than this article in *The Women's Bible Commentary*. And for those women who view Ephesians as the divinely inspired and inerrant Word of God, such interpretation is truly devastating. Do liberal scholars care about such women?

Why an Emancipative Approach Matters

Please note that my concern is not to defend the Bible, as evangelical feminists are sometimes accused of doing. It is true that my background is fundamentalist, that I still consider myself an evangelical liberationist, and that to this day I am an active member of the Evangelical and Ecumenical Women's Caucus.[56] It is also true that I spent many years of my life teaching college and graduate-level literature, and that I believe every book deserves to be approached affirmatively, meaning that the reader should assume a profound human connection with the author unless and until the author's values (embodied in choices of words, images, and structures) force the reader into an adversarial stance. Nevertheless, my concern is not to defend either the Bible or God Herself—both can take care of themselves. My concern is to defend the people in this world who are marginalized, oppressed, and brutalized. In the case of Eph. 5.21-33, that group is those religious women who have accepted an inferior status in marriage and even the abuse of themselves and their children on the basis of patriarchal interpretations of the sacred text.

Because domestic violence is so widespread, it is not enough to manifest a scholarly 'objectivity' in discussion of texts like Eph. 5.21-33, placing

---

56.   For information, write to the Evangelical and Ecumenical Women's Caucus, PO Box 3415, Wichita, KS 67201-3415, USA. For a sample copy of the organization's publication, write to *EEWC Update*, PO Box 11604, Norfolk, VA 23517. The website is at http://www.eewc.com

Contrary to Mary McClintock Fulkerson's statement that 'Evangelical feminist literature…documents [that] even the household code texts can be read to claim love and to contain fears' ('Contesting Feminist Canons: Discourse and the Problem of Sexist Texts', *JFSR* 7 [1991], pp. 55-73 [70]), I have seen no evidence of fearful rationalizations of male supremacy in EEWC. Perhaps Fulkerson is unaware of the 'Evangelical Left'.

them in their historical context and assuming that the author is fully in agreement with that context, so that the passage is unworthy of further discussion. As I was finishing this article, I received a manuscript that illustrates the approach I am urging as responsible feminist scholarship: Adrian Thatcher's *Marriage after Modernity: Christian Marriage in Postmodern Times*.[57] Thatcher acknowledges that post-Christian writers praise sexual relationships that celebrate equality and mutuality, yet notices that they have done little to foster enduring and spiritually profound relationships. So Thatcher calls for postmodern, yet Christian, marriages — equal partnerships that reject patriarchal norms, yet center upon a covenant of unconditional love. As Thatcher himself puts it:

> The end of patriarchy does not mean the end of unprovisional commitment; it merely removes the main obstacle in the way of exercising [unprovisional commitment]... The obligation [to love as Christ loved] is not diminished, but rather, intensified, because, after patriarchy, it becomes a shared one, and consequently one that is likely to have a higher chance of being carried out.[58]

While Thatcher might not agree with everything I have said about Ephesians 5, certainly he does more than simply stop after placing this text (and every other biblical text concerning marriage) into patriarchal context. He wrestles with the meanings, and wherever he sees them, extrapolates liberating insights that are instructive for meaningful partnerships (same-sex as well as hetero-sex) in a postmodern world. I hope that Thatcher's approach is indicative of a whole new trend in feminist biblical scholarship.[59]

Susan Thistlethwaite reports:

> In workshops for persons who work with abused women, I have found that most social workers, therapists, and shelter personnel view religious beliefs as uniformly reinforcing passivity and tend to view religion, both traditional Christianity and Judaism, as an obstacle to a woman's successful handling of abuse. Unfortunately, they also say that many strongly religious women cease attending shelters and groups for abused women when these beliefs are attacked.[60]

Such women need to hear Thistlethwaite's words of assurance: 'You have a right both to your religious beliefs and to your self-esteem.'[61]

57. A. Thatcher, *Marriage after Modernity: Christian Marriage in Postmodern Times* (New York: New York University Press, 1999).

58. Thatcher, *Marriage after Modernity*, p. 236.

59. See also Adrian Thatcher, ' "Crying Out for Discussion" — Premodern Marriage in Postmodern Times', *Theology and Sexuality* 8 (1998), pp. 73-95.

60. Thistlethwaite, 'Every Two Minutes', p. 100.

61. Thistlethwaite, 'Every Two Minutes', p. 100.

For the sake of those strongly religious women, I am grateful for the courage of Womanist scholars[62] and those feminist scholars such as Adrian Thatcher who will not only deplore the abuses of Scripture and patriarchal biblical backgrounds but then will also seek out and apply to current concerns the Bible's prophetic and liberating insights. I am calling on mainstream feminist Bible scholars to become similarly prophetic by manifesting a similar concern for how their work will fall upon the ears of religious women who desperately need to be shown a liberationist hermeneutic. For the sake of those whose trust in scholarship collapses as soon as the Bible is frontally attacked, Scripture should always be discussed in respectful tones, even when a necessary hermeneutic of suspicion is being taught and applied. And wherever there is an emancipative element in Scripture, it should be both detailed and emphasized.[63] In this way, Bible scholars can communicate to women the message that they have a right both to their religious beliefs and to their self-esteem.

---

62. See Renita J. Weems, 'Reading Her Way through the Struggle: African-American Women and the Bible', in Felder (ed.), *Stony the Road We Trod*, pp. 57-77; and Martin, 'The *Haustafeln*', pp. 206-31.

63. Another outstanding example of the approach I am calling for is Phyllis Trible's *God and the Rhetoric of Sexuality* (OBT; Philadelphia: Fortress Press, 1978). Even in *Texts of Terror* (Philadelphia: Fortress Press, 1984), p. 108, Trible encourages feminists to 'recover and reappropriate' those horrific stories.

(Re)Describing Reality?
The Transformative Potential of Ephesians
across Times and Cultures*

Elna Mouton

Introduction

The challenge of this essay is the continuing relevance or transformative potential of the biblical documents as ancient canonized texts originating from within patriarchal value systems. The epistle to the Ephesians provides a special case study for (re)describing the processes involved in textual communication. Its distinctiveness for this purpose is related to its explicit focus on the reinterpretation of power and its exigency of a deeply divided society as a possible analogy for the challenges facing South African churches at the beginning of the new century. The kaleidoscope of cultural systems represented in South Africa are all intrinsically characterized by values such as patriarchy, gender and racial stereotyping, and social stratification, which necessarily obscure respect for human dignity in general, and the role and talent of women and their participation in social institutions in particular. These values profoundly determine the economic, political, relational, mechanical, and electronic 'powers and principalities' in the marketplace, thereby influencing the quality of millions of people's lives. Moreover, our South African society is tortured by an exceptionally high incidence of power-related crimes such as murder and rape. The situation urgently challenges the integrity and relevance not only of the churches in South Africa, but also of theological education at large. It emphasizes the continuing need for the formation of a moral agency, the empowerment of Christian identity and ethos, and an accountable use of Scripture in Christian ethos.[1] The

---

*   This chapter is a reworked version of an earlier article, 'The Transformative Potential of Ephesians in a Situation of Transition', *Semeia 78* (1997) (= *Reading the Bible as Women: Perspectives from Africa, Asia, and Latin America*), pp. 121-43. Reprinted by permission.

   1.   Elna Mouton, 'The (Trans)formative Potential of the Bible as Resource for Christian Ethos and Ethics', *Scriptura* 62 (1997), pp. 245-57.

former often still functions as a justification of the 'submissive' role of women in church and society.

Categories and skills developed by such related disciplines as anthropology, sociology, literary science, classical and modern rhetoric, and hermeneutics support an examination of communication processes represented and stimulated by the Ephesians text. Its implied readers find themselves within a liminal or transitional phase characterized by an encompassing change in the attitude of their minds (4.23). This change is marked by shifts both from a view of God and humanity defined by exclusivity and separation (between people and God and between Jewish and Gentile believers) to an identity and ethos of inclusivity and unity, and from an emphasis on cultic activities (covenant, circumcision, law, temple) to an emphasis on relations in which people of different ethnic groups, gender, and social status have been united with Christ into one body or household. As the medium between radically contrasting elements, between different modes of existence, Ephesians functions as a threshold, a bridge, or a metaphor between the known and the unknown, between the 'already' and the 'not yet', and between remembrance and eschatological hope. It is particularly the dynamics of this 'betwixt-and-between' stage that provides its author and readers with the stimulus, values, and virtues to redefine their humanity and moral existence. The author facilitates these processes by *inter alia* utilizing metaphor and tradition as rhetorical strategies. These seem to have a paraenetic and transformative function analogous to that of ritual and rites of passage during liminal phases in the lives of individuals and groups, reflected in liturgical elements such as prayer, hymns, and references to the initiating rite of baptism in 4.5; 5.26-27.[2]

From Boundaries to Thresholds: The Dynamics of Liminality as Reconciliatory Strategy between Different Worlds

The concept of 'liminality' was introduced by the French anthropologist Arnold van Gennep, who uses the term 'rites of passage' in connection with the ceremonies and rituals performed at different stages in the life cycle of individuals and groups (birth, puberty, marriage, parenthood, retirement, and death). Van Gennep compares such events to the crossing of boundaries between territories. Like geographical boundaries that consist of stretches of land that function as neutral zones, a change from one phase of the life cycle to another often consists of a period of

---

2.   John C. Kirby, *Ephesians: Baptism and Pentecost. An Inquiry into the Structure and Purpose of the Epistle to the Ephesians* (London: SPCK, 1968).

time that functions as a neutral zone, where the person is neither in the one stage nor in the other. These rites or ceremonies serve principally to provide guidance for the responsibilities encountered in the new phase.[3] Van Gennep distinguishes three types of rites, namely rites of separation from a previous world, rites of transition, and rites of incorporation into a new world.[4] Using the Latin word *limen* (threshold), he respectively calls these rites preliminal, liminal, and postliminal.

In the fields of cultural anthropology and sociology the notion of liminality has since been developed further by several scholars, in particular by North American anthropologist Victor Turner. It has also been adapted and appropriated by theologians such as Gerald Arbuckle and Leo Perdue (both with reference to Turner), and Mark Kline Taylor,[5] with reference to anthropologist Paul Rabinow. Mindful of the resocialization of Christian communities into new roles and groups, Arbuckle[6] reworked Turner's social-anthropological model[7] by emphasizing three major phases during a time of change. The first involves a breach or separation from the known (often a well-structured, prosperous, and orderly situation, also known as a *societas* phase). The second is a liminal, often a crisis phase of transition, during which previous roles, regulations, structures, and certainties may be relativized and fundamentally rearranged. This phase is often a lengthy and complicated process, during which people feel an urgent need to discover meaning in what is happening, and to redefine their humanity. Turner refers to this as a *communitas* phase, a phase of 'reflexivity' and 'redressive action'.[8] A third phase is that of reintegration and reconstitution into new roles and groups, often by means of insights gained during the liminal phase. Taylor develops liminality, together with 'admiration', as a Christian reconciliatory strategy for dealing with human differences. He observes:

> *Liminality* is the term I reserve for the kind of life known 'betwixt and between' differentiated persons, groups or worlds. This is an experience of

---

3.   Arnold van Gennep, *The Rites of Passage* (trans. M.B. Vizedom and G.L. Caffee; London: Routledge & Kegan Paul, 1960), pp. 1-13, 21.

4.   Van Gennep, *The Rites of Passage*, pp. 15-25, 192-94.

5.   Mark K. Taylor, *Remembering Esperanza: A Cultural-Political Theology for North American Praxis* (Maryknoll, NY: Orbis Books, 1990), pp. 199-208.

6.   Gerald A. Arbuckle, *Grieving for Change: A Spirituality for Refounding Gospel Communities* (London: Geoffrey Chapman, 1991), pp. 31-37.

7.   Victor Turner, *Dramas, Fields, and Metaphors: Symbolic Action in Human Society* (Ithaca, NY: Cornell University Press, 1974), pp. 37-42; Leo G. Perdue, 'The Social Character of Paraenesis and Paraenetic Literature', *Semeia* 50 (1990), pp. 5-39 (9-11).

8.   Turner, *Dramas, Fields, and Metaphors*, pp. 45-57, 273-74.

the wonder, the disorientation and discomfort that can rise when one is suspended between or among different groups or persons.[9]

Taylor describes the liminal space between cultural boundaries as a difficult, fragile, risky, and trying experience, in which the ambiguities and strains are not easily tolerated. At the same time the liminal encounter represents a dynamic and dialectic process wherein no one remains static. As new alliances are constructed in the interaction between different worlds, people's moral identities and lifestyles are reconstituted. Despite their different time-frames and historical situations, and the different disciplines from which they write, both Van Gennep and Taylor emphasize the elements of risk and creativity extant within liminality.

The addressees of the epistle to the Ephesians are referred to as 'saints...the faithful in Christ Jesus' (1.1, 15). They seem mainly to originate from a Gentile background (2.11). The document presents its readers' movement and growth from one world to another, from a position outside Christ to being 'in Christ', as a continuous wrestling to understand, a risky process with significant analogies to Van Gennep's stages of separation, transition, and incorporation. However, the structure of the Ephesian rhetoric does not seem necessarily to resemble a linear pattern guiding its readers from a preliminal into a postliminal phase, but rather a cyclical movement of continuous reinterpretation and renewal within liminal space. Its implied readers have already accepted Christ, and the author wishes to guide them towards a better understanding of that honorable position. He therefore does not introduce a movement into or out of liminality, but within a liminality that he simply presupposes. The structure of this movement is a continual recycling of their life and world view — an ongoing reinterpretation of traditions, language, and behavior in terms of Jesus Christ. By inducing a process of continuous reorientation to Christ, Ephesians serves as a warning against any form of moral stagnation, false stability, absolute certainty, or closed ethical system. It is in this context that I believe its rhetoric and quest for moral identity and appropriate behavior has to be understood (1.4; 4.13; 5.27). In tandem with other disciplines, Van Gennep and Turner's analysis seem to be helpful in understanding the complex nature of liminality in a more nuanced way. In textual communication the movement within liminal space may be described in terms of the typical metaphorical processes of orientation, disorientation (alienation), and reorientation.[10]

---

9.   Taylor, *Remembering Esperanza*, p. 200.
10.   Paul Ricoeur, *The Rule of Metaphor: Multi-Disciplinary Studies of the Creation of Meaning in Language* (trans. R. Czerny, K. McLaughlin and J. Costello; Toronto:

Boundaries and Implied Shifts in the Moral Identity
and Ethos of the Ephesian Community

Ephesians is generally divided into four major sections, namely the opening (1.1-2), a first and second main section (1.3–3.21 and 4.1–6.20, respectively), and the ending (6.21-24).[11] Both the greetings at the beginning and the farewell wishes at the end contain the powerful blessing of χάρις and εἰρήνη, summarizing the document's view on humanity as one of wholeness in relation to God and fellow believers (1.6-7; 2.5-8, 14-17; 3.2, 7-8; 4.3; 6.15).[12] The eulogy of Eph. 1.3-14 (with the significant recurrence of εὐλογέω in 1.3) announces the thrust of the first main section—and also of the whole document—as a celebration of God's gracious blessings toward all people in Christ. That section contains various elements such as utterances of praise, thanksgiving, intercessory prayers, and confessions of faith. It is generally accepted that all these elements express the doxological exclamation or appeal to praise God, followed by the reasons why God has to be praised, that are related to the typical Jewish prayer form called the *berakah*.[13] Fundamentally, the *berakah* was an act of remembrance or orientation, where God was to be praised for the way God had worked in the past. By remembering God's deeds, the people were moved again to praise God.[14] In the case of Ephesians the act of remembering at the same time became an act of 'dismembering' or disorientation—a typical trait of liminality—because of the way in which previous traditions such as election, covenant, law, and the temple with its dividing wall had to be reinterpreted in the light of the Christ event (1.4; 2.11-18; 4.7-10).

These details point to a possible historical situation for Ephesians in the prejudice and underlying tension between the Jewish and Gentile

University of Toronto Press, 1977); Sallie McFague, *Metaphorical Theology: Models of God in Religious Language* (Philadelphia: Fortress Press, 1982), among others.

11. Elna Mouton, 'Reading Ephesians Ethically: Criteria Towards a Renewed Identity Awareness?', *Neot* 28/2 (1994), pp. 359-77 (363-68); *idem, Reading a New Testament Document Ethically* (Atlanta: Society of Biblical Literature; Leiden: E.J. Brill, 2002), pp. 53-87.

12. Greek references in this essay are from the third edition of the United Bible Societies' *Greek New Testament* (New York: United Bible Societies, 1975), and English references to the NIV.

13. Johnnie H. Roberts, *The Letter to the Ephesians* (Cape Town: Lux Verbi, 1991), p. 15; Rudolf Schnackenburg, *The Epistle to the Ephesians* (trans. H. Heron; Edinburgh: T. & T. Clark, 1991), pp. 44-47.

14. Luke T. Johnson, *The Writings of the New Testament: An Interpretation* (Minneapolis: Fortress Press, rev. edn, 1999), pp. 59-60.

Christian communities in western Asia Minor during the first century CE
(Eph. 2.11). Whether the document dates from an early period such as 58–
61 CE,[15] or a deutero-Pauline period,[16] the basic 'exigence'[17] in terms of
the struggle for identity among Jewish and Gentile Christians remained
acute and was intensified after the Roman–Jewish War (66–70 CE) when
the tension between Jews and Christians gradually led to a break between
the synagogue and the Christian communities around 85 CE. The thrust of
Ephesians thus reveals a serious flaw in the implied readers' understanding of God and themselves. However, although the relation between Jewish and Gentile Christians seems to be the main need which the author
wished to address, there were apparently also other (even more basic?)
features that distorted the Ephesian community's sense of humanity (e.g.
the inherently patriarchal structure seen in the household code in 5.21–
6.9). Taylor argues, 'The most fundamental form of otherness is male/
female otherness. If this otherness is marked by opposition and disdain, it
will be easier to oppose other others — be they black, Jewish, foreign, or
poor.'[18] Taylor continues by saying that only after reflection on this form
of dominance has been done may exploration of the whole tangle of
oppression's infrastructure begin. From a contemporary perspective, one
could therefore say that a complex set of issues probably contributed to
the exigence behind Ephesians, namely, the confirmation of the readers'
identity and ethos in relation to Christ and one another. Within this
context the power of Christ's sacrificial love is emphasized as a reconciliatory strategy through which any 'dividing wall' between people had
been abolished.

Another significant trait of the first main section is that its different
elements are arranged in an A-B-C-B-A chiastic pattern. This means that
not only the recurring elements of the eulogy in 1.3-14 and the doxology
in 3.20-21, and the two intercessory prayers in 1.15-21 and 3.1, 14-19 are
emphasized by the particular structure, but specifically the confession of
faith in 1.22-23 (with its three illustrative explanations in 2.1-22) as a non-
repeating middle section.[19] The dramatic consequences of 1.22-23 are
particularly described in transitional terms: Those who were dead have

15. Markus Barth, *Ephesians 1–3* (AB, 34; New York: Doubleday, 1974), pp. 10-12;
Roberts, *Ephesians*, p. 13.
16. Paul J. Sampley, 'Scripture and Tradition in the Community as Seen in Ephesians 4.25ff.', *ST* 26 (1972), pp. 101-109 (102); Schnackenburg, *Ephesians*, pp. 24-29;
Andrew T. Lincoln, *Ephesians* (WBC, 42; Dallas: Word Books, 1990), pp. xxxv-lxxiii.
17. Lloyd F. Bitzer, 'The Rhetorical Situation', *Philosophy and Rhetoric* 1 (1968), pp.
1-14.
18. Taylor, *Remembering Esperanza*, p. 82.
19. Roberts, *Ephesians*, pp. 14-19.

been made alive (2.1-10); those who were far away, excluded from citizenship in Israel, have been brought near (2.11-18); and those who formerly had been power- and statusless foreigners and aliens (ξένοι καὶ πάροικοι) have been made fellow citizens with God's people and members of God's household (2.19-22). By destroying the barrier of hostility through his cross (2.14-16), Christ gave birth to a new creation, a new humanity.

The pivotal confession of 1.22-23, which summarizes the preceding prayer (1.12-21), deals with two closely related matters: the exalted position of Jesus as resurrected and sovereign lord, and his significance as a gift of salvation to the believers as liminals. The second aspect defines the first in a profound and surprising way. In the context of Ephesians, Christ's magnificent power and honor (as lord and head) is decisively yet paradoxically defined in terms of his sacrificial love, humility, and care as servant (1.7; 2.13, 16; 4.32; 5.2, 25, 29). This position is characterized particularly by the memory of his cross—the rite of passage par excellence, which he performed on behalf of his followers. His cross, resurrection, and ascension guaranteed their salvation through faith in him, and yet would throw them into a permanent state of liminality. The metaphors of head, body and fullness thus function as shifting devices in thrusting the readers' thoughts towards a full understanding of their new humanity in Christ.[20]

Two factors accomplish this linking of the experience of Christ to the identity of the believers in their situation of liminality. First, the images of head (1.10; 4.15-16; 5.23, 29-30), body (4.12-16; 5.29-30), and fullness (3.19; 4.13; 5.18) in 1.22-23 stress the close and inseparable relationship between God's people and Christ. As head, Christ incorporated all who belong to him into one body when he accomplished their salvation. What has happened to him has happened to them. When he was raised from the dead, they were raised with him. When he was seated at God's right hand, they were seated with him (2.4-6). The structure of 2.6 is syntactically parallel to that of 1.20, which is of major rhetorical significance (note the two aorist indicatives συνήγειρεν and συνεκάθισεν in 2.6, and the two aorist participles ἐγείρας and καθίσας in 1.20). The second factor is the symbol of the cross. Within the Mediterranean sociological world of the first century, death on a cross was considered as an extremely shameful event.[21] In Ephesians this symbol is reinter-

20. G. Daan Cloete and Dirk J. Smit, 'Preaching from the Lectionary: Eph 1.20-23', *JTSA* 63 (1988), pp. 59-67.

21. Saul M. Olyan, 'Honor, Shame, and Covenant Relations in Ancient Israel and Its Environment', *JBL* 115 (1996), pp. 201-18 (214 n. 43).

preted and becomes, through the resurrection, an honorable deed for the benefit of those who adhere to Christ by faith.[22] It is the memory of these glorious yet strange events which was meant to shape the moral identity and ethos of the readers of Ephesians during the liminal process.

The second main section of the letter consists primarily of paraenetic elements directed to the church. These are interwoven with theological and christological motivations, and intrinsically linked to and informed by the first main section. The structural and semantic coherence between the two main sections is indicated by such conjunctions as οὖν, τοῦτο οὖν and διό in 4.1, 17, 25 and 5.15, which indicate the particular sections they introduce as a direct and logical consequence of what had been said before.[23] The essence of Ephesians 1–3 (a new humanity in relation to Christ and fellow believers) is thus explicated in terms of a life worthy of their calling (4.1). In fact, it was particularly the *communitas* experience of reconciliation between Jewish and Gentile Christians that opened their eyes to recognize their full potential in Christ. Ephesians 4–6 contains the radical implications of this insight. They should be 'kind and compassionate to one another, forgiving each other, just as in Christ God forgave you' (4.32). They should live a life of love, 'just as Christ loves you and gave himself up for you' (5.2; 4.2). They were to 'put on the new self, created to be like God in true righteousness and holiness' (4.24). Within the covenant vocabulary of the Hebrew Bible, honor was closely connected with justice, righteousness, and peace.[24] Consequently, the virtues and values characteristic of their new paradoxical status in Christ were also meant to redefine the traditionally patriarchal relations described in the domestic code of 5.21–6.9. The husband, for instance, hears that he is the head of the wife 'as Christ is the head of the church' (5.23). Christ's headship is characterized by the power of his love—a power which is paradoxically revealed in the 'weakness' of his suffering. The husband also has to submit to his wife (5.21), and to love her 'just as Christ loved the church and gave himself up for her' (5.25). The domestic code likewise encourages the wife to claim her primary identity in Christ and to be empowered by his example. Her role implies submission to a husband whose humanity is implicitly modeled on the example of Christ.

---

22. Wayne A. Meeks, *The Origins of Christian Morality: The First Two Centuries* (New Haven: Yale University Press, 1993), pp. 14-15, 61-65, 131-35.

23. Mouton, *Reading a New Testament Document Ethically*, pp. 70-75; Holland Hendrix, 'On the Form and Ethos of Ephesians', *USQR* 42 (1988), pp. 3-15.

24. Olyan, 'Honor, Shame, and Covenant Relations', p. 202 n. 3.

The Structure of the Ephesian Rhetoric as an
Ongoing Movement within Liminal Space

The continuing, risky process by which the Ephesian readers had to learn to match their new identity to a lifestyle (and language) worthy of their calling occurred in the creative, imaginative, liminal tension between remembrance and hope. While remembering not only their former way of living as Gentiles (2.11, 12), but especially what God has done for them in Christ (1.3–3.20; 4.20-24; 5.8), they were looking forward to the 'day of redemption' when they would inherit their full salvation (1.14; 4.30). In the interim their hope would be kept alive by their memory of the Christ event and through their response to the ongoing encounter with the risen Christ and the Spirit (2.22; 3.17; 4.6, 10, 30; 5.18). Amid the danger of evil powers (6.10-13), it was particularly from within the liminal space that they would be transformed and energized to grow toward their full potential in Christ (4.1, 12-16; 5.23-24, 32; 5.1-2; 6.10).

The Ephesian author facilitates this process by continuously reminding his readers of the privilege and associated ethos of their new position in Christ, in contrast to who they were before. In this way he maintains the cyclical movement within their liminal situation. Significant in this regard is the present imperative μνημονεύετε introducing 2.11-19 ('Remember that formerly you who are Gentiles by birth…were separate from Christ, excluded from citizenship in Israel and foreigners to the covenants of the promise… But now in Christ Jesus you…have been brought near'). It denotes a continuous redeeming of the past, while confirming the readers' new beginning in Christ.[25]

The cyclical structure of the rhetoric in the intercessory prayer of 1.15-23 is emphasized by the author's introduction in 1.16-18. The main verb οὐ παύομαι is followed by two present participles (εὐχαριστῶν ὑπὲρ ὑμῶν and μνείαν ποιούμενος), as well as a purpose clause in the perfect tense (εἰς τὸ εἰδέναι ὑμᾶς), implying a continuous effect in the present ('I have not stopped giving thanks for you, remembering you in my prayers. I keep asking the God of our Lord Jesus Christ… that you may know…'). The rest of the first main section pictures the grace of God — the basic motivation for the believers' new identity — in terms of a continuous present activity (1.19, 23; 2.4, 8, 10, 18-19, 21-22; 3.6, 12-13, 15, 20).

It is especially in the paraenetic section of Ephesians (chs. 4–6) that the cyclical pattern of its rhetoric comes to the fore. Within the broad

---

25. Bernard C. Lategan, 'Imagination and Transformation: Ricoeur and the Role of Imagination', *Scriptura* 58 (1996), pp. 213-32 (229).

structure of the document,[26] the present imperatives in 4.17, 23, 25, 30, 32; 5.1-2, 8b, 10, 18-21 (as well as other present tense forms in those two chapters) indicate a process of continuous moral formation in accordance with the community's new identity in Christ. The imperatives following 5.18 ('Be filled with the Spirit…') in the domestic code and the armor of God passage confirm the rhetorical pattern of continuous action in the present as the only proper ethos worthy of their calling (5.24-25, 27-29, 33; 6.1-10, 16, 18).

In this open-ended movement within liminality, the question may arise as to what extent the rhetoric of Ephesians allows for the existence or formation of boundaries. How, for instance, would a community of faith whose understanding of God and reality is characterized by a cyclical movement of reinterpretation deal with the continual confrontation with and assimilation of strangers, and with new knowledge, new experiences, and new situations? From within the context of Ephesians it is clear that any structures and boundaries (necessary though they may be under given circumstances) would only be justifiable in so far as they impel movement, communication, healing, reconciliation, and moral formation.[27] Where they inhibit movement, stop communication, or absolutize differences, they have to be dismantled. The rhetorical processes in Ephesians resemble an ongoing interaction between the identity awareness and ethos of followers of Christ. The document thus considers the creativity, tension, paradox, and risk of liminal spaces as the optimal context for moral formation and growth.

Within the movement of the Ephesian rhetoric mentioned above, the nature of Christ's power in 1.22 and its relation to wifely submission in 5.22 deserve special attention. It is rhetorically significant that the strategic verb ὑποτάσσω in 1.22 (as part of the faith confession) recurs in its middle form ὑποτάσσομαι in the paraenetical section of the document (5.21, 24). In both instances it is surrounded and nuanced by a context referring to the fullness or wholeness of the body of Christ. The verb ὑποτάσσω, meaning 'to subject to' or 'to bring under the control of someone',[28] was used as a military term in the first-century Mediterranean context, referring to the acknowledgment of a person's status, dignity, and authority embodied in others' obedience, loyalty, and

---

26. Mouton, *Reading a New Testament Document Ethically*, pp. 54-75; Roberts, *Ephesians*, pp. 14-21.

27. Taylor, *Remembering Esperanza*, p. 207.

28. Johannes P. Louw and Eugene A. Nida (eds.), *Greek–English Lexicon of the New Testament* (Cape Town: Bible Society of South Africa, 1989), p. 476.

submission to that person's directives and wishes.[29] The verb ὑποτάσ-σεται in 5.24 likewise means 'to take a subordinate role in relation to that of another'.[30]

As a general injunction and motivation, respectively, Eph. 5.21 and 6.9b frame the household code by reinterpreting its patriarchal structure from a christological perspective. Eph. 5.21 is a transitional verse 'completing the series of participles which are dependent on the verb πληροῦσθε, "be filled", from v. 18, while itself providing the verbal form on which the first injunction in the…household code is dependent'.[31] The idiomatic expression in 6.9b (καὶ προσωπολημψία οὐκ ἔστιν παρ᾽ αὐτῷ, from λαμβάνω πρόσωπον) literally means 'He does not lay hold of someone's face' — in other words, 'He does not esteem anyone according to face value', as in Deut. 10.17; 16.19; Lev. 19.15; Mt. 22.16; Mk 12.14; Lk. 20.21; Acts 10.34; Rom. 2.11; Gal. 2.6; Col. 3.25.[32] It probably originated in the context of slavery, where slaves were chained to one another while waiting to be sold on the market. As inferiors they were not allowed to lift up their heads until a potential buyer would do so, sometimes brutally, in order to examine their teeth and general health. In Eph. 6.9, as well as parallel expressions in Deut. 10.17; 16.19, and Lev. 19.15, this phrase occurs in a context that emphasizes God's sovereignty and almighty power. In contrast to the often abusive power of contemporary authorities, the essence of God's power is defined in terms of loving care and concern for people, and particularly by God's restoring what was lost to them, namely, their dignity and humanity. The Ephesians author thus seems radically to reverse the patriarchal connotation of ὑποτάσσω (as imposed loyalty and obedience) to reflect not only the essence of the relationship between Christ and the church (in terms of willing honor and reverence), but also among the members of the body itself. On this point, note also the semantically related terms φοβέομαι in 5.33, ὑπακούω in 6.1, 5, and τιμάω in 6.2, which all relate to the guiding principle for wise living in the Old Testament covenant, namely the 'fear of YHWH'. This profound reverence for the God of Israel is reinterpreted here as the overriding motivation for wise Christian living (1.8, 17; 5.15) and for relationships within the new community. It is an attitude that looks to Christ in awe at his overwhelming love

29. Louw and Nida (eds.), *Greek–English Lexicon*, p. 468.
30. Lincoln, *Ephesians*, p. 367.
31. Lincoln, *Ephesians*, p. 365.
32. Louw and Nida (eds.), *Greek–English Lexicon*, p. 768; Mouton, *Reading a New Testament Document Ethically*, pp. 72-73.

and power[33] — as paradoxical expressions of his obedience, humility, and submission to God's will. These expressions implicitly resemble the thrust of the document as a radical reinterpretation of human relations in the light of the Christ event.

However, read from a twenty-first-century feminist perspective, and reading from within the current sociopolitical context in South Africa, the patriarchal language that expresses and constitutes the christologically reinterpreted notion of mutual submission in the domestic code (5.21) creates tension and a sense of inconsistency and distance, particularly with regard to the role of wives and slaves, and therefore runs a serious risk of being abused by later readers. Its *Wirkungsgeschichte* indeed very often tragically witnesses to the contrary of its intended rhetorical effect of wholeness, peace, and righteousness. Walls of separation have been rebuilt, the submissive role of wives has often been overemphasized, and as a result the church's vision of God, itself, and its mission in society has been seriously obscured and blurred.[34]

Nowhere in Ephesians is the vulnerability of the hermeneutical process better illustrated than by the relation between its liberating vision of reconciliation, unity, and mutuality, and the typical patriarchal language that describes that vision by notions such as 'sonship' (1.15), Christ as 'head' (1.22; 4.15; 5.23), 'one new man' (2.15), 'wifely submission' (5.22), and slaves' obedience with 'respect and fear' toward their masters (6.5). The paradigm used for Christian marriage in 5.22-33 is the relation between Christ and the church. Wives are made the image of the church, whereas husbands are made the image of Christ, which gives a theological basis to an inferiority of the female to the male in terms of a divinely willed order. In spite of the radical reinterpretation of patriarchal domination by the paradoxical example of Christ, the language structure of Eph. 5.21–6.9 raises serious questions for later readers: Does the language (of mutuality and submission) challenge, reinterpret, or reassert the conventional connotations and contexts of a hierarchichally ordered morality? Does it serve as a prophetic vision for the relationship between Christ and the church? Or does it — at this point — reinforce a cultural-patriarchal pattern of subordination by describing (instead of *redescribing*) reality, and thereby modifying the received Pauline baptismal tradition of Gal. 3.28?

Schüssler Fiorenza argues that this theological paradigm:

33.   Lincoln, *Ephesians*, pp. 365-68.

34.   Elna Mouton, 'Die Verhaal van Afrikaanse Christenvroue', *Scriptura* 63 (1997), pp. 475-90; *idem*, 'Remembering Forward and Hoping Backward? Some Thoughts on Women in the Dutch Reformed Church', *Scriptura* 76 (2001), pp. 77-86.

reinforces the cultural-patriarchal pattern of subordination, insofar as the relationship between Christ and the church clearly is not a relationship between equals, since the church-bride is totally dependent and subject to her head or bridegroom. Therefore, the general injunction for all members of the Christian community, 'Be subject to one another in the fear of Christ', is clearly spelled out for the Christian wife as requiring submission and inequality.[35]

For Schüssler Fiorenza, the christological modification of the husband's role 'does not have the power, theologically, to transform the patriarchal pattern of the household code, even though this might have been the intention of the author. Instead, Ephesians christologically cements the inferior position of the wife in the marriage relationship.'[36] She concludes that the author was not able to Christianize the code: 'The gospel of peace has transformed the relationship of gentiles and Jews, but not the social roles of wives and slaves within the household of God.' It therefore seems that the radical and moral instruction of Jesus gradually was eroded by compromises with the dominant world view. The Ephesians text shows 'a community experimenting, growing, wrestling and ultimately failing to embody the vision of its founder'.[37] Although the author of Ephesians does not seem to find these aspects incompatible,[38] the tension between the document's dynamic, complementary perspective and its hierarchical language may inhibit its transformative potential for later readers.

Although the constricting structures of patriarchy and slavery are not directly addressed in Ephesians, radically new values and attitudes are introduced — their radicality and newness being embodied in the example of Christ. Though it is even doubtful whether its intended effect made a dramatic difference in, for example, the subordinate role of women in the first centuries CE,[39] it appears that the document was meant to

35.   E. Schüssler Fiorenza, *In Memory of Her: A Feminist Theological Reconstruction of Christian Origins* (New York: Crossroad, 1983), p. 269.

36.   Schüssler Fiorenza, *In Memory of Her*, p. 270; cf. E. Elizabeth Johnson, 'Ephesians', in C. Newsom and S. Ringe (eds.), *Women's Bible Commentary* (Louisville, KY: Westminster/John Knox Press, expanded edn, 1998), pp. 428-32; Cynthia B. Kittredge, *Community and Authority: The Rhetoric of Obedience in the Pauline Tradition* (HTS; Harrisburg, PA: Trinity Press International, 1998).

37.   Jonathan A. Draper, 'Oppressive and Subversive Moral Instruction in the New Testament', in Denise Ackermann, Jonathan A. Draper and Emma Mashinini (eds.), *Women Hold Up Half the Sky: Women in the Church in Southern Africa* (Pietermaritzburg: Cluster, 1991), pp. 37-54 (50).

38.   Lincoln, *Ephesians*, p. 366.

39.   Pieter J.J. Botha, 'Folklore, Social Values and Life as a Woman in Early Christianity', *South African Journal for Folklore Studies* 3 (1992), pp. 1-14; Wayne Meeks,

reorient both Jews and Gentiles, and both men and women, according to their previous social status of either power or powerlessness. How would such a process work epistemologically in terms of experience and explanation?

The Transformative Potential of Ephesians: The Moral Function of its Rhetorical Strategies

The (re)orienting potential of metaphor is an essential element of liminality and of the rhetorical and transformative aspects of canonized texts. Like rites of passage, the rhetorical strategies in Ephesians function to shape and to remind its readers of their identity and appropriate ethos during a time of fundamental change. In this context our interest in metaphors particularly lies in their referential (redescriptive) and relational nature.[40] Lategan rightly claims that a 'better understanding of the function of reference in all its forms holds the key to unlock the transformative potential of (biblical) texts in contemporary situations'.[41] According to Ricoeur,[42] the referential or transformative power of a text lies in its ability to suggest, to open up, to facilitate, to mediate, to make possible, to produce a 'world in front of it', a 'proposed world' which readers may adopt or inhabit. In this way it discloses a possible new way of looking at things. The transformative potential of a text concurs with the notion of the implied reader as 'a device to engage the real reader by offering a role to be played or an attitude to be assumed'.[43] It is 'the reader we have to be willing to become in order to bring the reading experience to its full measure'.[44]

The First Urban Christians: The Social World of the Apostle Paul (New Haven: Yale University Press, 1983), pp. 23-25; *idem, The Origins of Christian Morality: The First Two Centuries* (New Haven: Yale University Press, 1993), pp. 49-50, 138-47.

40.   Bernard C. Lategan, 'Reference: Reception, Redescription and Reality', in Bernard C. Lategan and Willem S. Vorster, *Text and Reality: Aspects of Reference in Biblical Texts* (Philadelphia: Fortress Press, 1985), pp. 67-93; *idem,* 'Revisiting Text and Reality', *Neot* 28.3 (1994), pp. 121-35; *idem,* 'Imagination and Transformation', pp. 226-28; Wentzel van Huyssteen, *The Realism of the Text: A Perspective on Biblical Authority* (Pretoria: University of South Africa, 1987).

41.   Lategan, 'Revisiting Text and Reality', p. 134; *idem,* 'Imagination and Transformation', p. 229.

42.   Paul Ricoeur, 'Biblical Hermeneutics', *Semeia* 4 (1975), pp. 29-148; *idem, Interpretation Theory: Discourse and the Surplus of Meaning* (Fort Worth: Texas Christian University Press, 1976), pp. 89-95; *idem, The Rule of Metaphor*, pp. 216-56.

43.   Bernard C. Lategan, 'Introduction: Coming to Grips with the Reader', *Semeia* 48 (1989), pp. 3-17 (10).

44.   Willem S. Vorster, 'The Reader in the Text: Narrative Material', *Semeia* 48 (1989), pp. 21-39 (25).

Metaphor in particular can help people to integrate and to redescribe their experiences by changing the (meaning of the) language they use. Metaphors are heuristic devices for the redescription of reality or lived experience which break up inadequate interpretations of the world and open the way to new, more adequate interpretations.[45] By means of comparison, a metaphor creates a relation of meaning between two things in such a surprising way that something new comes to the fore about the unknown factor in the comparison. It is especially this important observation that metaphors redescribe reality that brings about a better understanding of our knowledge and experience of reality.[46] Sallie McFague deals with the interactional and referential function of metaphor as an element basic to the understanding of human thinking and language in general, and to the communicative processes of reinterpretation and liminality in particular.[47] As an act of remembrance and dismembrance, then, metaphors as well as story and tradition as extended metaphors become crucial instruments for survival in the liminal space — a possible way of decoding 'the traces of God's presence in history'.[48] For these reasons it has been suggested above that the exigence or rhetorical situation presented by the Ephesians document (the position from which the author wished to guide his readers' thoughts and behavior through discourse) be investigated as an imperfection in the readers' concept of God and humanity. To persuade Gentile Christians of their equal status with Jewish Christians, and wives and husbands, children and parents, slaves and masters of their mutuality in Christ, the author utilizes a network of metaphors and of traditions as metaphorical expressions.

The Genre of Ephesians as Reinterpreted Tradition

The genre of the document functions metaphorically to affirm the readers' new identity and ethos. According to Holland Hendrix, the document's structure shows remarkable parallels to the typical honorific

---

45.   Bernard C. Lategan, 'Textual Space as Rhetorical Device', in Stanley E. Porter and Thomas H. Olbricht (eds.), *Rhetoric and the New Testament: Essays from the 1992 Heidelberg Conference* (Sheffield: JSOT Press, 1993), pp. 397-408 (404-407); *idem*, 'Aspects of a Contextual Hermeneutics for South Africa', in Johann Mouton and Bernard Lategan (eds.), *The Relevance of Theology for the 1990s* (Pretoria: Human Sciences Research Council, 1994), pp. 17-30 (21).

46.   Ricoeur, *Interpretation Theory*, pp. 45-69; *idem*, *The Rule of Metaphor*, pp. 239-46; *idem*, *Essays on Biblical Interpretation* (ed. L.S. Mudge; Philadelphia: Fortress Press, 1980), pp. 25-27.

47.   McFague, *Metaphorical Theology*, pp. 14-29.

48.   Ricoeur, *Essays on Biblical Interpretation*, p. 26.

decrees found on monuments and inscriptions in Greco-Roman antiquity.[49] In the moral world of first-century Asia Minor, honors for bene-
factors were a well-known phenomenon:

> As with many decrees, Ephesians is a prescription of reality. The author
> adapts a pervasive social reality, the benefactor-beneficiary phenomenon,
> and through his adaptation prescribes a new network of benefaction. What
> is achieved is a powerful reinforcement of Christian identity and cohesion.
> Christians are those who honor their divine benefactor through moral
> behavior, animated by love as expressed in mutual benefit.[50]

The purpose of ancient honorific decrees was constantly to remind bene-
ficiaries of their inheritance and to persuade them toward specific action.
Hendrix emphasizes the ethos associated with a specific social identity
and again finds a striking parallel in Ephesians:

> An ethos of reciprocal benefactions and honor for the common good of the
> people and the glory of her patrons was the social premise of the benefactor-
> beneficiary phenomenon. It is precisely this ethos which is articulated in a
> 'Christianized' form in Ephesians. As the ultimate benefactors, God and
> Christ are honored through moral behavior that mutually benefits God's
> people.[51]

Understanding the Ephesians document as a reinterpreted 'honorific
decree' embedded in the epistolary genre illuminates its overwhelming
emphasis on Christ's lordship and the author's and recipients' exalted
position of power (1.10, 19-23; 2.5, 6). This understanding also clarifies
the document's alternative ethos of praise-giving (1.6, 12, 14; 3.20-21;
5.20), unity (4.1-16), and mutual submission (5.21) associated with those
who believe that what God did was for their benefit (1.19; 5.25). Within
the liminal phase of their 'becoming', the author acts as mediator and
reminder of the universal gifts of God's beneficence in Christ (1.3-14)
and calls his readers to appropriate honor of God and mutual caring for
one another (4.25-32; 5.1-21) as expressions of this 'common good of the
people and the glory of her patrons'.

Temporal and Spatial Indicators
Functioning like metaphors, various persuasive techniques or *topoi* are
embedded within the encompassing device of the Ephesians genre, by
means of which the author wishes to shift his audience from one posi-

---

49.   H. Hendrix, 'On the Form and Ethos of Ephesians', *USQR* 42 (1988), pp. 3-15.
50.   Hendrix, 'On the Form and Ethos of Ephesians', p. 10.
51.   Hendrix, 'On the Form and Ethos of Ephesians', p. 10.

tion to another. These refer to aspects of people, time, and place.[52] *Topoi* necessarily reflect the value system of a group or society, and can therefore not be separated from the socio-historical and moral world within which they function.[53]

Deeply concerned about his audience's perception of their primary status 'in Christ' as the result of God's radical presence in this world, the Ephesians author uses every possible means to contrast their previous (shameful, powerless) position and behavior with that of their present (honorable, powerful) situation and corresponding ethos. In different ways temporal and spatial indicators mark the decisive periods 'before' and 'after' the readers' coming to faith (2.1-6, 11-13, 19-22; 4.17-24; 5.8). The period of their present status is seen as fundamentally different from their previous status. Their position of dishonor has been replaced by a position of honor. In contrast to a shameful and powerless position where they had been looked down upon by the Jews (2.11-13), excluded from citizenship in Israel and viewed as aliens to the covenant (2.12, 19), they are now depicted as fellow citizens of God's people and members of God's household — a dwelling in which God lives by God's Spirit (2.22).

The temporal and spatial indicators in Ephesians function on two important levels. First, they are used to identify different dispensations and preferred or non-preferred positions. Second, they are used as a rhetorical strategy 'to effect the shifting of position'.[54] Indicating preferred and non-preferred positions is one thing. To achieve a shift in the right direction is, however, quite another matter. How does the author go about ensuring the desired result? How does he influence his readers to accept their new, advantageous position, even after they have come to faith (1.1, 15)? How is their change of attitude and behavior supposed to take place?

For the Ephesians author the key to change is provided by the interrelated communication processes of orientation, disorientation, and reorientation,[55] alienation and re-identification,[56] association and disassociation,[57] or distanciation and appropriation.[58] These processes essen-

---

52. Johannes N. Vorster, 'Toward an Interactional Model for the Analysis of Letters', *Neot* 24.1 (1990), pp. 107-30 (123).

53. Bruce J. Malina, *The New Testament World: Insights from Cultural Anthropology* (Louisville, KY: Westminster/John Knox Press, 1993), pp. 28-62, specifically with regard to honor and shame as pivotal values of the first-century Mediterranean world.

54. Lategan, 'Textual Space', p. 402.

55. Ricoeur, 'Biblical Hermeneutics', pp. 122-28; *idem, Interpretation Theory*, pp. 46-53; *idem, The Rule of Metaphor*, pp. 65-100; McFague, *Metaphorical Theology*, pp. 46-48.

56. Andrie B. Du Toit, 'Alienation and Re-identification as Pragmatic Strategies in Galatians', *Neot* 26.2 (1992), pp. 279-95.

57. Lategan, 'Textual Space', p. 402.

tially reveal the (re)orientating or transformative potential of metaphorical language, which forms the heart of (biblical) hermeneutics as a boundary-crossing subject.

The Persuading Potential of Jesus Christ as Metaphor

The Ephesians metaphors serve as windows (albeit hazy) through which the processes of identification, estrangement, and reorientation, typical of the image-making capacity of the human mind in a situation of liminality, can be viewed. Any creative act of interpretation, discovery, decision-making, transition, or transformation can be recognized as the imaginative combination and synthesis of the familiar into new wholes,[59] which is a redescription of reality.[60] With reference to McFague,[61] Christ's role in Ephesians may be described as an extended 'metaphor or parable for God' and a 'model for Christian behavior'. These notions have the potential to impact on biblical readers (especially in times of *communitas*) by continuously reorienting and transforming their self-understanding and ethos as disciples of Jesus Christ. As with metaphors, the essence of parable is that it works by indirection, through the ordinary, mundane, and secular, to bring about new insight. This means that we start with the more familiar work of Jesus from 'below', and move indirectly to his person, and to the invisible, unfamiliar God whom Jesus represents. The whole network of Jesus' life — his words and deeds and particularly his death, resurrection, and exaltation — thus provides a grid or screen through which the understanding of God can be realigned.[62]

How does Jesus' designation as parable of God realign, redefine, or reorient people's understanding of God?[63] As a true and novel metaphor, Jesus as parable always reorders, shocks, and upsets familiar, conventional preconceptions and understandings of God. In Jesus God is found in places where God would not be perceived. In Jesus God is particularly

58.   Patrick J. Hartin, 'Ethics and the New Testament: How Do We Get from There to Here?', in Mouton and Lategan (eds.), *The Relevance of Theology for the 1990s*, pp. 511-25 (514-16).

59.   McFague, *Metaphorical Theology*, pp. 35-36.

60.   Ricoeur, 'Biblical Hermeneutics', pp. 122-28; *idem, Interpretation Theory*, pp. 45-69; *idem, Essays on Biblical Interpretation,* p. 26.

61.   McFague, *Metaphorical Theology*, pp. 31-66, 90-194.

62.   McFague, *Metaphorical Theology*, pp. 49-54; Richard B. Hays, 'Scripture-Shaped Community: The Problem of Method in New Testament Ethics', *Int* 44 (1990), pp. 42-55 (45-50).

63.   Ricoeur, 'Biblical Hermeneutics', pp. 122-28; *idem, Interpretation Theory*, pp. 89-95; *idem, The Rule of Metaphor*, pp. 216-56.

and dramatically present at the margins of human existence. Not to say that God is not at the center of life, but in Jesus the center *shifts* to marginal people and places. Jesus is born in a place where no child was meant to be born; Jesus dies at a place where criminals were executed. Jesus dies violently as an innocent victim of human sin (brought about by men who were threatened by his message and behavior).[64] Through this trauma of horror, humiliation, and shame, a shocking vision of God is presented. The ultimate site where God would *not* be perceived, paradoxically *becomes* the site of God's presence.

This radical reversal of divine power reveals not only who God is, but also what it means to be human, with radical implications for all forms of life. In showing compassion to women, children, tax-collectors, Samaritans, Jesus subverts the established values of power in the moral world of first-century Palestine. In shifting the center to the margins, and the margins to the center, God's concrete presence in Jesus becomes a radical moment of shock and surprise, inviting people inside and outside those texts to look differently, to adopt new roles, to reorient their understanding of God and their traditions in the light of God's liberating presence in Christ.

McFague believes that the heart of the drama of Jesus' life and death is the tension that it manifests between accepted ways of relating to God and to others and a new way of living in the world. As such, Jesus' life and especially his death and resurrection have to be viewed as radical and iconoclastic, continuously calling into question the comfortable and secure homes that our interpretations of God have built for us.[65] In this sense the church finds itself in a constant situation of liminality: like Christ we are called to a life *in* but not *of* the world, and to lives that always stand in criticism of the status quo and that press toward fulfillment of the body of Christ.

The ultimate purpose of the Ephesians author's use of Christ as metaphor and parable is to provide a basis for the readers' new self-understanding and perspective on reality.[66] A major strategy he uses in accomplishing this is to emphasize his own and the readers' identification with Christ. He reminds them that their own dramatic change was not self-initiated, but rather was effected by the closest possible association with Christ, in his death and resurrection, and especially in his

---

64. Elizabeth A. Johnson, *She Who Is: The Mystery of God in Feminist Theological Discourse* (New York: Crossroad, 1992), pp. 158-59.

65. McFague, *Metaphorical Theology*, pp. 51-54.

66. Lategan, 'Textual Space', pp. 404-406.

exaltation to the right hand of God (1.18-21).[67] 'Change cannot be achieved on one's own or in isolation—only in union with Christ and solidarity with fellow-believers.'[68] In this way Christ functions not only as a parable, but also as a model inducing specific behavior. This means that specific virtues and values associated with him are generated toward those who identify with him. In the context of Ephesians these include humility, love, forgiveness, righteousness, peace, and hope.

Through various strategies the Ephesians author encourages his readers to think of themselves in terms of the new position they ought to assume—as fellow citizens with God's people, as one body in Christ, as a new humanity. The preferred position indicated by persuasive strategies in the document is the continuous renewal of their spirit and ethos in accordance with God's righteousness and holiness (4.23-24). By inviting humankind to assume its honorable status in Christ, Ephesians offers its readers a new self-understanding, leading to a new ethos, new attitudes and actions.

To summarize, one may say that the starting point of all persuasive strategies is the delicate, liminal tension among identification, alienation, and reorientation. For later readers these processes hold the key to the transformative potential of the biblical documents. To inhabit their strange, alternative world is not only a gift of God's grace (Eph. 2.5, 8-10), but also a faithful hermeneutical choice: 'In a co-operative shared work, the Spirit, the text, and the reader engage in a transforming process, which enlarges horizons and creates new horizons.'[69]

Revisioning the Liminal Encounter between Ephesians and Contemporary Readers

It has become clear that the Ephesian epistle is characterized by the dynamic, liminal process of the early Christian communities' search to understand human existence in the light of the Christ event.[70] The unique hallmark of this process is their continuous and radical reorientation to the alien, completely other, yet for them truthful story of Jesus Christ. However, the document's christological-ecclesial perspective does not only orient the interpretive processes implied by the text itself, but

---

67. Lincoln, *Ephesians*, p. 61.
68. Lategan, 'Textual Space', p. 405.
69. Anthony C. Thiselton, *New Horizons in Hermeneutics: The Theory and Practice of Transforming Biblical Reading* (Grand Rapids: Zondervan, 1992), p. 619.
70. Meeks, *The Origins of Christian Morality*, pp. 1-17, 109-10.

implicitly also those activated and facilitated by it.[71] An ethically responsible reading of Ephesians by subsequent readers thus calls for a continuous wrestling, for imaginative, Spirit-filled, and critical reflection on the active presence and will of God in ever changing times and circumstances. The processes and obstacles involved in such a journey are implied and anticipated in the Ephesians text itself. Amid its glorious 'in Christ' vision and powerful human potential for the good, it also reckons with the fragile realities of human cultural limitations and fallibility and its inclination to evil impulses. This gives pause to all hopes that character and virtue can be created instantly so as to guarantee good. However, the epistle assures its readers that they are not left alone in their struggle for the good. Rather, God provides Christ and his body as the full armor of God's protection against the powers and principalities, the spiritual forces of evil in the heavenly realms (Eph. 6.10-20). The memory of Christ's story, and of the faith community's story in the light of it, is meant to remain a source of living hope in the present. In this way liminality may lead to deepened faith experiences and reflection on God.

For these reasons, professional and ordinary readers of the Bible share the moral obligation to engage in the creative tension of the liminal space between the dynamics of the biblical texts and the multiple needs and suffering, fears, dreams, and hopes of contemporary readers.[72] The question is *how* the culturally bound alternative world of Ephesians may be brought into relation with, and impact on, present-day moral challenges. In accordance with its relational nature, the authority of Ephesians for subsequent readers first of all resides in the continuing encounter with the living God mediated and stimulated by the text.[73] The transformative potential of Ephesians lies in its referential power, in its ability to point beyond itself to a reality that it could only describe in a limited and provisional manner, namely, the full story of Christ. The authority of Scripture therefore has to be refocused and restructured within the dynamic site of continuous interaction among God's life-giving Spirit, contemporary faith communities, and the biblical texts. It is within this creative space where the revelatory power of these documents comes to the fore. Such an approach would embrace the many dimensions of the full hermeneutical circle, and would be truthful to the dynamic nature of these

71. Allen Verhey, *The Great Reversal: Ethics and the New Testament* (Grand Rapids: Eerdmans, 1984), pp. 179-87.

72. E. Schüssler Fiorenza, 'The Ethics of Biblical Interpretation', *JBL* 107 (1988), pp. 3-17 (13).

73. Bernard C. Lategan, 'Hermeneutics', *ABD*, III, pp. 149-54 (154); *idem*, 'Revisiting Text and Reality', pp. 131-33.

documents and the continuous processes of interpretation and reorientation that they represent. Surprisingly, such a spiral movement among Spirit, text, and readers is crucial for the unlocking of the liberating meaning of those ancient texts. In this way Ephesians invites later readers to commemorate its story liturgically — in their practical daily life — with awe and admiration.

To respond faithfully and with sensitivity to the rhetorical function of Ephesians is to account for its transformative potential amid its cultural-historical biases[74] — that is, the typically human process of redescription in the light of new knowledge and experience underlying it. Involvement in the liminal space therefore asks for an open-endedness which humbly recognizes the provisional nature of all faith utterances. Thus, to allow for explanations and experiences of a living God who is constantly revealed in new and surprising ways,[75] later readers of Ephesians are challenged to account for its patriarchal language, and to create the inclusive language needed to express and construct their experiences. The document does not bind us in a rigid, legalistic way, but liberates us toward the imaginative appropriation of the mighty, healing power of God's love in new circumstances. In spite of its patriarchal embeddedness, the document invites contemporary readers to identify with Christ in the paradoxical triumph of his resurrection and exaltation and to grow beyond all limited and stereotypical views of humanity.

We have seen how the dynamics of liminality function in Ephesians as a reconciliatory strategy between different moral worlds, providing for its readers the vision, values, and artistic skills to redefine their understanding of God and humanity. Therefore, to respect its revelatory power is to dedicate oneself to accomplishing the full potential of the body of Christ. Anything less would confine the God of Ephesians to the boundaries of an ancient text in a way contradictory to its own nature, and can therefore not be considered as normative. Committed to the authority of Scripture as liberating practice for all people — in ever changing times and circumstances — interpretive communities are called to critically examine their exegetical and theological traditions in terms of the ethical *effects* which they had and still have in the lives of people. As a necessary critical tool, feminist rhetorical inquiry elucidates 'the ethical consequences and political functions of biblical texts and scholarly discourses in their historical as well as contemporary sociopolitical contexts', and

---

74. Cf. Malina, *The New Testament World.*
75. Richard B. Hays, *Echoes of Scripture in the Letters of Paul* (New Haven: Yale University Press, 1989), pp. 32-33; Meeks, *The Origins of Christian Morality*, pp. 217-19.

asks: 'What does a reading of the Bible "do" to someone who submits to its world of vision?'[76]

For me as a white South African woman from within the Reformed tradition, this poses a formidable challenge. Reading Ephesians has become both a liberating and frightening experience to me. Liberating, because of the Christian story's potential to enable all people to become mature persons in Christ, yet also frightening because of the power of our ideologically based interpretive frameworks and presuppositions, and the reality of our moral world which in many, many respects seems to be so far away from this vision.

In South Africa, many significant sociopolitical changes have been accomplished since the country's miraculous first democratic elections in 1994, as embodied in the Constitution of 1996 with its far-reaching bill of rights. However, these changes have often not been accompanied by anticipated attitudinal and behavioral changes. For the purpose of my argument it is important to distinguish between these structural changes on the one hand, and the *collective consciousness* of people on the other. The latter has to do with emotions, assumptions, convictions, and values. At this level the personal and collective scars of a *deeply divided society*— such as poverty, power abuse, violence, crime, and corruption—are still part of our daily lives, and are for sure not going to disappear easily. It is clear that the evil forces of separation, 'dividing walls of hostility' (Eph. 2.14), have deeply distorted the sense of humanity, dignity, and identity of *all* people in South Africa, even those who may not realize it—the poor and the rich, women and men, black and white. In the final analysis these distortions have to be observed within the context of an encompassing cosmic evil and its profound influence on the quality of all forms of life.

Of all the possible features of the complex South African moral situation at the moment, I single out three brief observations with regard to the recent past of the country's history—each with positive and negative sides—which deeply influence the way in which South Africans think and act, and which pose tremendous challenges to the churches and theological education in the process of transition.

As a general observation regarding the present political agenda in South Africa, one may say that a wide concern exists with moral issues and processes redefining the country's moral vision and fibre. A remarkable number of initiatives have been taken by the government toward the moral reconstruction of society, *inter alia* the Truth and Reconciliation

76. Elisabeth Schüssler Fiorenza, *But She Said: Feminist Practices of Biblical Interpretation* (Boston: Beacon Press, 1992), p. 47.

Commission, the Gender Commission, a Public Protector, various Moral Summits and Anti-Corruption Conferences, and a National Religious Forum. One would expect the churches — by their very nature and identity — to be whole-heartedly interested and involved in the renewal of the whole of life, including the political and public social order. Ironically, however, this does not seem to be the case. Initiatives for moral reconstruction are more driven by the state than by the churches.[77]

My second and third observations respectively relate to some major hermeneutical and societal shifts in the recent past of the country's history. With regard to general hermeneutical trends (and the use of the Bible in particular), the relationship between various forms of theology and faith and the immoral ideology of apartheid in South Africa has always been very complex. What cannot be ignored, however, is the overall impression that (a particular form of so-called and self-acclaimed) *Reformed* Christianity played a major role in the justification of apartheid.[78] There have been significant shifts away from this hermeneutical stance — particularly during the past two decades. However, in spite of the Dutch Reformed and other churches' explicit and repeated confession of their role in this sad history, and particularly their repressive use of (certain aspects of) the Bible:

> it cannot be denied that, both within the Reformed communities and from the perspective of outsiders, apartheid has given the Reformed tradition, and even Christianity itself, a bad reputation in South Africa and has caused a lack of credibility and even self-confidence.[79]

One can hardly overestimate the negative effects of this history on the self-image of Afrikaans-speaking Reformed Christians.

In the process many black people and women in particular have become deeply suspicious of the often repressive readings of the Bible that were imposed on them and which caused them to feel like second- and third-class citizens not only in society, but also in the kingdom of God. Very often they, as well as those who were privileged by the system, feel disillusioned and deceived by the many 'successful' ways in which Scripture has been used to justify and solidify racial and gender apartheid. For such people to be surprised (again) by Scripture's transformative and liberative vision of reconciliation, and to be persuaded by virtues

---

77. Cf. Dirk J. Smit, 'Can We Still Be Reformed? Questions from a South African Perspective' (paper read at international conference on 'Reformed Theology: Identity and Ecumenicity', Heidelberg, Germany, 18–22 March 1999), pp. 1-3.

78. Smit, 'Can We Still Be Reformed?', pp. 3-7.

79. Smit, 'Can We Still Be Reformed?', p. 4.

such as truthfulness, authenticity, and integrity (while lacking appropriate role models), have become an enormous challenge.[80]

A third trend that profoundly influences the way in which South Africans think and act is the radical transformation with numerous societal shifts that are taking place at the moment. In many ways these are closely related to and intertwined with the previous point, and ironically strengthen the already deeply entrenched sense of alienation in people's minds. With very broad strokes this can be characterized as an overnight transformation from a basically (homogeneous) 'premodern' society to a typically (pluralistic, democratic, secular) 'modern' society, and in many ways even a 'postmodern' one.[81] A potentially constructive yet also dangerous consequence of the latter is that it leads to a breakdown of the hegemony of truth claims. In a secular postmodern society no institution, including Christianity with its Truth claims (with a capital T and in the singular) and authoritative biblical texts, has any privileged status. For many people this means that all truth claims merely become a matter of opinion, and that morality is a matter of personal preference. The emphasis is often on *different* rationalities and viewpoints, with little regard for that which binds people together. Instead of celebrating the richness of plurality and complementarity as a gift, the postmodern attitude for many people becomes synonymous with a certain disintegration, to a loss of orientation and cohesion, a loss of identity and community, a lack of responsibility and involvement, to a general attitude of apathy, of 'who cares?' These tendencies go against the distinctive nature of Christianity as a life-giving *community*.

This leads to a further implication for the role of religion in a secularized society. In such a society religion still has an important and even increasingly popular place. However,

> it must restrict itself to playing its so-called proper role, which means it must restrict itself to the private sphere of the individual's personal, intimate life. Religion is privatized. It loses its place in public life... Its connections to other subsystems, like politics, economic life, the public media, the legal system, and public education, are seriously threatened, and often made impossible by walls of separation.[82]

Again these trends of alienation and disorientation go against the very heart of the biblical claim that the presence of God should be proclaimed

---

80. E. Mouton, 'Die Verhaal van Afrikaanse Christenvroue: Uitnodiging tot Morele Vorming', *Scriptura* 63 (1997), pp. 475-90.

81. Dirk J. Smit, 'Morality and Individual Responsibility', *JTSA* 89 (1994), pp. 19-30 (20-21); *idem*, 'Can We Still Be Reformed?', pp. 4-5.

82. Smit, 'Can We Still Be Reformed?', p. 5.

and honored in every sphere of life. The situation undoubtedly suggests a potential crisis for the Christian community because it implies an uncertainty about our very *identity*, our calling, mission, and purpose in society. For Christians, the notion of God's radical presence in every sphere of life is not something that we can choose to ignore while retaining our identity. For Reformed people this conviction is deeply embedded in our particular form of faith in the living Triune God as the God of history and creation, and our lives *coram Deo*.[83] It is primarily based on the status and authority of the Bible as representative of a huge chorus of (often repressed) voices, speaking from various times, places, and circumstances, witnessing about a dynamic relationship between a living, speaking, acting God and living, speaking, acting human beings in the everyday concrete reality of their lives. This primary conviction counteracts any possible form of fragmentation, disconnectedness, and alienation in God's world.

As much as this may be an extremely general and superficial perspective on South Africa's moral situation at the moment, its one-sidedness may perhaps help us to understand some of its implications for the churches and theological education in the country.

Both the above-mentioned processes or shifts hold tremendous potential. They bear the promise of a new, more accountable hermeneutical awareness as well as the celebration of plurality and the resistance of any form of hegemony. However, both are being accompanied (and often ironically so!) by a deep sense of *loss*—the loss of wholeness, integration, and integrity, the loss of a collective moral identity, memory, and destination (who we are, where we come from, where we would like to be going), the loss of trust in all forms of leadership, including church leadership, the loss of trust even in the truth and truthfulness of God's word, and as a logical result, the loss of a corresponding corporate ethos of dignity and respect for life. As far as Christianity is concerned, these symptoms tragically but definitively point toward the essence of the problem. It is clear that the churches in South Africa need a new sense of mission and purpose. To have lost our sense of calling means that we have lost our *orientation*, our primary identity as Christians—the most basic conviction of who we are and who we are supposed to be. This is essentially a *theological* problem, which manifests itself as a so-called '*moral* crisis', but in actual fact goes much deeper. It therefore calls for a careful *theological* response.[84]

---

83.   Smit, 'Can We Still Be Reformed?', p. 11.

84.   Smit reiterates this observation: 'The most serious reason for concern about the state of Reformed Christianity in South Africa…is not the alarming proportions of our

Some serious implications in terms of threats, temptations, and challenges for South African churches in general, and religious education and (Reformed) theological training in particular, have become evident. Complex questions arising from these conclusions are *inter alia*: How can an apartheid-oriented (shame-based) perspective on difference be transformed into a community-oriented perspective (of self-worth) which would not be threatened by plurality but appreciate and celebrate it instead? What kind of moral discourse would impact on members of such a society (including those who have lost their trust in the church and the Bible as the Word of God)? Would the theological and moral rhetoric of (re)conciliation — so essential to the biblical tradition — still be desirable, or at all possible? What are the underlying motives, visions, and values of such language supposed to be — in order to be conducive to social transformation?

It is clear that an effective rhetoric of (spiritual) *orientation* is needed: orientation to a Reality bigger and more powerful than ourselves, to an accountable view of biblical authority as liberating practice, to a new sense of communal identity. All these have serious implications for how we read and interpret the Bible, for how we read the South African context, for the particular images (of God) that we choose for this moment in history, for how we define church, liturgy, spirituality, morality…

In the transitional process in South Africa, racial oppression has understandably been prioritized as the primary sin to be eradicated. However, 'the instructured mechanisms of race, gender and class in the oppression of people have not been adequately understood'.[85] The major crisis arising from this situation for me is the relative *silence* of many churches on these issues:

> An appalling and too often unacknowledged side of the endemic violence in our society is the sexual violence inflicted on women and children. Even if this fact is acknowledged, it is often not understood that sexual violence is essentially an evil abuse of power. As such, it is a *theological* problem. Racism and sexism are structures of domination which create conditions for the abuse of power… A number of churches and certain church leaders have been justly vocal in their condemnation of apartheid. Few…have spoken out against sexism. [86]

moral crisis and our lack of responsibility, but the integrity of our own identity and the credibility of our own life and witness. We face a theological — not primarily a moral — crisis and we need a theological response.' Smit, 'Can We Still Be Reformed?', p. 11.

85. Denise M. Ackermann, 'Faith and Feminism: Women Doing Theology', in John De Gruchy and Charles Villa-Vicencio (eds.), *Doing Theology in Context: South African Perspectives* (Maryknoll, NY: Orbis Books, 1994), pp. 197-211 (201).

86. Ackerman, 'Faith and Feminism', p. 205; emphasis mine.

There have been significant changes. However, the memory of nearly two thousand years of a male-dominated church, backed by theology that is derived from mainly Western male scholarship, has left us with enormous challenges. The most serious part of this heritage is its implicit and explicit theological justification. As in the case of Eph. 5.22, the patriarchal language of the biblical documents often still serves to legitimate the secondary role of women in the home, church, and society. Even more acute is the theological problem that is created when humanity and the nature of God are predominantly represented in terms of male images.

To deal with the situation creatively, I propose a 'hermeneutic of liminality' that reclaims the transformative potential of the biblical writings as an invitation to accomplish a healed and full body of Christ. In terms of the Ephesian perspective, such a vision invites Christians to develop what H.R. Niebuhr calls a 'common memory', in which persons not only share the present life, but also adopt as their own the past history of others. 'Where common memory is lacking, where men [sic] do not share in the same past, there can be no real community, and where community is to be formed common memory must be created.'[87] This means that we will have to be (even more) open to listen to the stories of all the people in South Africa, particularly those who have not been considered as important in the past, and to adopt the past—including the past sins—of other groups as our own, and to risk forgiving them and ourselves for what we have done to each other. This will allow us the opportunity to lament the loss of our full humanity for such a long time, and to grow from *remembering* our inherited traditions of alienation to *dismembering* them in the light of Christ's healing love. In this sense the present liminal context may be conducive to understanding Christ's inclusive and relational view of humanity in a new way. It will hopefully be a *kairos* moment, a rebirth, a resurrection in terms of rethinking and redefining our humanity.

In concurrence with Ackermann's relational anthropology[88] and feminist theology as liberating praxis,[89] the key words in a hermeneutic of liminality are 'relationality' and 'risk'. 'Relationality as basis for a transformative view of humanity is...concerned with our relationships with

---

87. H. Richard Niebuhr, *The Meaning of Revelation* (New York: Macmillan, 1941), p. 86.

88. Denise M. Ackermann, 'Being Woman, Being Human', in Ackermann, Draper and Mashinini (eds.), *Women Hold Up Half the Sky*, pp. 93-105 (100-103); *idem*, 'Defining Our Humanity: Thoughts on a Feminist Anthropology', *JTSA* 79 (1992), pp. 13-23 (16-23).

89. Ackermann, 'Faith and Feminism', pp. 201-208.

ourselves, with one another, with God and with our environment.'[90] It is the opposite of alienation, apathy, and exclusion. 'Risk' refers to the courage, energy, and commitment required to deal with the deeply entrenched power of patriarchy and other forms of oppression.[91] Christ is our model with regard to this stereoscopic vision of transformation. Ephesians witnesses that Christ is able to translate different stories into one new story (1.10), into a new common memory, which might become a common hope for the future. In terms of Taylor's vision of a 'postmodern trilemma', it challenges us to respect and where necessary creatively to reinterpret tradition, to celebrate plurality, and to resist any form of domination.[92]

A hermeneutic of liminality does not allow for final, unalterable answers, decisions, and certainties. It rather challenges us to live patiently and humbly with the tension of risk (the risk to remember, to love, to forgive, to hope), and the tensions of paradox, ambivalence, pain, and even ridicule. Appropriating the perspective of Ephesians in terms of the formation of moral people, the transformation of a moral society, and the information of moral action is a slow, lifelong, more often than not cumbersome process. It nevertheless continues to encourage followers of Christ towards the realization of the full potential of his body. There is no instant way toward accomplishing it. It is a narrow road which calls for a hermeneutic of trust, hope, and commitment.

90. Ackermann, 'Being Woman, Being Human', p. 102.
91. Ackermann, 'Faith and Feminism', p. 207.
92. Taylor, *Remembering Esperanza*, pp. 40-45.

THE EPISTLE TO THE CONGREGATION IN COLOSSAE AND THE INVENTION OF THE 'HOUSEHOLD CODE'*

Angela Standhartinger

Ever since feminists began their theological interpretation of the epistle to the Colossians, its role in the Christian history of oppression has been observed. The so-called household code of Col. 3.18–4.1 is the first and oldest of a series of New Testament texts that call on women, children, and slaves to submit to men, fathers, and lords. Especially within Protestantism, the 'household codes' were interpreted as a divine commandment that regulated the roles of family members and established marriage and family to be the fundamental task of a woman's Christian life.

How could something like that have come about in Pauline congregations among whom, according to Gal. 3.28, the community of equals was lived out? What led to the demand for women's submission in congregations that elected women to be leaders, envoys, and Apostles?[1] Before examining the introduction of the household code into the epistle to the Colossians and thus into the Pauline tradition, I examine first the origin of the epistle.[2]

Sender and Addressee

There is now a broad consensus among exegetes that the epistle to the Colossians was not written by Paul himself. In several places, the letter that alleges to have been composed by Paul in prison implies that Paul's death had been known for some time. What is subject to debate among scholars is whether the male or female authors—I shall refer to them

---

*   Translated by Barbara Rumscheidt and Martin Rumscheidt. Originally published as 'Der Brief an die Gemeinde in Kolossä und die Erfindung der "Haustafel" ', in Luise Schottroff and Marie-Theres Wacker (eds.), *Kompendium Feministische Bibelauslegung* (Gütersloh: Gütersloher Verlagshaus, 1998), pp. 635-45. Reprinted by permission.
1.   See Phil. 4.2-3; 1 Cor. 1.11; Rom. 16.1-16.
2.   See the extensive treatment in Angela Standhartinger, *Studien zur Entstehungsgeschichte und Intention des Kolosserbriefs* (NovTSup, 94; Leiden: E.J. Brill, 1999).

from now on as Pauline—were in possession of concrete information about Colossae. However, the letter is addressed not only to Colossians but to all human beings and to the whole earth. For that reason, I judge the mention of the address 'to the Colossians' to be part of what the epistle intends to achieve. The choice of that address shows that the gospel propagates itself relentlessly to the farthest corners of the Roman Empire.

Colossians was written for all who were interested in the correspondence of Paul. But why did Pauline write an epistle in the name of Paul and Timothy rather than in her own? Many exegetes assume that Pauline wanted to endow her theological opinion and her admonitions with the authority of Paul.[3] I find this thesis is problematic because it has to presuppose two assumptions that in my view cannot be proven. One is that in his generation Paul enjoyed undisputed authority in his congregations. The second is that he claimed such a role as head of the congregations for himself. Yet, according to texts such as 1 Corinthians 12, Paul himself was decisive in opposing hierarchical structures. The composition of pseudepigraphical letters need not be traced back to a loss of authority in the subsequent generation. Several schools of philosophy in antiquity understood the idea of copyright rather differently than we do today. They published their thinking on principle under the name of the actual originator of their ideas and not under that of the author.[4] In addition, ancient literary tastes found it important to enrich significant passages of speeches and narratives with fictive texts of important personalities. This was practised in the schools themselves, for example, by sketching the speech of the tortoise before outwitting the hare or by composing a letter to his wife. What Paul might have said or written, had he composed a letter to a newly established congregation shortly before his death, could perhaps be one of the ideas behind Pauline's epistle to the Colossians.

The Colossian Community as a Model Community

Pauline begins her epistle in the plural 'we'. Who stands behind the 'we' remains open. She reports that the 'word of truth, the gospel' (1.5) has reached the addressees as it has people 'throughout the world' so that it bears fruit and grows among them as in the whole cosmos (1.6). For a

---

3.   E.g. Mary Rose D'Angelo, 'Colossians', in Elisabeth Schüssler Fiorenza (ed.), *Searching the Scriptures: A Feminist Commentary* (New York: Crossroad, 1994), II, pp. 313-24.

4.   Iamblichus, *De Vita Pythagorica* 158 and elsewhere; Seneca, *Epistulae* 33.4.

letter, written presumably in the sixties of the common era, this is a daring if not to say an exaggerated claim.

The end of the opening paragraph mentions Epaphras, 'our very dear fellow slave' and 'trustworthy deputy' of Christ, and identifies him as the one who had provided the information about the congregation. But he cannot have been the head or leader of that congregation for he was not in Colossae (4.12-14). Imprisoned with Paul, he struggles like Paul for the congregation and its neighbours (1.29–2.1). In Epaphras Pauline has created Paul's 'double' or counterpart. Both are called envoys or servants (διάκονοι) of God (cf. Col. 1.23, 25). Epaphras is not the only 'trustworthy deputy' and 'dear fellow slave' (1.7). Pauline speaks in similar terms about Tychicus (4.7-8), Onesimus (4.9), and Archippus (4.17). She calls Onesimus 'a dear brother' (Phlm. 16), someone much more so 'to you'. That he is or was a slave, as it is reported in Philemon, is not mentioned by Pauline. Behind these fictive reports there is no hierarchical but a collective understanding of leadership that includes the whole community. Like Epaphras, Tychicus, and Onesimus all addressees belong to the 'faithful brothers [and sisters]' (1.2). Epaphras is called explicitly 'your fellow citizen' (4.12).

With this list of greetings Pauline develops a different understanding of congregation than, for example, the Pastoral Epistles. Contrary to Paul's epistles, the exhortation to greet one another is missing. Other than in Romans 16 or 1 Cor. 16.19, for example, only one woman, Nympha, is mentioned. The numerous (fictive) reports Pauline uses to embellish the list of names in Philemon create the impression that the congregation consists only of men, making it well-nigh impossible to remember the 'famous' women.

It was perhaps coincidental, but Pauline has contributed to the remembering of women in Paul's congregations. At the end of her epistle she asks that after having been read to the whole congregation, the epistle should be made available to the congregation in Laodicea and that the — presumably fictive — letter *from* that congregation be read out 'in Colossae' (4.16). Pauline, it appears, wants to collect the epistles of Paul's group and duplicate them. But neither in her time nor in late decades was this something to be taken for granted. With this idea Pauline allows us to reconstruct today a more differentiated picture of Paul's group.

Theological Foundations 1.9-23

After her opening paragraph, Pauline delivers theological assurance, using the style of a hymn. Her important terms are fullest knowledge, wisdom,[5] and insight (1.10). She calls on her addressees to thank God, the father, that he has made 'us' heirs to the saints in light and transformed us from the power of darkness into the kingdom of the son of his love (1.12). Pauline emphasizes that salvation and redemption are already heavenly reality now.

The Colossian hymn of 1.15-20 is part of Pauline's theological position and its determination. This hymn or poem describes extensively the son that God loves. However, the hymn leaves open who this 'he' is that it celebrates. If one substitutes the male pronouns with female pronouns, one comes upon an original wisdom hymn that is at the root of this passage. Wisdom is celebrated here as the creator of the cosmos, the woman leader of the heavenly world and the beginning of all that is. Editing and interpreting a wisdom hymn as a hymn to Christ is nothing unusual in the Jesus movement.[6] In the present case this occurs chiefly in the passage of v. 20b, 'by making peace through his death on the cross'. The theological idea of this passage is that the death of individual righteous persons brings to an end the disunion between God and God's people, making peace in the world by washing away with their blood the sins of the people (e.g. *4 Macc.* 17.22–18.4a). Such a theology is alienating today. At a time when the cross was no piece of decorative art but a horrible instrument of torture and execution, and death was the order of the day, this was *one* theological interpretation of the death of God's friends.

Reports about Paul and the Congregation(s)

Marked by the language of prayer and hymnic thanksgiving, the beginning of the epistle describes the addressees' participation in the new cosmic reality. This is where Pauline could well have ended her epistle. Instead, what follows is something restraining: 'as long as you persevere and stand firm in the solid base of the faith (πίστις)…'(1.23). Such calls for perseverance and endurance (cf. 1.11; 2.6-7) and steadfastness (4.2) are repeated, pointing to one of the congregations' greatest problems. They seem to have fallen apart and to have turned away in disappointment.

Pauline names one reason why the congregation fell apart; she does this in 1.24, the formulation of which is difficult to understand. 'Now I [Paul] rejoice in my sufferings for your sake, and in my flesh I complete what is lacking in Christ's afflictions.' The end of the story of Christ's afflictions is surely known to all addressed in this epistle. Paul's own

---

5. This term occurs particularly often in Colossians.
6. Cf. Phil. 2.6-11; Jn 1.1-18.

death is referred to obliquely. His death, which the Second Testament does not report, has caused uncertainty among his friends. Even though Paul had to reckon a number of times with impending execution, he was convinced that he would experience the end of the world and Christ's return.[7] His violent death, which the first epistle of Clement hints at (*1 Clem.* 5.5-7), must have shaken and endangered Paul's group. Is it still worthwhile to seek baptism if the promised life has failed to arrive? Ought one not rather to conclude from Paul's death that such a life was too dangerous? And would it not be more reasonable, therefore, to abandon the sinking ship and make friends anew with the world?

Pauline retorts that Paul's death was not senseless but that it happened for the sake of Christ's body, the congregation (cf. 1.18). Here Pauline develops a new ecclesiology. Unlike Paul, she does not speak of many communions (ἐκκλησίαι) of the saints in diverse locations but only of one communion which is in his body (1.24). It comes into being through holding fast to the head, who is Christ (2.19). This hierarchical image is taken from Roman philosophy of state.[8] Pauline's ecclesiology depicts the relation between Christ and the community as the mirror image of the relation between the emperor and his body, the Roman Empire.

Pauline holds up the heavy struggle that Paul wages for the addressees of this letter, for their neighbours and all who have not seen or no longer see him (ἑόρακαν, 1.29–2.1). In so doing she alludes to Paul having been martyred. And even if Paul is (now) absent in the flesh, he is present to those addressed in the spirit, sees and rejoices about them (2.5). In a manner of speaking, her letter is a heavenly letter in which the dead Paul assures those who receive it of his spiritual presence. With this letter, Pauline wants to comfort and unite in love all who hear it.[9]

Admonitions

Paul's (heavenly) epistle is not only to give consolation, unite people, and to persuade them to remain in their community; it also has a long list of admonitions. Already in the personal reports Pauline has her fictive author declare: 'I say this in order that no one may delude you with beguiling speech' (2.4). The admonition to let nobody sow uncertainty is expanded in the second chapter (2.8, 16, 18). The largest amount of energy spent to this day in the study of Colossians has been

---

7.   1 Thess. 4.15; Rom. 13.11.
8.   Seneca, *De Clementia* 3.2.1-3; Curtius Rufus, *Historia Alexandri Magni* 10.9.1-5.
9.   Col. 2.2; cf. 2.19; 3.14-15, 18.

devoted to the question of who this 'no one' was. In my view, the point was to protect the congregation from being rendered uncertain by pessimism and by arguments that had the appearance of being logical. Pauline knows that the congregation does not enjoy a position of superiority; rather, she fears that it may be pillaged and subject to internal dissension, everyone judging everyone else.

She seeks to give courage to the congregation by calling upon its members to set their 'minds on things that are above' (3.2). She makes a number of suggestions of how this new reality may and should affect the life of the congregation. She contrasts putting off the 'old human being' and what that being does with putting on the new, the renewed human being who has been transformed and enabled to live the reality that is celebrated in the hymn (1.15-20). This is made concrete through her adoption of the baptismal confession of Gal. 3.28: 'Here there cannot be Greek and Jew, circumcised and uncircumcised, barbarian, Scythian, slave, free, but Christ is all, and in all'. However, Pauline does let her sisters disappear in silence. The doublet 'neither male nor female' from Gal. 3.28 is missing from Col. 3.11. All the groups named can be represented by men alone. In the doublet 'no barbarian, no Scythian' Pauline depicts the utopian idea that the abolishing of social differences also includes the differences between 'locals' and 'foreigners'.

Thus, Pauline asserts that in Christ's space there are no longer any ethnic and social differences. And yet, the epistle contains the 'household code'. How do these two things fit together?

The 'Household Code' of 3.18–4.1

The verses 3.18–4.1 form a self-enclosed section that formally sticks out of the context. All of a sudden, it is no longer the whole congregation that is addressed in the plural, but different social groups; women, children, slaves are specified and called upon to submit themselves to the specifically corresponding group of men, fathers, and masters.

The substance of this section is neither new nor specifically Christian.[10] Numerous documents and tracts of ancient political economy and money matters that touch upon the relationship between masters and slaves, husbands and wives, fathers and sons. Here it is particularly the works of economics of the Roman imperial period that view the home (οἶκος) as the nucleus of the state.[11] According to the ideology presented

---

10.   Elisabeth Schüssler Fiorenza, *In Memory of Her: A Feminist Theological Reconstruction of Christian Origins* (New York: Crossroad, 1983), pp. 251-59.

11.   Arius Didymus; Josephus, *Apion* 198–210.

in such works, the peace, security, and well-being of the state can be vouchsafed only by a proper order in the home.

These economic works are thematic treatises and not collections of admonitions. Nor do they address individual groups.[12] That is why scholarly research has been divided to date in this area. Some researchers maintain that the 'household codes' are specifically Christian constructions. Others argue that this text is really not a christological or theological argument.

Because Col. 3.18 is the oldest Second Testament text called a household code and also the formally most cohesive, some scholars have suggested that behind the household code of Col. 3.18–4.1 there lurks a later addition or gloss of a different author. The fact that the context does not lead one to expect this self-contained passage would support such a view. In addition, Col. 3.18–4.1 spends not one word on the problem of mixed relationships that virulently occupied the Jesus movement.[13] The admonitions remain non-specific and unrealistic as far as 'unbelieving' husbands or masters are concerned.[14] But in my judgment, this passage is no gloss. However, the correctly noted impression that it appears to be a gloss gives a few hints as to Pauline's intentions behind the text.

There are indeed legal codes that list a bundle of duties to God as well as duties of the old and the young, the ruled and the rulers, of men and women. These codes are addressed to most groups in the cities and to their homes (ὄικος), and the respective specific duties to the correlative groups are stated in the imperative and in certain cases substantiated briefly. Unfortunately it is difficult to determine the *Sitz im Leben* of every individual legal code, its objective and purpose. One such legal code does in my view reveal something about its *Sitz im Leben*.

A second- or first-century BCE stele that had been found in Philadelphia (Asia Minor) lists conditions for admission into a mystery-cult sanctuary:

> For good fortune…the instructions, given in his sleep to Dionysius who gives open access to his house to men and women, free and slave… Other than his wife a man shall not defile a strange woman, whether free or slave, who has a husband, nor a boy nor a virgin, and shall not commend others to do so… A free woman shall be holy and not know the bed or company of a man other than her own… The gods will show favour to those who follow [this rule].[15]

12.   Ulrike Wagener, *Die Ordnung des 'Hauses Gottes': Der Ort von Frauen in der Ekklesiologie und Ethik der Pastoralbriefe* (WUNT, 2.65; Tübingen: J.C.B. Mohr [Paul Siebeck], 1994).

13.   1 Cor. 7.12-23 and elsewhere.

14.   This is addressed differently, e.g., in 1 Pet. 3.1-6.

15.   *SIG*² III no. 985. The translation is that of K. Berger and C. Colpe (eds.),

Like the household codes of Colossians, this stone document lists admonitions addressed to two socially related groups: men and women, and gives a brief substantiation. The purpose of this inscription is twofold. For one, it obliges men and women to obey these instructions on specific feast days. For another, it makes plain to all outsiders what goes on in this sanctuary. The point of this seemingly is to protect the community of the mystery cult. Many non-initiates and especially Roman officials viewed these cults with suspicion since one of their features was precisely that they were not public. They were suspected—partly for good reason—of celebrating the abolition of social order, women taking on the roles of men, slaves those of the free. It is small wonder that for a long time the introduction of mystery cults was prohibited in Rome. With the publication of this inscription, Dionysius protects the mystery cult-sanctuary in Philadelphia against such suspicions. All who pass by are informed that here too, especially in this place of secrecy, everything is in 'good order', that this mystery cult constrains its members to adhere with particular zeal to their traditional social roles.

What did Pauline want to accomplish by introducing her household code into the epistle to the Colossians? She puts in a kind of legal code the substance of which is determined by political economy. This makes for contradictions with the congregation's concrete situation and the context of the epistle. If putting on the human being made new abolishes the differences between slaves and free (3.10-11), why should slaves submit to their worldly masters? Why does she deal with earthly things at all after having so eloquently described the heavenly reality of those addressed?

Relations between socially different groups of people are not spoken to in Colossians apart from the household code. The only social group that is mentioned in Col. 3.18–4.1 as well as in the rest of the epistle are 'fellow slaves' Epaphras and Tychicus. This 'title', known only from Colossians, refers to Paul's self-appellation 'slave of Christ' (Gal. 1.10; Phil. 1.1 and elsewhere). At the same time, the section on slaves is the longest within the household code. It contains a number of peculiarities. In the ancient world, slaves were not legal persons. But here they are promised an inheritance (3.24). They are also warned against doing what is unjust for there is not partiality toward persons (3.25). What advantages were slaves supposed to expect from partiality toward their persons?

On the literary level the slave-parenesis relates explicitly to Tychicus and Epaphras, the latter being depicted as one of the addressees (4.12).

Religionsgeschichtliches Textbuch zum Neuen Testament (NTD, 1; Göttingen: Vandenhoeck & Ruprecht, 1987), nos. 512, 274-75.

What attracts attention not least is that in the admonition to the masters, the keyword ἰσότης is used, which in this context is ill-placed. Ἰσότης means equality, a concept used, for example, by the Essenes against slavery.[16] Verse 4.1 may be translated as follows: 'You masters, show your slaves what is just and equality' (ἰσότης). In my view, this is Pauline's hint to read the household code against the grain.

Like the stele in Philadelphia, the household code informs outsiders who take cognizance of it what goes on inside ('in the Lord'): no subversive overturning at all but the solidification of patriarchal social orders, a communication that in view of Col. 3.11 had a calming effect not least upon Roman officials. But there are reasons to assume that at least part of Pauline's addressees uncovered her intentional action of concealing the real issue and decoded the 'household code' that she had conspicuously made to stand out from the context and read it in the sense of the new reality of Christ, the abolishing of class differences and creating a community of mutually encouraging fellow slaves.

Pauline and the Epistle to the Congregation in Colossae

I have tried to reconstruct Pauline's interests that caused her to compose this epistle. Whether Pauline was a woman or a man can scarcely be determined. Many may be more inclined to think of a male author. But let us assume that Pauline was in fact a woman or a group of women; she would have done something typical of many women today. She gave comfort to frustrated friends, female and male, who had been robbed by Paul's death of all hope. She wrote a heavenly letter for her friend Paul, a testament so to speak, explaining his death and calling the congregations to stay together. She decisively developed the theology of her friends further, rescued them from a deep crisis but kept her own name hidden. But she also kept her sisters hidden, making their cohesion, solidarity, and steadfastness to a large extent invisible. That is her biggest mistake. More still: she sacrificed them for an easier, perhaps the only possible way of the group's short-term survival in a time of much threat. She chose to forego the use of female images for God and for divine reality. She saw the relationship among God, the son of God, and the world in strictly hierarchical terms, as an image of earthly conditions. In so doing she let a part of her sisters' and brothers' utopias fall into oblivion. With the invention or introduction of the household code she became an accomplice in the history of the oppression of women, girls, and slaves. It may be said that she overestimated the critical understanding of her hearers and read-

16. Philo, *Omn. Prob. Lib.* 79; cf. also *Spec. Leg.* 2.68.

ers. It may also be that some of her sisters and brothers saw through her tactics, exposed the contradiction between household code and context, and unmasked it for what it could perhaps have been intended as: a writing to cover up and protect the congregation against persecution. However, others could use her epistle as Paulinic legitimation of their own writings that oppress women and slaves. But it is to the credit of Pauline and her sisters that this was felt to be necessary subsequent to the appearance of the epistle to the Colossians.

1 TIMOTHY 2.9-15 AND THE PLACE OF WOMEN IN THE CHURCH'S MINISTRY*

David M. Scholer

Evangelicals who oppose or limit the participation of women in preaching, teaching, or exercising authority in the church consider 1 Tim. 2.11-12 the clearest and strongest biblical text in support of their position.[1] Although 1 Cor. 14.34-35 appears to be absolute on prohibiting women from speaking in the church and cites 'the law' as sanction for this view, this text is not cited as frequently and forcefully, probably because it is obvious that 1 Cor. 11.5, indicating that women do pray and prophesy, in some way qualifies the prohibition of 1 Cor. 14.34-35.[2] In contrast, 1 Tim. 2.11-12 appears to have no qualification of any kind and a sanction is provided by a clear allusion to Genesis 2–3 (1 Tim. 2.13-14). This passage has been addressed in numerous articles stemming from the evangelical communities, both from those who oppose or limit the participation of women in ministry[3] and from those who support full participation of women in ministry.[4]

*   Originally published in Alvera Mickelsen (ed.), *Women, Authority and the Bible* (Downers Grove, IL: InterVarsity Press, 1986), pp. 193-219. Reprinted by permission.
     1.   See, e.g., G.W. Knight III, *The New Testament Teaching on the Role Relationship of Men and Women* (Grand Rapids: Baker Book House, 1977), p. 29, who lists this text as the one 'which most clearly gives both the apostle Paul's verdict and his reason'; and the space given to this passage in J.B. Hurley, *Man and Woman in Biblical Perspective* (Grand Rapids: Zondervan, 1981), pp. 195-233.
     2.   For further comments on this, see D.M. Scholer, 'Women in Ministry, Session 6: 1 Corinthians 14.34, 35', *Covenant Companion* 73.2 (1984), pp. 13-14.
     3.   Evangelical articles that oppose or limit the participation of women in ministry are: G.L. Archer, 'Does 1 Timothy 2.12 Forbid the Ordination of Women?', in *Encyclopedia of Bible Difficulties* (Grand Rapids: Zondervan, 1982), pp. 411-15; G.W. Knight III, 'ΑΥΘΕΝΤΕΩ in Reference to Women in 1 Timothy 2.12', *NTS* 30 (1984), pp. 143-57; D.J. Moo, '1 Timothy 2.11-15: Meaning and Significance', *Trinity Journal* 1 (1981), pp. 62-83; *idem*, 'The Interpretation of 1 Timothy 2.11-15: A Rejoinder', *Trinity Journal* 2 (1982), pp. 198-222; C.D. Osburn, 'ΑΥΘΕΝΤΕΩ (1 Timothy 2.12)', *Restoration Quarterly* 25 (1982), pp. 1-12; A.J. Panning, 'ΑΥΘΕΝΤΕΙΝ—a Word Study', *Wisconsin Lutheran Quarterly* 78 (1981), pp. 185-91; B.W. Powers, 'Women in the Church: The Application of 1 Timothy 2.8-15', *Interchange* 17 (1975), pp. 55-59.

This essay provides exegetical and hermeneutical considerations on 1 Tim. 2.9-15 that are crucial to a responsible, contextual interpretation of this Pauline text and to its consistent application to the place of women in the church within the context of faith and commitment to biblical authority.[5]

To carry out this purpose, this essay focuses on (1) the historical context of the passage gained by using the often-neglected 1 Tim. 2.15 as a key to uncovering the social-historical context and (2) the particular arguments of those who see this text as a primary basis for excluding or limiting women in ministry.

The approaches that neglect this text[6] or dismiss it because it does not

---

4.   Evangelical articles that support full participation of women in ministry are: J.J. Davis, 'Ordination of Women Reconsidered: Discussion of 1 Timothy 2.8-15', *Presbyterian Communique* 12.6 (1979), pp. 1, 8-11, 15 (repr. in R. Hestenes [ed.], *Women and Men in Ministry* [Pasadena, CA: Fuller Theological Seminary, 1980], pp. 37-40); N.J. Hommes, 'Let Women Be Silent in the Church: A Message Concerning the Worship Service and the Decorum to Be Observed by Women', *Calvin Theological Journal* 4 (1969), pp. 5-22; K.W. Hoover, 'Creative Tension in 1 Timothy 2.11-15', *Brethren Life and Thought* 22 (1977), pp. 163-66; C.C. Kroeger, 'Ancient Heresies and a Strange Greek Verb', *Reformed Journal* 29.3 (1979), pp. 12-15 (repr. in Hestenes [ed.], *Women and Men in Ministry*, pp. 60-63); R. Kroeger and C.C. Kroeger, 'May Women Teach? Heresy in the Pastoral Epistles', *Reformed Journal* 30.10 (1980), pp. 14-18; V.R. Mollenkott, 'Interpreting Difficult Scriptures', *Daughters of Sarah* 5.2 (1979), pp. 16-17 (repr. in *Daughters of Sarah* 7.5 [1981], pp. 13-16); P.B. Payne, 'Libertarian Women in Ephesus: A Response to Douglas J. Moo's article, "1 Timothy 2.11-15: Meaning and Significance"', *Trinity Journal* 2 (1981), pp. 169-97; M.D. Roberts, 'Woman Shall Be Saved: A Closer Look at 1 Timothy 2.15', *TSF Bulletin* 5.2 (1981), pp. 4-7; D.M. Scholer, 'Exegesis: 1 Timothy 2.8-15', *Daughters of Sarah* 1 (1975), pp. 7-8 (repr. in Hestenes [ed.], *Women and Men in Ministry*, p. 74); *idem*, 'Women in Ministry, Session 7: 1 Timothy 2.8-15', *Covenant Companion* 73.2 (1984), pp. 14-15; *idem*, 'Women's Adornment: Some Historical and Hermeneutical Observations on the New Testament Passages', *Daughters of Sarah* 6.1 (1980), pp. 3-6; A.D.B. Spencer, 'Eve at Ephesus (Should Women Be Ordained as Pastors according to the First Letter to Timothy 2.11-15?)', *JETS* 17 (1974), pp. 215-22; *idem*, 'Paul, Our Friend and Champion', *Daughters of Sarah* 2.3 (1976), pp. 1-3.

5.   In spite of genuine historical, literary, and theological problems, I remain convinced that the Pastoral Epistles (1 and 2 Timothy, Titus) are best accounted for as coming from Paul or from someone under his general supervision. This is not the place to rehearse the arguments. In any event, 1 Tim. 2.9-15 is part of the church's New Testament canon and must be dealt with as such; I reject the view (e.g. Powers, 'Women in the Church', and Hommes, 'Let Women Be Silent') that 1 Tim. 2.9-15 deals only with the marriage relationship and not the place of women in the church. For me, the specific language and the context make this clear.

6.   E.M. Tetlow, *Women and Ministry in the New Testament* (New York: Paulist Press, 1980), for example, does not mention this text at all in the book.

correspond well with one's 'genuine' Pauline 'canon within a cannon'[7] are rejected here. Such approaches usually see 1 Tim. 2.9-15 as a post-Pauline critique of the 'genuine' Paul on women's place in the church. My approach assumes much more complexity both for Paul's thought and for the variety of situations that he addresses.

Exegetical Considerations

1 Timothy 2.15 – the Heresy at Ephesus and the Purpose of 1 Timothy
The discussion of 1 Tim. 2.9-15 and its bearing on the place of women in the church often focuses immediately or only on vv. 11-12 (or vv. 11-14) to the exclusion of vv. 9-10 and especially of the notoriously difficult v. 15. For example, George W. Knight's book, which considers 1 Tim. 2.11-15 the clearest biblical evidence for his position, never discusses v. 15 per se.[8] Susan Foh ends her discussion of 1 Tim. 2.8-15 by saying: 'The last verse (v. 15) in this section is a puzzle and a sort of non sequitur.'[9] Such neglect shows an irresponsible and symptomatic neglect of reading texts in their contexts.

Verse 15 is clearly the climactic resolution of the whole unit.[10] The subject introduced in v. 9 is 'likewise *women*'. The explicit noun (*woman* or *women*) is repeated in vv. 10, 11, and 14 and is implied throughout. The sentence of v. 15 is connected with the preceding by δέ ('yet') and the opening verb depends on the previous sentence for its subject ἡ γυνή ('the woman'). One frequently mentioned problem with v. 15 is that the first verse verb σωθήσεται ('will be saved') is singular, whereas the second verb μείνωσιν ('to abide or remain') is plural. This demonstrates the obvious connection between vv. 15 and 2.9-14 — Eve (v. 13) represents woman (v. 14) or women (vv. 9, 10, 11); thus, the grammatically

---

7.   See, e.g., R. Scroggs, 'Paul and the Eschatological Woman', *JAAR* 40 (1972), pp. 283-303: 'To separate the establishment Paul from the historical Apostle is reasonably simple… The Pastorals are thus immediately discarded and, for our purposes, hopefully forgotten' (p. 284). Scroggs (and others) also reject 1 Cor. 14.34-35 as non-Pauline. At least two scholars have argued, further, that it is thus logical to regard 1 Cor. 11.3-16 as non-Pauline as well and do so regard it: W.O. Walker, Jr, '1 Corinthians 11.2-16 and Paul's Views Regarding Women', *JBL* 94 (1975), pp. 94-110; and G.W. Trompf, 'On Attitudes toward Woman in Paul and Paulist Literature: 1 Corinthians 11.3-16 and Its Context', *CBQ* 42 (1980), pp. 196-215.

8.   Knight, *The New Testament Teaching*.

9.   S.T. Foh, *Women and the Word of God: A Response to Biblical Feminism* (Grand Rapids: Baker Book House, 1980), p. 128.

10.   In spite of the punctuation in *NovTGr*[26] and the arguments of some, I reject the view that 1 Tim. 3.1a ('This is a faithful saying') is the conclusion of 2.9-15 or any part of it. I understand it to be the introduction to 3.1b.

natural shift in v. 15 from the singular (woman as womankind) to the plural (individual women).

Not only is v. 15 clearly part of the 2.9-15 unit, but it is also its climax. It provides, within the structure of Paul's argument, a positive conclusion to the negative statements in 2.11-14. Therefore, until v. 15 is adequately addressed, there is no legitimate entrée to the rest of the paragraph (2.9-14).

The opening clause, 'woman will be saved through childbirth' (v. 15a) often reads with great difficulty for Protestant evangelical interpreters; thus, the New International Version translates it: 'But women will be kept safe through childbirth.' Of course, σώζειν ('to save') can have a range of meanings, but in such Pauline contexts the virtually inevitable sense is that of the salvation of God in Christ. This sense of salvation is confirmed by the next clause, 'if they continue in faith, love and holiness with propriety' (NIV), which would make little sense otherwise.

One relatively common attempt to resolve the difficulties is to assume that the singular subject of 'will be saved' is Eve and the 'childbearing' is the birth of the Messiah Jesus, implying that Eve's sin (2.14) is reversed with the coming and work of Christ.[11] Such a view, however, founders on the most likely meaning of τεκνογονία ('childbearing and child-rearing'; see 1 Tim. 5.14) and the inapplicability of this reading of 2.15 with reference to 2.13-14.[12]

In view of the vocabulary, structure and contextual location of 2.15, this conclusion to the discussion of the place of women in the church must mean that women find their place among the saved (assuming, of course, their continuation in faith, love, and holiness) through the maternal and domestic roles that were clearly understood to constitute propriety (σωφροσύνη) for women in the Greco-Roman culture of Paul's day.[13]

The concern for propriety in v. 15 appears also in v. 9 at the beginnings of this paragraph in connection with women's dress and adornment. This concern in vv. 9-10 is another aspect of a woman's domestic role of decency and propriety in Greco-Roman society at that time.

These concerns in 2.9-15 for propriety in women's behavior imply that in 1 Timothy and, more generally, in the Pastoral Epistles, Paul is addressing a challenge to their behavior. This is confirmed by the context of similar passages. These other texts focus on what is appropriate behavior

11. See, e.g., Spencer, 'Eve at Ephesus', and Roberts, 'Woman Shall Be Saved'.

12. For significant lexical data, see C. Spicq, *Les épîtres pastorales* (2 vols.; EBib; Paris: Gabalda, 4th edn, 1969), I, pp. 382-83; see also Moo, '1 Timothy 2.11-15', p. 71.

13. For the cultural context see S.B. Pomeroy, *Goddesses, Whores, Wives and Slaves: Women in Classical Antiquity* (New York: Schocken Books, 1975); and D.L. Balch, *Let Wives Be Submissive: The Domestic Code in 1 Peter* (SBLMS, 26; Chico, CA: Scholars Press, 1981).

for women and for domestic life, particularly with reference to the opposition (heresy) that Timothy and Paul faced and in terms of Paul's concern for the church's social reputation within Greco-Roman society.

The emphasis in 2.15 takes on a special focus when it is noted that the opponents, against whom Paul is writing and warning Timothy, forbid marriage (1 Tim. 4.3). Thus, it is not surprising that Paul dwells on marriage concerns in his long paragraph on widows in the church (1 Tim. 5.3-16). He stresses that widows under 60 years of age should not be put on the roll of widows (5.11) but should marry, have children and manage their homes (5.14). This appeal is explicitly set against an alternative behavior: 'They get into the habit of being idle and going about from house to house. And not only do they become idlers, but also gossips and busybodies, saying things they ought not to' (5.13 NIV).[14] Paul finds such behavior so unacceptable that he describes it as following Satan (5.15). The widows 60 years of age and older can be placed on the roll of widows provided that their lives have been marked by good works (5.10), a characteristic explicitly called for in 2.9-10 and implied in 2.15.

The concern is also explicit in Tit. 2.3-5. Older women are to be exemplary in behavior and committed to teaching younger women what is good (2.3-4). What the younger women are to be taught corresponds to what is said in 1 Tim. 2.5, 9-10 and 5.9-15: they are to love their husbands and children, be subject to their husbands and be domestic.[15] The concern for propriety is also expressed (2.4-5).

Concern for proper domestic life is also noted in texts directed to male leaders within the church. Bishops (1 Tim. 3.4-5), deacons (1 Tim. 3.12), and elders (Tit. 1.6) must be persons whose home and family life are respectable and in order.

These texts and others express concern for the reputation of the church within the larger Greco-Roman society:[16] 'a good reputation with outsiders' (1 Tim. 3.7); 'to give the enemy no opportunity for slander' (1 Tim. 5.14); 'so that...our teaching may not be slandered' (1 Tim. 6.1); 'so that no one will malign the word of God' (Tit. 2.5); 'so that those who oppose you may be ashamed because they have nothing bad to say about us' (Tit. 2.8); and 'so that in every way they [slaves] will make the teaching about God our Savior attractive' (Tit. 2.10). Certainly this concern lies behind Paul's first agenda item in 1 Timothy in which the rationale is

14. See a similar concern in Philo, *Spec. Leg.* 3.169-71.

15. On the meaning of the term see BAGD, p. 561; note that this is a Hellenistic term.

16. Biblical quotations are from the NIV with occasional alterations to make the language inclusive.

'that we may live peaceful and quiet lives in all godliness and holiness. This is good, and pleases God our Savior, who wants all persons to be saved' (2.2-4).

This concern for public reputation, model domestic life, and appropriate decorum and maternal-domestic roles for women clearly implies that the opposition (heresy) that Paul and Timothy faced in Ephesus constituted an assault on marriage and what were considered appropriate models for women in that society. As noted above, the heresy prohibited marriage (1 Tim. 4.3). Apparently, the false teachers encouraged women to leave their homes and meet together (see 1 Tim. 5.13-15 and the implied converse of Tit. 2.4-5). Part of the heresy evidently involved what Paul called 'worldly old wives' tales' (τοὺς βεβήλους καὶ γραώδεις μύθους, 1 Tim. 4.7).[17] This accounts for Paul's emphasis on godly living and right teaching for older women in 1 Tim. 5.9-10 and Tit. 2.3-4.

Such inferences are confirmed by the description of the false teachers and their methods in 2 Tim. 3.1-9. They 'worm their way into homes and gain control over weak-willed women (γυναικάριον),[18] who are loaded down with sins and are swayed by all kinds of evil desires, always learning but never able to acknowledge the truth' (3.6-7).

1 Tim. 2.15, then, in its immediate and larger context within the Pastoral Epistles, opens the way for understanding the paragraph on the conduct of women in the church in 1 Tim. 2.9-15. It addresses a particular situation of false teaching in Ephesus that assaulted and abused what was considered appropriate and honorable behavior for women.[19]

To see 1 Tim. 2.9-15 as addressing a particular heresy focused on women and women's roles raises the whole issue of the purpose of 1 Timothy (as well as 2 Tim.). The purpose of 1 Timothy is to combat the Ephesian heresy that Timothy faced. Paul addresses this heresy immediately

17. The translation is that of BAGD, p. 138. Note that the term γραώδης (characteristic of old women) is a Hellenistic and Stoic term and is only here in the New Testament (BAGD, p. 167).

18. See BAGD, p. 168. This term is a relatively uncommon word found almost entirely within the Hellenistic period.

19. The heresy is some type of ascetic-Gnosticizing movement within the church (1 Tim. 1.3-7; 6.20-21) but cannot be more specifically defined. There is no clear or particular evidence that connects this heresy with any pagan worship in Ephesus and its sexual activities and connotations. For background on the Artemis/Diana cult in Ephesus see the references given in Moo, '1 Timothy 2.11-15', p. 81 n. 118. Two especially useful articles bearing on the heresy and women in the Pastoral Epistles are R.J. Karris, 'The Background and Significance of the Polemic of the Pastoral Epistles', *JBL* 92 (1973), pp. 549-64; and J.M. Bassler, 'The Widows' Tale: A Fresh Look at 1 Timothy 5.3-16', *JBL* 103 (1984), pp. 23-41. See also the earlier study of J.M. Ford, 'A Note on Proto-Montanism in the Pastoral Epistles', *NTS* 17 (1970–71), pp. 338-46.

after the formal beginning of the letter (1.3-7). Apart from the final 'grace be with you' (6.21b), the letter ends with explicit concern about the false teaching (6.20-21). Paul mentions false teachers frequently throughout the letter (1.18-20; 4.1-8; 5.16; 6.3-10; see also 2 Tim. 2.16-18; 3.1-9; 4.3-4, 14-15).[20]

It is within this understanding of the purpose of 1 Timothy that 1 Tim. 3.14-15 should be understood: 'I am writing you these instructions so that...you will know how people ought to conduct themselves in God's household...'

Scholars such as George Knight and James Hurley understand 1 Tim. 3.14-15 as *the* purpose of 1 Timothy and infer from it that Paul is giving a suprasituational 'church manual'. Thus, Hurley begins his chapter on 1 Tim. 2.8-15 with a unit entitled 'The Announced Purpose of 1 Timothy' and writes that Paul 'considered what he said normative beyond the immediate situation' and 'indicates that his instructions should have a general rather than closely limited application'.[21] Knight also begins his treatment of 1 Tim. 2.8-15 by noting that 1 Tim. 3.14-15 determines its character.[22]

Yet it is presumptuous to take 1 Tim. 3.14-15 out of the context of the whole letter and make it the proof of a transsituational reading of 1 Timothy. Rather, 3.14-15 should be seen as a summary statement of the specific directions given for meeting a particular problem of heresy that Timothy was facing in Ephesus at that time.[23]

Therefore, 1 Timothy should be understood as an occasional *ad hoc* letter directed specifically toward enabling Timothy and the church to

---

20.   See G.D. Fee, *1 and 2 Timothy, Titus* (Good News Commentary; San Francisco: Harper & Row, 1984) for a presentation of 1 Timothy as an *ad hoc* letter dealing with a particular problem of heresy.

21.   The unit is in Hurley, *Man and Woman*, pp. 195-97; the quotations are from p. 196.

22.   Knight, *The New Testament Teaching*, pp. 29-30.

23.   The understanding of the purpose of the Pastorals and the heresy faced by them is different from the situation proposed in the intriguing book by D.R. MacDonald, *The Legend and the Apostle: The Battle for Paul in Story and Canon* (Philadelphia: Westminster Press, 1983). In brief, MacDonald argues that the complexity of Paul led in two post-Pauline directions on women in the church. The Pastorals represent the domestication of the gospel; the *Acts of Paul* represent the 'socially radical' Paul on women. In fact, MacDonald argues that the Pastorals are directed against the traditions that ultimately surface in the *Acts of Paul* and that, therefore, what is 'heresy' from the Pastorals' perspective is what is the 'positive' view of women in the *Acts of Paul*. In spite of the difference between MacDonald's and my assessment of the opponents of 1 Timothy and the Pastorals, his book is useful in getting at the particular social-historical context of the Pastorals.

avoid and combat the false teachers and teaching in Ephesus. This false teaching appealed strongly to women and led them so astray that traditional values of marriage and the home were seriously violated.

1 Timothy 2.9-10
The paragraph on the place of women in the church begins with 1 Tim. 2.9. The opening clause is somewhat unclear, although it is related to 2.8 by ὡσαύτως ('likewise'). In 2.8 Paul instructs men on the proper posture and attitude for prayer. This relates to the theme of prayer introduced in the previous paragraph (2.1-7). Whether v. 9 should be understood specifically as an instruction to women at prayer or as general instruction on women's adornment and dress cannot be resolved, although the latter may be slightly more likely.[24] In any event, the context is the church.

With the perspective of 1 Tim. 2.15 and the purpose of the entire epistle seen as combating false teaching, 2.9-10 is clearly as serious a set of injunctions in the context as 2.11-12.[25] The instructions regarding women's dress and adornment are given without qualification. Most important, 2.9-10 is similar to 2.15 in affirming high standards of cultural decency so that the church will be above reproach. These standards contrast the values encouraged by the opposing heretical teachings.

This assumption is confirmed when the injunctions regarding women's adornment and dress are seen within the larger societal contexts of the church, in terms of both Jewish and Greco-Roman cultures.[26] The extra-biblical literature from these cultural contexts also favors modesty and rejects expensive clothing, hair styling, gold jewelry, and pearls. These Jewish and pagan passages regularly condemn such external adornment and argue that a woman's inner beauty and chastity should be her real adornment.

24. See Moo, '1 Timothy 2.11-15', p. 63.

25. Contrast this with S.B. Clark, *Man and Woman in Christ: An Examination of the Roles of Men and Women in Light of Scripture and the Social Sciences* (Ann Arbor: Servant Books, 1980), p. 194: 'We should not place too much emphasis on the exhortation to women to adorn themselves modestly and sensibly. This exhortation is not the heart of the passage.' This certainly begs the issues at hand and decides on grounds totally apart from the text or 1 Timothy that the 'heart' of the passage is elsewhere (i.e. 2.11-12).

26. For more extensive treatment of this point with the citation of numerous primary texts, see Scholer, 'Women's Adornment'. This article provides the detailed evidence for this section on 1 Tim. 2.9-10 in this essay. The texts include *1 En.* 8.1-2; *T. Reub.* 5.1-5; *Pseudo-Phintys* and *Pseudo-Perictione* (Neo-Pythagorean texts from about the second century BCE); Seneca, *To Helvia on Consolation* 16.3-4; Musonius Rufus 3.17-20; Juvenal, *Satires* 6.457-59, 501-503, 508-509; Plutarch, *Advice to the Bride and Groom* 26, 30-32; and *Sentences of Sextus* 235, 513.

More important, in virtually all the Jewish and pagan texts, the rejection of external adornment was part of a woman's submission to her husband and a recognition of her place among men in general. Using external adornments such as pearls, gold jewelry, hair styling, and expensive, provocative clothing indicated two undesirable characteristics — material extravagance and sexual infidelity.

Thus, the progression of thought in 1 Tim. 2.9-15 moves from concern for women's adornment (vv. 9-10) to concern for women's submission and silence in public worship (vv. 11-12). These are two sides of the same coin in the cultural settings of the first century CE, which assumed male dominance and a belief in women's subordination and inferiority.

In view of this unity of 2.9-12 and the conclusion in 2.15, there is no exegetical, historical, and hermeneutical basis to regard 2.9-10 as normatively different from 2.11-12. Nevertheless, most evangelicals, including those who see 2.11-12 as warrant for limiting women in ministry, take the injunctions against women's adornment in 2.9-10 to be culturally relative and do not seek to apply them in the unqualified terms in which they are stated. Furthermore, many who discuss 2.11-12 as warrant for limiting women in ministry do not even consider 2.9-10 in their discussion, or they treat it rather briefly.[27]

The point is that 2.9-10 is intended to protect women from the enticements of the false teachers (see esp. 1 Tim. 4.1-3; 6.3-10) and the temptations of sexual infidelity within Greco-Roman culture to which the false teaching could lead. Thus, 2.9-10 is part of Paul's specific response to the false teaching in Ephesus that had been directed especially at women who had been made vulnerable by their treatment as inferior or marginal in their society. Paul encourages dress and adornment for women that correspond to the 'high moral standards' of Jewish and pagan society and, therefore, present the church as of good reputation and without offense.

1 Timothy 2.11-12 and the Pauline Context of Women's Participation in the Church's Ministry
To the degree that 2.15 and 2.9-10 are limited to the threat and presence of the false teachers in Ephesus and are set within particular cultural

27. Note that Moo, '1 Timothy 2.11-15', and Knight, *The New Testament Teaching*, include only 2.11-15 in their discussions. Foh's section entitled '1 Timothy 2.8-15' (*Women and the Word*, pp. 122-28) does not, in fact, treat 2.9-10. Hurley's chapter on 1 Tim. 2.8-15 (*Man and Woman*, pp. 195-233) includes only a page and a half on 2.9-10 (pp. 198-99). In my judgment, Hurley understands to some degree the 'culturally conditioned' character of 2.9-10, but he is not consistent in understanding the whole of 2.9-15 on the same model.

values, so also are the injunctions to silence and submission in 2.11-12.[28] All are part of the same paragraph.

The injunctions of 2.11-12 correspond with the generally accepted norms of behavior and expectations for women in both Jewish and Greco-Roman cultures.[29] Thus, the statements of 2.11-12 reinforce honorable patterns of behavior in response to the false teaching and its abusive use of women. The statements of 2.9-10 and 2.15 do the same.

The statements of 2.11-12 are thus *ad hoc* instructions intended for a particular situation in Ephesus of false teaching focused on women. These statements are not to be understood as universal principles encoded in a suprasituational 'church order manual' that limit women in ministry in all times and places. Rather, the instructions of 2.11-12 are directed against women who, having been touched or captivated by false teachings, are abusing the normal opportunities women had within the church to teach and exercise authority.

This interpretation is grounded in three basic perspectives. First, the immediate context (2.9-15) and the larger context of 1 and 2 Timothy show that the fundamental issue being addressed throughout 1 Timothy is the false teaching plaguing the church in Ephesus. This false teaching and its teachers had women as a particular focus and encouraged them to radically violate appropriate and honorable behavior patterns for women. Thus, it is reasonable to assume that this situation occasioned the specific remarks of 2.11-12.

Those who see 2.11-12 as excluding or limiting women in ministry usually object to such a historical reconstruction. They argue that if Paul had intended 2.11-12 to mean that women who were involved in the false teachings should be prohibited from teaching or exercising authority in the church, he could easily have said so at this very point. Moreover, Paul could have mentioned cultural values of importance to the church.[30]

---

28. I reject the suggestion that Paul's 'I do not permit' (οὐκ ἐπιτρέπω, 2.12) is a basis for limiting 2.11-12 because it is only opinion. Paul often expresses his apostolic authority in personal terms (e.g. 1 Cor. 7.40, 12). See the 'debate' over ἐπιτρέπω in Payne, 'Libertarian Women', pp. 170-73, and Moo, 'Interpretation', pp. 199-200. I side with Moo and do not rest my case for a limited application of 2.11-12 on Payne's observations on this point.

29. For the cultural context of the customary prohibition on women's public speaking, see the citations in nn. 13, 14, 19, and 26. The contention of Moo, '1 Timothy 2.11-15', p. 81, that due to trends in the Hellenistic period and especially the presence of the cult of Artemis/Diana in Ephesus, women engaging in public teaching would not be offensive is too simplistic and too narrow a view of all the evidence regarding the place of women in Greco-Roman culture.

30. See, e.g., Moo, 'Interpretation', p. 203; Knight, *The New Testament Teaching*, pp. 31-32; Hurley, *Man and Woman*, p. 203.

Such an objection does not take seriously the character of 1 Timothy as an occasional letter or the full context of 1 and 2 Timothy. Such an objection assumes that 2.11-12 is one unit in a series of timeless, universal principles set within a document on church order. The commands of 2.11-12, however, occur within a specific paragraph, the climax of which (2.15) already indicates a specific situation. The larger context of 1 and 2 Timothy confirms this. Thus, 2.11-12 must always be understood within these contexts, as well as the larger Pauline context. To assert that Paul did or could have easily written for the sake of twentieth-century interpreters begs the whole question of the contextual and historical situation addressed in 1 Timothy. Paul is not obligated to give a full account of the whole social context shared by him and his original readers. Paul did not do that in his complex discussion of eating meat offered to idols and abuses in church worship directed to Corinth (1 Cor. 8–10; 12–14). Those texts also have interpretive ambiguities that must be resolved by social-historical reconstruction. The complete literary context and the shared experience and knowledge of author and first readers made such discussion unnecessary.

Another objection is that if Paul's purpose was to stop heretical teaching within the church's worship, then the male false teachers should have been included within the injunctions of 2.11-12.[31] This assumes that the male false teachers participated in the church's regular worship at the same level as the women who were touched by the false teachings. Nevertheless, the context of 1 and 2 Timothy suggests that the women involved were special targets of the male false teachers and were probably used by them as a means of infiltration. Certainly Paul does not condone or ignore false teachers simply because they are men; the rest of 1 and 2 Timothy makes that clear. Furthermore, this objection does not recognize that 2.11-12 is part of a paragraph (2.9-15) that is devoted exclusively to the issue of women in the Ephesian church. The abuses of men are handled elsewhere in the letter.

Another factor basic to the interpretation of 2.11-12 concerns Paul's use of the unusual word αὐθεντεῖν (translated 'to have authority over' RSV) in the second injunction (2.12). This is the only occurrence of this word in Paul's writings and, indeed, in the entire New Testament. The word is not frequently used in ancient Greek literature. The precise meaning of αὐθεντεῖν and its use in 2.12 cannot be completely resolved at this time; scholars are currently in an extended debate on the issue.[32]

---

31. See, e.g., Moo, 'Interpretation', p. 203.
32. See the articles devoted to this term listed in nn. 3 and 4, by Knight,

Traditionally, αὐθεντεῖν has been understood to connote a sense of 'to domineer' or 'to usurp authority' and the term is even associated with murder.³³ Although not all of the evidence and arguments have been fully assessed, two points seem relatively certain. First, the term is unusual. If Paul were referring to the normal exercise of authority, his otherwise constant ἐξουσία/ἐξουσιάζω ('authority/to exercise authority') vocabulary would most likely have been used. The choice of such an unusual term itself indicates that Paul intended a different nuance of meaning. Second, in spite of Knight's efforts to the contrary, many uses of the term seem rather clearly to carry the negative sense of 'domineer' or 'usurp authority'.³⁴ Thus I see the injunctions of 2.11-12 as directed against women involved in false teaching who have abused proper exercise of authority in the church (not denied by Paul elsewhere to women) by usurpation and domination of the male leaders and teachers in the church at Ephesus.³⁵

The most crucial factor in understanding 2.11-12 is the matter of Paul's practice with regard to women's ministry in the church. Careful analysis of Acts and Paul's letters demonstrates that women engaged in the gospel ministry in Paul's churches just as men did.³⁶ Scholars such as Moo and Hurley argue that since none of the Pauline texts explicitly states that women 'taught' or 'exercised authority', the case for women in ministry at this level has not been established and the supposed evidence is irrelevant. This approach does not take seriously the depth of evidence available.³⁷ For example, even though Phil. 4.2-3 does not say that Euodia and Syntyche 'taught', Paul's description of their ministry implies that they taught and did so with authority.

'ΑΥΘΕΝΤΕΩ'; Panning, 'ΑΥΘΕΝΤΕΙΝ; Osburn, 'ΑΥΘΕΝΤΕΩ'; and Kroeger, 'Ancient Heresies'.

33. See Osburn, 'ΑΥΘΕΝΤΕΩ', pp. 2-8, for a brief summary of the evidence with primary text reference.

34. See Osburn, 'ΑΥΘΕΝΤΕΩ'; Kroeger, 'Ancient Heresies'.

35. If it were ever established that the term means only neutral or positive authority, the interpretation of 2.11-12 argued here would not be lost; the first and third perspectives would still establish the case.

36. For detail on all these texts, see D.M. Scholer, 'Paul's Women Co-Workers in the Ministry of the Church', *Daughters of Sarah* 6.4 (1980), pp. 3-6; *idem*, 'Women in Ministry, Session 3: Its Basis in the Early Church' and 'Women in Ministry, Session 4: Its Basis in Paul (Part One)', *Covenant Companion* 73.1 (1984), pp. 12-13; and *idem*, 'Women in Ministry, Session 5: Its Basis in Paul (Part 2)', *Covenant Companion* 73.2 (1984), pp. 12-13.

37. For one example, cf. Scholer (articles cited in n. 36) on Junia as apostle in Rom. 16.7 with Hurley, *Man and Woman*, pp. 121-22; and Moo, '1 Timothy 2.11-15', p. 76; *idem*, 'Interpretation', pp. 207-208. This would apply to all the women noted in Rom. 16.1-16 and Phil. 4.2-3.

Moo, Hurley, and others also discount the evidence on women in the ministry in Paul's churches on another ground. Their approach posits two levels of authority. They insist that the women noted in Rom. 16.1-16 and Phil. 4.2-3 and the activity indicated in 1 Cor. 11.5 show that women participated in the ministry of the church, but not at the level of authority prohibited by 1 Tim. 2.11-12. Such an approach imposes on the New Testament a concept of two levels of authority that is never indicated in the Pauline texts. Furthermore, this approach assumes that the structures reflected in 1 and 2 Timothy were normative in all Paul's churches. This assumption is rendered virtually untenable by 1 Corinthians alone, not to mention other letters of Paul.[38] For example, Hurley and Moo allow that even if Junia (Rom. 16.7) were a woman designated as an Apostle, she would not be an example of a woman having authority (in the sense of 1 Tim. 2.12) in the church because it would be clear that the use of the term 'apostle' here would have a very general, nonauthoritative sense![39]

Other unwarranted means have been used to maintain 1 Tim. 2.11-12 as a 'timeless absolute' prohibiting or limiting women with regard to teaching and exercising authority. One argument, noted first by Origen in his commentary on 1 Corinthians, says that 1 Tim. 2.12 does not exclude *private* instruction women give to men, with Priscilla's teaching of Apollos in Acts 18.26 as the example.[40] Such an argument does not address the fact that even such private teaching was certainly authoritative.

A final matter concerns the debate over whether women's engaging in prophecy (1 Cor. 11.5, 14; Acts 2; 21.8-9) indicates that women taught with authority in the church. Hurley and Moo, for example, sharply distinguish between prophecy and teaching, claiming that prophecy does not constitute the authoritative teaching ruled out by 1 Tim. 2.11-12.[41] Defining 'prophecy' is difficult, but recent major studies of prophecy in the early church, such as those by David Hill and David Aune, clearly indicate that prophetic utterances and prophecy did function as authoritative teaching within Paul's churches.[42] This is certainly how

---

38. For an extended critique of these two arguments against the significance of the Pauline data on women in ministry, see D.M. Scholer, 'Hermeneutical Gerrymandering: Hurley on Women and Authority', *TSF Bulletin* 6.5 (1983), pp. 11-13.

39. Hurley, *Man and Woman*, p. 122; Moo, 'Interpretation', p. 208.

40. Origen, *Commentary on 1 Corinthians* 74 (the text of this fragment is in C. Jenkins, 'Origen on 1 Corinthians', *JTS* 10 [1908–1909], pp. 41-42).

41. Hurley, *Man and Woman*, pp. 120-21, 188-94; Moo, '1 Timothy 2.11-15', pp. 73-75; *idem*, 'Interpretation', pp. 206-207.

42. D. Hill, *New Testament Prophecy* (New Foundations Theological Library; Atlanta: John Knox Press, 1981); D. Aune, *Prophecy in Early Christianity and the Ancient Mediterranean World* (Grand Rapids: Eerdmans, 1983); see also T.W. Gillespie, 'Proph-

prophecy should be regarded in 1 Cor. 11–14, where Paul extols prophecy as the most desirable gift and activity for the edification of the church. Paul's definition of prophecy in 1 Cor. 14.3 makes it, along with the whole argument of 1 Cor. 14.1-25, a functional equivalent of authoritative teachings.[43]

A recent study by James Sigountos and Myron Shank adds a new argument to the relationship between prophecy and teaching. These scholars argue that Paul could allow women to prophesy and to pray and yet forbid them to teach because such a distinction was common in Greco-Roman society.[44] Although there has not yet been time to evaluate carefully the evidence they cite, it is dubious that they have made their case with respect to the Pauline literature. In some of the Greco-Roman texts they cite, prophecy is distinct from teaching because prophecy is mindless or beyond rational control. This analysis, however, does not fit Paul, since the Apostle argues vigorously (1 Corinthians 14) that prophecy *was* edifying speech that appealed to the rational thought of both speakers and hearers.

1 Timothy 2.13-14

The rationale for the injunctions stated in 2.11-12 is given in 2.13-14 in two parts: (1) Adam was created prior to Eve; and (2) it was Eve, not Adam, who was deceived and who transgressed. Those who believe that the statements in 2.11-12 are general and universal and that they limit women in ministry usually place great stress on the allusions to Genesis 2–3 found in 1 Tim. 2.13-14.[45] Several issues arise in assessing the meaning and significance of Paul's use of Genesis 2–3 at this point.

The discussion is introduced with γάρ ('for'). It is unclear whether the term here is meant to be causal (the position favored by Moo and others)

---

ecy and Tongues: The Concept of Christian Prophecy in Pauline Theology' (PhD dissertation, Claremont Graduate School, 1971).

43.   I find it telling that Hurley does not cite 1 Cor. 14.3 or deal with Paul's positive emphasis on prophecy for edification in his book; see Scholer, 'Hermeneutical Gerrymandering', and the excellent critique of Moo in J.G. Sigountos and M. Shank, 'Public Roles for Women in the Pauline Church: A Reappraisal of the Evidence', *JETS* 26 (1983), pp. 283-95 (the critique is found on pp. 285-86). These authors conclude that prophecy was at least as authoritative in Paul as was teaching.

44.   Sigountos and Shank, 'Public Roles', pp. 283-95. For the record, Sigountos and Shank do not see 1 Tim. 2.11-12 as prohibiting or limiting women in ministry today (p. 294).

45.   See, e.g., Knight, *The New Testament Teaching*, p. 32 ('No more basic and binding reason could be cited'); Moo, '1 Timothy 2.11-15', pp. 68-71; and Hurley, who has 'an excursus on Gen.1–3 and Paul's use of it' in the midst of his chapter on 1 Tim. 2.8-15 (*Man and Woman*, pp. 204-21).

or explanatory (the position that I favor). One's reading of the flow of the entire paragraph is the ultimate factor in deciding the meaning.

Those who find the allusion to Genesis 2–3 a reason for giving 1 Tim. 2.11-12 timeless validity assume that any injunction followed by a scriptural allusion is absolute. There is, however, no internal Pauline evidence that a Genesis allusion for the injunctions of 2.11-12 gives them greater universal significance than, for example, injunctions about widows in 1 Tim. 5.3-16, which do not include a Genesis allusion.

Furthermore, the Genesis allusion in 1 Tim. 2.13-14 is often considered to be an especially authoritative sanction because it derives from so-called creation ordinances. Of course, this applies only to the first sanction (2.13); the second sanction (2.14) is drawn from the account of the sin that violated the original situation. An argument drawn from the Genesis 3 account of sin does not necessarily give a Pauline injunction universal validity. After all, Paul's allusion to Genesis 1 in Gal. 3.28 must mean that, among those in Christ, the original mutuality and equality and the shared authority established in creation (Gen. 1.26-28) is restored.

The allusion in 1 Cor. 11.7-9 to Genesis 2 (which is before sin enters) indicates that arguments from the so-called creation ordinances can be used by Paul to support an injunction with clear historical-cultural limitations. The purpose of 1 Cor. 11.3-16 (seen esp. in vv. 4-5, 6, 7, 10, 13 and in the climax in 16) is to argue that women ought to have their heads covered in worship whenever they engage in prayer or prophecy. The purpose of this passage is not a presentation of male headship;[46] rather, that point is one of the several arguments used (along with nature, church practice, Genesis, and Christ's subordination to God) for the point that women should have covered heads in worship. The majority of evangelicals subscribing to biblical authority (including those who find in 1 Tim. 2.9-15 a basis for excluding or limiting women in ministry) understand the specific point of 1 Cor. 11.3-16 to be no longer directly applicable in our culture, at least in practice if not also in formal interpretation.[47] Such recognition indicates that Genesis 2 can be used by Paul to argue for a command that is historically and culturally limited.

It is important, however, in understanding 1 Tim. 2.13-14 to examine the specific data that Paul uses from Genesis. What seems overwhelmingly clear is that Paul is *selective* in his use of Genesis material.

---

46. See, e.g., Knight, *The New Testament Teaching*, pp. 32-34; Hurley, *Man and Woman*, p. 182 ('The basic command...at issue is the appointive headship of men', p. 184).

47. As implied in this paragraph, some persons who concede this limitation for 1 Cor. 11.3-16 have then attempted to argue that the headcovering for women was never the main point of the passage anyway.

That Adam was created prior to Eve (2.13) is drawn from Genesis 2; and the creation account in Genesis 1 does not set priorities in the creation of the two sexes.[48] Gal. 3.28 establishes that Paul knew the language of Genesis 1.27. Paul also selected Genesis 2 rather than Genesis 1 in his discussion in 1 Cor. 11.7-9. There, too, Paul asserts that Adam was created before Eve. In the 1 Corinthians text, Paul is even more selective in asserting that the man 'is in the image and glory of God; but the woman is the glory of man' (11.7). Although Paul does not deny that woman also was created in the image of God (Gen. 1.26-27; 5.1-2), he deliberately chooses to mention only that the man is in God's image in order to more clearly buttress his argument for head coverings for women. Paul, however, does qualify his Genesis argument in 1 Cor. 11.7-9 by his parenthetical, strong counterassertion in 11.11-12 of the mutual interdependence of man and woman in the Lord, a text parallel to Gal. 3.28.

In 1 Tim. 2.13, Paul selects data from Genesis 2 which state that man was created before woman. In contrast to 1 Cor. 11.3-16, 1 Tim. 2.9-15 has no qualifying assertion. Nevertheless, Paul clearly selected his Genesis material explained in 2.11-12.

More complex is Paul's selectivity with regard to Eve's deception and sin (2.14) drawn from traditional Jewish interpretation of Genesis 3. The account in Genesis 3 allows for different emphases. Gen. 3.1-7 makes it clear that woman and man sin together: the serpent addresses the woman with the plural 'you', and Gen. 3.6 states that the man was with the woman in the event.[49] On the other hand, Genesis 3 has the woman eat the fruit first, and she alone acknowledges deception (v. 13).[50]

In the Jewish tradition, Genesis 3 was usually understood to emphasize Eve's culpability for sin and death. One of the better known texts, Sir. 25.24, asserts: 'From a woman sin had its beginning, and because of her we all die' (RSV). Philo says that the serpent speaks to the woman because she 'is more accustomed to be deceived than man… She easily gives way and is taken in by plausible falsehoods which resemble the truth' (*Quaest. in Gen.* 3.3 [LCL]). Various other Jewish texts make similar statements about Eve.[51]

---

48. On the interpretation of Genesis 1–3 itself, see D.M. Scholer, 'Women in Ministry, Session 1: Its Basis in Creation', *Covenant Companion* 72.22 (1983), p. 14; and P. Trible, *God and the Rhetoric of Sexuality* (OBT; Philadelphia: Fortress Press, 1978).

49. The phrase about the man's presence with the woman has been omitted, without warrant, in some Bible translations.

50. Philo, *Leg. All.* 3.61, made this observation.

51. See, e.g., Philo, *Op. Mund.* 156, 165; *4 Macc.* 18.6-8; *The Life of Adam and Eve.*

That Paul is selective in his use of Eve in 1 Tim. 2.14 seems clear from at least three other Pauline texts. In 2 Cor. 11.3, Eve's deception is a negative model, warning all Corinthian believers — men and women — against false teaching. This shows that Paul did not limit Eve's deceivability to women. In both Rom. 5.12-14 and 1 Cor. 15.21-22, the Apostle attributes sin and death to Adam, not Eve. This emphasis is also known, although to a lesser extent, in Judaism (*2 Bar.* 23.4). Clearly, the contextual needs of the argument determine what part of the Genesis narrative Paul uses and emphasizes.

Paul's selective and wide range of arguments is well known. He even uses some that may have reflected beliefs and practices he did not approve. In 1 Cor. 11.3-16, Paul uses at least five arguments to buttress his point. In 1 Cor. 15.12-57, Paul employs several arguments for the future bodily resurrection, including one based on a practice and belief in baptism for the dead (v. 29), with which he could have hardly agreed. In 2 Cor. 11–12, he rhetorically uses an argument against his opponents of personal boasting in spite of his own objections to doing it. Paul consciously gathered and used arguments that suited the point he wished to make.

Thus, 1 Tim. 2.13-14 should be understood as an explanatory rationale for vv. 11-12 that uses data from Genesis 2–3 selectively to suit the needs of the argument at hand.[52] The women who were falling prey to the false teachers in Ephesus were being deceived and were transgressing as Eve did.[53] The rationale using Eve's deception in v. 14 is, therefore, *ad hoc* and occasional and is no more a 'timeless' comment about women than the use of the same point in 2 Cor. 11.3. In both cases, Paul is warning against false teachers and false teaching.[54]

If one assumes that 1 Tim. 2.11-12 is a 'universal, timeless absolute' and that 2.13-14 as a scriptural allusion is an 'absolute' authority, one faces the uneasy possibility that 2.14 implies that women are by nature deceivable in a way that men are not.

---

52. I would paraphrase the beginning of 1 Tim. 2.13-14 as follows: 'For the scripture provides a way of supporting these injunctions [2.11-12] in that Adam...'

53. There is not sufficient evidence, in my judgment, to identify the false teaching in Ephesus as Gnosticism in a complete enough sense to hold that, as in some forms of developed Gnosticism, Eve was a 'hero' of the false teachers and thus account for Paul's statements about Eve here.

54. Moo, '1 Timothy 2.11-15', p. 70, e.g., gives indirect consent to the selective nature of 2.13-14 by commenting that 'in attributing blame to woman here, Paul in no way seeks to exonerate man...he concentrates upon the woman because it is her role which is being discussed'.

The ancient Jewish traditions current in Paul's time did hold that women were inherently more deceivable. From this came numerous consequences about the inferiority and subordination of women.[55] Both Moo and Hurley struggle with this. In his first article on 1 Timothy 2, Moo had written that 'it is difficult to avoid the conclusion that Paul cites Eve's failure as exemplary and perhaps causative of the nature of women in general and that this susceptibility to deception bars them from engaging in public teaching'.[56] After being criticized for this remark, Moo claims misrepresentation but admits that 'the difficulties with viewing v. 14 as a statement about the nature of women are real'.[57] Moo then endorses Hurley's resolution, that it is 'very unlikely that Paul meant to say...that all women are too gullible to teach'.[58] Rather, Hurley argues that Paul's point is that Adam sinned deliberately, thus demonstrating that God had given to him (thus to men) the capacity to be a religious leader. Actually, this appears simply to be another way to say that, conversely, women do not have this capacity and are thus more deceivable than men. The implications are disturbing and contradict the reality of the whole of biblical teaching, church history, and human experience.[59]

Hermeneutical Considerations

I will briefly identify five specific hermeneutical considerations that are crucial to the interpretation and application of 1 Tim. 2.9-15, especially within the evangelical traditions.

1. *Starting Points and Balance of Texts.*[60] Two hermeneutical axioms have wide, general acceptance: (1) clearer texts should interpret less clear or ambiguous texts and (2) any viewpoint that is claimed to be 'biblical' should be inclusive of all the texts that speak to that particular issue. We

---

55. Here see esp. L. Swidler, *Women in Judaism: The Status of Women in Formative Judaism* (Metuchen, NJ: Scarecrow, 1976).

56. Moo, '1 Timothy 2.11-15', p. 70.

57. Moo, 'Interpretation', p. 204; cf. Payne, 'Libertarian Women', pp. 175-76.

58. Hurley, *Man and Woman*, pp. 214-16, esp. p. 215.

59. Clark, *Man and Woman*, pp. 201-205, is an example of another attempt to cope with Eve's deception in 2.14 as a rationale for 2.11-12. He argues for a typological interpretation that, he claims, does not hold that women are necessarily deceivable but Eve as a type who was deceived has set the scriptural pattern for the subordinate, nonteaching place of women. The explanation seems strained and also has disturbing implications.

60. See D.M. Scholer, 'Women in Ministry, Session 8: Summary—Consistency and Balance', *Covenant Companion* 73 (1984), p. 15.

need to recognize, however, that these axioms are often used with assumptions that are not explicit.

One such assumption that underlies most uses of 1 Tim. 2.11-12 to exclude or limit women in ministry is that this is *the* clear text through which all other New Testament texts on women in the church must be read. If 1 Tim. 2.11-12 is the starting point, the conclusion is inevitable. But the New Testament does not specify particular starting points for many issues. For example, on the matter of the so-called eternal security of believers, does one read Heb. 6.4-6 'through' Rom. 8.28-39, or should the Romans text be read 'through' the one from Hebrews?

Why should we assume that 1 Tim. 2.11-12 is the controlling text through which other texts on women must be read? That passage cannot be divorced from its immediate paragraph of vv. 9-15. If one reads the whole paragraph, the 'simple clarity' of 1 Tim. 2.11-12 is called into question. F.F. Bruce writes on Gal. 3.28: 'Paul states the basic principle here: if restrictions on it are found elsewhere in the Pauline corpus [e.g., 1 Tim. 2.11-12]…they are to be understood in relation to Gal. 3.28, and not *vice versa*'.[61]

The balancing of texts is especially crucial for interpreting 1 Tim. 2.9-15 because the larger Pauline context and practice with regard to women in the ministry of the church confirm the understanding that the 1 Timothy text is limited to a problematic situation and is not a denial of Pauline practice.

2. *The Danger of Equivocation.* Anyone who argues for the 'timeless', absolute character of any scriptural injunction should be prepared to take such a text without qualification or equivocation. For those who use 1 Tim. 2.11-12 to exclude or limit women in ministry, the passage often seems to 'prove too much'. Those who claim its absoluteness began to equivocate as early as Origen and John Chrysostom.[62]

Hurley, for example, argues that 1 Tim. 2.11-12 clearly prohibits women from authoritatively teaching men. Yet he would allow women to teach on the mission field, in regular worship if under the authority of an elder, and in Bible study groups and the like.[63] He assumes that the only teaching of men prohibited to women in vv. 11-12 is that committed to the

---

61.   F.F. Bruce, *The Epistle to the Galatians: A Commentary on the Greek Text* (NIGTC; Grand Rapids: Eerdmans, 1982), p. 190.

62.   Origen, *Comm. on 1 Cor.* 74; John Chrysostom, *Homily* 3.1 (on Rom. 16.6); see J. LaPorte, *The Role of Women in Early Christianity* (Studies in Women and Religion, 7; Lewiston, NY: Edwin Mellen Press, 1982), pp. 122-23.

63.   Hurley, *Man and Woman*, pp. 242-52.

office of elder. Others who see the passage as prohibiting women from teaching men often see no problem in women writing theological books or teaching in theological seminaries.[64]

Yet 1 Tim. 2.11-12 is not directed at only a certain level of persons (ordained elders rather than missionaries, a distinction that would be very difficult to maintain within Paul's churches) or at only one form of teaching (such as preaching in distinction from writing). It is rather an unqualified prohibition, the limits of which are found only in its specific sociohistorical purpose.

3. *Consistency.* Forced consistency is not a desirable hermeneutical axiom. Instead, one must achieve interpretive consistency through giving each text its integrity. Such consistency demands that 1 Tim. 2.9-10 and 15, for example, be taken with the same seriousness and be interpreted with the same procedures as 2.11-12.

The issue of consistent interpretation throughout 1 Timothy needs to be addressed. Foh's *Women and the Word of God*, for example, has a chapter entitled 'What the New Testament Says about Women', which discusses 1 Tim. 2.8-15 but never touches 1 Tim. 5.3-15, a passage nearly twice as long, which is devoted exclusively to the place of women in the church. Similarly, Hurley's *Man and Woman in Biblical Perspective* devotes 39 pages to 1 Tim. 2.8-15 but only 29 lines on three scattered pages to 1 Tim. 5.3-16. Certainly, those who see the purpose of 1 Timothy as a 'timeless' church manual should hold that 1 Tim. 5.3-16 be applied as literally and absolutely as 2.11-12. Such inconsistency suggests that their agenda is much more than a concern for biblical authority and for accurate biblical teaching.

4. *The Cultural Conditioning of the Text and the Interpreter.*[65] The concept of genuinely objective biblical interpretation is a myth. All interpretation is socially located, individually skewed, and ecclesiastically and theologically conditioned. Nowhere is all of this more clear than on the issue of understanding biblical teaching on the place of women in the church's ministry. Generally, persons raised within Holiness, Pentecostal, and certain Baptist traditions experienced women teaching authoritatively in the church long before they were equipped to interpret 1 Tim. 2.11-12 and never found that passage a problem. Conversely, persons raised in

64. See Payne, 'Libertarian Women', pp. 174-75, for comments on this.

65. My concerns here are developed much more fully in D.M. Scholer, 'Unseasonable Thoughts on the State of Biblical Hermeneutics: Reflections of a New Testament Exegete', *American Baptist Quarterly* 2 (1983), pp. 134-41. Some of the language in this section is taken verbatim from this article.

many Reformed traditions knew long before they were equipped to interpret 1 Tim. 2.11-12 that women were to be excluded from authoritative teaching in the church. They grew up finding the verses clear support for what they believed.

All biblical interpreters, regardless of where they now stand on the issues of women in ministry, have been deeply influenced by both the sexism and misogyny of our culture and also the currents of nineteenth-century women's rights and twentieth-century feminist movements.[66]

One should not despair over the reality of the cultural conditioning of interpreters. Rather, all interpreters should openly recognize this and proceed with caution, humility, and a commitment to as high a level as possible of interpretive integrity and consistency as well as sensitivity to the historical settings of the biblical texts.

Not only are interpreters conditioned. The authors of biblical texts also lived and thought within particular historical-social settings. The biblical texts themselves are addressed to various historical settings for many different purposes. Thus, the Bible as God's Word is God's communication *in* history, not above it or apart from it. In this sense, the entire Bible consists of historically conditioned (i.e. culturally conditioned) texts.

Such an understanding of the Bible does not deny that many biblical texts are statements or contain principles of a directly transcendent or universal character, even if they have a particular setting in history and culture that *can* be explored and explained.

It is not easy to determine which biblical texts are so relative to their own cultural settings or are so limited to their own historical circumstances that they do not have or cannot have transcultural claims as normative texts. The task is complex, but unless we struggle to develop consistent principles for making such determinations, our inherited traditions, theological presuppositions, or personal prejudices will dictate what is and what is not culturally relative.[67]

5. *History of Interpretation.* Those who interpret 1 Tim. 2.9-15 as a historically limited, *ad hoc* text and who support full participation of women in every aspect of ministry are often charged with theological flaws or deviations. First, they are accused of capitulating to the influence of

---

66. One certainly ought to read the searching critique of androcentric biblical interpretation found in the first section of E. Schüssler Fiorenza, *In Memory of Her: A Feminist Theological Reconstruction of Christian Origins* (New York: Crossroad, 1983), pp. 1-95.

67. Elsewhere (Scholer, 'Unseasonable Thoughts', pp. 139-40), I have developed eight guidelines for attempting to distinguish between what is culturally relative and what is transculturally normative in Scripture texts.

secular feminism. Second, they are accused of denying or weakening biblical authority.

A few vignettes and a quick look at the history of the interpretation of 1 Tim. 2.9-15 show the inappropriateness of such charges. Such an approach to 1 Tim. 2.9-15 is hardly novel. The first book published in English defending full and equal participation of women in ministry was written by a Quaker, Margaret Fell, in 1666.[68] Fell argued that 1 Tim. 2.11-12 was directed only against the deviating women described in 1 Tim. 5.11-15.

In the nineteenth century, at least 36 defenses of women in ministry were published in English.[69] Probably the most significant of these for 1 Tim. 2.9-15 are those of Antoinette L. Brown, Luther Lee, Phoebe Palmer, Catherine Booth, and A.J. Gordon.[70] They all argued, within a context of commitment to biblical authority, that 1 Tim. 2.9-15 was limited to a particular situation. They all noted the significance of the verb αὐθεντεῖν in 1 Tim. 2.12 and the importance of other Pauline data that showed women as participants in ministry. Although none developed these observations on 1 Tim. 2.9-15 fully, they noted these points within the context of biblical exegesis that sought to be faithful to biblical theology and authority.

Early in the twentieth century, two books by women had considerable

---

68. M. Fell, *Women's Speaking Justified, Proved and Allowed by the Scriptures* (London, 1666; repr. Amherst: Mosher Book and Tract Committee, New England Yearly Meeting of Friends, 1980).

69. N.A. Hardesty, *Women Called to Witness: Evangelical Feminism in the 19th Century* (Nashville: Abingdon Press, 1984), pp. 162-64.

70. A.L. Brown, 'Exegesis of 1 Corinthians xiv, 34, 35; and 1 Timothy ii, 11, 12', *Oberlin Quarterly Reviews* 3 (1849), pp. 358-73. Brown wrote this as a paper at Oberlin, where she was the first woman to complete the theological course there (in 1850), although the school would not grant her the degree. L. Lee, *Woman's Right to Preach the Gospel* (Syracuse, NY: self-published, 1853). This was the sermon preached at A.L. Brown's ordination on 15 September 1853, at South Butler, New York. Brown was the first woman ordained by a standard church body in the United States. This sermon has been reprinted in D. Dayton, *Luther Lee: Five Sermons and a Tract* (Chicago: Holrad House, 1975). P. Palmer, *Promise of the Father; or A Neglected Specialty of the Last Days* (Boston: Henry V. Degen, 1859; repr. Salem, OH: Schmul, 1981), pp. 24-25, 48-50. Palmer was a prominent Methodist evangelist. C. Booth, *Female Ministry; or, Woman's Right to Preach the Gospel* (London, 1859; repr. [partially] New York: Salvation Army Supplies Printing and Publishing Department, 1975). Booth and her husband founded the Salvation Army. A.J. Gordon, 'The Ministry of Woman', *Missionary Review of the World* 7 (1894), pp. 910-21; repr. in [Fuller] *Theology, News and Notes* 21.2 (1975), pp. 5-9; *Gordon College Alumnus* 8.1 (1978), pp. 3-4, 8-9; *Equity* 1.1 (1980), pp. 26-31; and as *Gordon–Conwell Theological Seminary Monograph* 61 (1974). Gordon was a Baptist pastor in Boston, who founded what became Gordon College and Gordon Divinity School (later Gordon–Conwell Theological Seminary).

influence on the issues of women in ministry. Katherine Bushnell published a series of one hundred Bible studies in book form, which was, to a large extent, summarized and popularized by Jessie Penn-Lewis.[71] Both stressed that, because of the evidence that women did engage in ministry in Pauline churches, 1 Tim. 1.11-12 was a temporary prohibition due to the perilous situation for women in society at that time and place.

In our own time, a staggering number of evangelical scholars and writers — many of whom are especially known for their defense and support of biblical authority — have understood 1 Tim. 2.9-15 as a limited text. The following representative list includes men and women in scholarly and popular works with a wide range of publishers, denominations and theological traditions: Paul K. Jewett, Leon Morris, Robert K. Johnston, John J. Davis, Donald G. Bloesch, F.F. Bruce, Dorothy Pape, Patricia Gundry, Dennis Kuhns, Don Williams, Shirley Stephens, Margaret Howe, Myrtle Langley, Mary J. Evans, Ward Gasque, Klyne Snodgrass, Alvera and Berkeley Mickelsen, Philip Siddons, and Aida Spencer.[72]

71.   K.C. Bushnell, *God's Word to Women: One Hundred Bible Studies on Woman's Place in the Divine Economy* (place and date uncertain; repr. North Collins, NY: Ray B. Munson, c. 1975); J. Penn-Lewis, *The 'Magna Charta of Woman' according to the Scriptures* (Bournemouth: Overcomer Book Room, 1919; repr. Minneapolis: Bethany Fellowship, 1975).

72.   Paul K. Jewett, *Man as Male and Female: A Study in Sexual Relationships from a Theological Point of View* (Grand Rapids: Eerdmans, 1975); Leon Morris, 'The Ministry of Women', in R. Hestenes and L. Curley (eds.), *Women and the Ministries of the Church* (Pasadena, CA: Fuller Theological Seminary, 1979), pp. 14-25; Robert K. Johnston, 'The Role of Women in the Church and Family: The Issues of Biblical Hermeneutics', in *idem, Evangelicals at an Impasse: Biblical Authority in Practice* (Atlanta: John Knox Press, 1979), pp. 48-76; Davis, 'Ordination of Women Reconsidered'; D.G. Bloesch, *Is the Bible Sexist? Beyond Feminism and Patriarchalism* (Westchester: Crossway, 1982) (Bloesch does see 1 Tim. 2.9-15 as a limited text, but for other reasons he qualifies the degrees to which women should participate in ministry); Bruce, *Galatians*, p. 190; *idem*, 'Women in the Church: A Biblical Survey', *Christian Brethren Review* 33 (1982), pp. 7-14; D.R. Pape, *In Search of God's Ideal Woman: A Personal Examination of the New Testament* (Downers Grove, IL: InterVarsity Press, 1976), pp. 149-208; P. Gundry, *Woman Be Free!* (Grand Rapids: Zondervan, 1977), pp. 74-77; D.R. Kuhns, *Women in the Church* (Focal Pamphlets, 28; Scottdale, PA: Herald Press, 1978), pp. 48-52; D. Williams, *The Apostle Paul and Women in the Church* (Van Nuys: BIM Publishing Co., 1977), pp. 109-14; S. Stephens, *A New Testament View of Women* (Nashville: Broadman, 1980), pp. 145-47; E.M. Howe; *Women and Church Leadership* (Grand Rapids: Zondervan, 1982), pp. 45-53; M. Langley, *Equal Woman: A Christian Feminist Perspective* (Basingstoke: Marshall, Morgan & Scott, 1983), pp. 55-56; M.J. Evans, *Woman in the Bible* (Downers Grove, IL: InterVarsity Press, 1984), pp. 84-105; W.W. Gasque, 'The Role of Women in the Church, in Society, and in the Home', *Crux* 19.3 (1983), pp. 3-9; K. Snodgrass, 'Paul and Women', *Covenant Quarterly* 34.4 (1976), pp. 3-19; A. and B. Mickelsen, 'May Women Teach Men?', *Standard*

This demonstrates that the approach advocated in this essay and by many other persons grows out of deep respect and concern for sound biblical exegesis and a vital commitment to biblical authority for the church. Only the ill-informed could suggest that such exegesis depends on or even takes its initiative from secular feminism or that this 'cloud of witnesses' is 'soft' on biblical authority.

Conclusion

Through the exegetical and hermeneutical considerations offered here, four basic conclusions have emerged:

1. 1 Tim. 2.9-15 should be understood as a unified paragraph on the place of women in the church in Ephesus. It provided instructions for and was limited to a particular situation of false teaching.

2. 1 Tim. 2.11-12 cannot legitimately be divorced from its immediate context of 1 Tim. 2.9-15 or its larger literary context of 1 and 2 Timothy, including significant texts such as 1 Tim. 5.11-15 and 2 Tim. 3.6-7. Paul's words in 1 Tim. 2.9-15 must also be placed in the context of all other Pauline data on the participation of women in ministry.

3. It should be acknowledged within the evangelical communities that the type of interpretation of 1 Tim. 2.9-15 offered here and by many others is a completely acceptable and legitimate option within the framework of evangelical theological and ecclesiastical traditions and institutions. Those who see in 1 Tim. 2.11-12 an exclusion or limitation of women in ministry cannot with integrity say or imply that those who understand 1 Tim. 2.9-15 as a historically conditioned and limited text have thereby denied or weakened a strong commitment to biblical authority or to responsible biblical interpretation.

4. All persons concerned with biblical interpretation must admit the reality of agenda other than simply a commitment to biblical authority and biblical teaching. Faithfulness to Scripture and desire to interpret accurately what the Bible teaches are genuine. Nevertheless, commitment to biblical authority and the sheer existence of particular texts, such as 1 Tim. 2.11-12, do not account for all that is happening within the evangelical discussion. The virtual neglect of 1 Tim. 5.3-16, equivocations in the application of 1 Tim. 2.11-12, and the very nature of the controversies over women in ministry within the evangelical communities demonstrate that there are many motivations and interests that deeply touch our interpretations of Scripture.

74.4 (1984), pp. 34, 36-37; P. Siddons, *Speaking Out for Women: A Biblical View* (Valley Forge, PA: Judson, 1980), pp. 82-85; Spencer, 'Eve at Ephesus'.

LIMITS AND DIFFERENTIATION:
THE CALCULUS OF WIDOWS IN 1 TIMOTHY 5.3-16

Jouette M. Bassler

The logic and objectives of 1 Tim. 5.3-16 are difficult to grasp. Why does
the letter devote so much space to instructions and observations regarding widows? What did it mean to 'honor' widows? What did it mean to
put them on the list? What did the listed widows gain? What did unlisted
widows lose? What sense can be made of the criteria for putting widows
on the list? What was the author trying to accomplish with his detailed
instructions? And what was the widows' response to all of this? The more
one ponders the text, the more the questions proliferate.

Much of the blame for this confusion lies with the author of this letter, who conceals the reality of the lives and motivations of the widows
behind demeaning stereotype, obfuscating rhetoric, and confused syntax, just as he conceals his own circumstances and motives behind the
claim of Pauline authorship. To determine what was really going on
requires aggressive interpretation. In what follows I attempt to reconstruct the nature of the widows' circle, the motivations of those who
participated in it, and the purpose of the restrictions imposed on the
widows in this passage. I am guided by the presupposition that the letter
does not necessarily represent how things actually were in the church,
but how the author wanted things to be. To get behind the rhetoric to the
reality requires equal measures of critical exegesis and imaginative
historical reconstruction.[1] The first step is to determine what we can

---

1.   This is a revision of an essay that first appeared in 1984 ('The Widows' Tale: A
Fresh Look at 1 Tim. 5.3-16', *JBL* 103 [1984], pp. 23-41). This revised attempt at critical
exegesis and historical reconstruction is significantly enhanced by the recent meth-
odological work of scholars such as Elizabeth A. Castelli, 'Paul on Women and Gen-
der', in Ross Shepard Kraemer and Mary Rose D'Angelo (eds.), *Women and Christian
Origins* (Oxford: Oxford University Press, 1999), pp. 221-35; Cynthia Briggs Kittredge,
'Corinthian Women Prophets and Paul's Argumentation in 1 Corinthians', in Richard
A. Horsley (ed.), *Paul and Politics: Ekklesia, Israel, Imperium, Interpretation* (Festschrift
Krister Stendahl; Harrisburg, PA: Trinity Press International, 2000), pp. 103-109;
Lucinda A. Brown, 'Asceticism and Ideology: The Language of Power in the Pastoral

plausibly assume about the self-understanding and social situation of the women whom the author addresses as widows.

The Background: Paul and Celibate Women

The Pastoral Letters are pseudonymous with regard to both their author and their addressees.[2] We know neither who wrote them nor to whom they were written. This means that we also cannot locate them precisely in time or geographical space. All we can say with certainty is that they were written to a church (or churches) somewhere in the Pauline mission field sometime before the end of the second century CE, when explicit references to these letters begin to appear.[3] This is not much, but it is a start, for it suggests that to grasp the issues at stake in the instructions to and about the widows, we need to ask about the theological self-understanding and religious lifestyle nurtured among women in Pauline churches.

One round of evidence comes from the number of women Paul mentions by name in his letters, most of whom have significant leadership roles in the church.[4] Prisca, a well-traveled Christian missionary who,

Epistles', in Vincent L. Wimbush (ed.), *Discoursive Formations, Ascetic Piety and the Interpretation of Early Christian Literature* (*Semeia*, 57; Atlanta: Scholars Press, 1992), pp. 77-94; Elisabeth Schüssler Fiorenza, 'Paul and the Politics of Interpretation', in Horsley (ed.), *Paul and Politics*, pp. 40-57; and especially Antoinette Clark Wire, *The Corinthian Women Prophets: A Reconstruction through Paul's Rhetoric* (Minneapolis: Fortress Press, 1990).

2. A few scholars continue to defend Pauline authorship (most notably, perhaps, George W. Knight III, *Commentary on the Pastoral Epistles* [NIGTC; Grand Rapids: Eerdmans, 1992] and Luke Timothy Johnson, *1 Timothy, 2 Timothy, Titus* [Atlanta: John Knox, 1987]), but the overwhelming majority regard the letters as pseudonymous. A full discussion of the issue can be found in Jerome D. Quinn, *The Letter to Titus* (AB, 35; New York: Doubleday, 1990), pp. 2-22. It is generally, but not universally, assumed that the same author wrote all three letters (see, however, Jerome Murphy-O'Connor, '2 Timothy Contrasted with 1 Timothy and Titus', *RB* 98 [1991], pp. 403-18).

3. Asia Minor is usually assumed (with varying degrees of confidence) to be the point of origin and intended destination of the letters, though Rome is occasionally proposed. Usually a date in the first decades of the second century is assumed. No proof on any of these issues is possible.

4. On leadership roles of women in Pauline churches, see, e.g., Elisabeth Schüssler Fiorenza, *In Memory of Her: A Feminist Theological Reconstruction of Christian Origins* (New York: Crossroad, 1983); Margaret Y. MacDonald, 'Reading Real Women Through the Undisputed Letters of Paul', in Kraemer and D'Angelo (eds.), *Women and Christian Origins*, pp. 199-220; Carol Meyers (ed.), *Women in Scripture* (New York: Houghton Mifflin, 2000); Karen Jo Torjesen, *When Women Were Priests: Women's Leadership in the Early Church and the Scandal of their Subordination in the Rise of Christianity* (San Francisco: HarperSanFrancisco, 1993).

with Aquila, established and led a number of house churches (1 Cor. 16.19; Rom. 16.3-5; see also Acts 18); Junia, a prominent Apostle (Rom. 16.9);[5] Phoebe, a minister and benefactor of the church in Cenchreae (Rom. 16.1-2);[6] Tryphena and Tryphosa, missionary partners (Rom. 16.12);[7] Persis, another worker 'in the Lord', probably in the mission field (Rom. 16.12); Mary, a prominent worker in Rome's churches (Rom. 16.6); Euodia and Syntyche, missionary partners in Philippi (Phil. 4.2-3).[8] In addition, Apphia was a prominent member and probably a leader (with Philemon) of the church in Colossae (Phlm. 2), and Nympha hosted a church in her house and probably had some leadership role in it (Col. 4.15).

Paul mentions these women casually, with no indication that he (or anyone else) found their presence and status in the churches remarkable. Clearly women were accepted without question in a variety of leadership roles in the Pauline mission field and mission churches. Yet it is likely that many, perhaps most, of the women whom Paul acknowledges in these roles came from the more privileged ranks of the church—women with enough wealth and independence to travel, to host a church in their homes, or to serve as patrons.[9] Not all women could aspire to these occasional, usually trans-local, leadership roles, nor would women of means in these roles have been particularly distinctive in the Roman world.[10] Local 'ideological leadership', the teachers and prophets in the

---

5. On Junia, see especially Bernadette Brooten, 'Junia…Outstanding among the Apostles (Rom. 16.7)', in Leonard Swidler and Arlene Swidler (eds.), *Women Priests: A Catholic Commentary on the Vatican Declaration* (New York: Paulist Press, 1977), pp. 141-44; Elisabeth Schüssler Fiorenza, 'The Apostleship of Women in Early Christianity', in Swidler and Swidler (eds.), *Women Priests*, pp. 135-40.

6. On Phoebe, see Elisabeth Schüssler Fiorenza, 'The "Quilting" of Women's History: Phoebe of Cenchreae', in Paula M. Cooey, *et al.* (eds.), *Embodied Love: Sensuality and Relationship as Feminist Values* (San Francisco: Harper & Row, 1987), pp. 35-49.

7. On these women, see Mary Rose D'Angelo, 'Women Partners in the New Testament', *JFSR* 6 (1990), pp. 65-86.

8. On these two women, see D'Angelo, 'Women Partners', and Cynthia Briggs Kittredge, *Community and Authority: The Rhetoric of Obedience in the Pauline Tradition* (HTS; Harrisburg, PA: Trinity Press International, 1998), esp. pp. 53-110.

9. See Wayne A. Meeks, *The First Urban Christians: The Social World of the Apostle Paul* (New Haven: Yale University Press, 1983), pp. 51-73; see also Halvor Moxnes, 'Social Integration and the Problem of Gender in St. Paul's Letters', *ST* 43 (1989), pp. 99-113, esp. 106; Schüssler Fiorenza, *In Memory of Her*, pp. 168-73.

10. So M.Y. MacDonald, 'Reading Real Women', p. 218; see also Bernadette J. Brooten, *Women Leaders in the Ancient Synagogue: Inscriptional Evidence and Background Issues* (BJS, 36; Chico, CA: Scholars Press, 1982) and Mary Taliaferro Boatwright, 'Plancia Magna of Perge: Women's Roles and Status in Roman Asia Minor', in Sarah

local churches, was a more democratic option, available to more women, and potentially more disruptive of cultural values and expectations.[11] On what basis, though, did women exercise this leadership?

It has long been assumed that Gal. 3.28 provided the early church with a theological basis for transcending socially inscribed hierarchies, insofar as it seems to promote a radical egalitarian vision: 'There is no longer Jew or Greek, there is no longer slave or free, there is no longer male and female, for all of you are one in Christ Jesus.'[12] According to a prevalent interpretation, this formula expresses Paul's firm conviction that 'in Christ' hierarchical gender differences (as well as ethnic and class differences) were abolished, and men and women were established as equal. Furthermore, this equality was not simply an eschatological hope; Paul strove to actualize it within his fledgling churches. On occasion he was forced to compromise this ideal, for example, when he was confronted with excessive enthusiasm that threatened the church's internal stability and missionary goals (e.g. 1 Cor. 11.2-16). At heart, though, a theologically grounded egalitarian impulse pervaded the early Pauline churches only to be extinguished by later, reactionary generations.[13]

This reading has, however, been seriously challenged on the grounds that the wording of the baptismal formula refers to sexual differentiation rather than to gender equality.[14] It is clear, for example, that the third

B. Pomeroy (ed.), *Women's History and Ancient History* (Chapel Hill: University of North Carolina Press, 1991), pp. 249-72.

11. The term 'ideological leadership' is that of Moxnes ('Social Integration', p. 106); the phenomenon has been most extensively investigated, however, by Wire, *Corinthian Women Prophets*.

12. The groundbreaking work on this verse is Wayne A. Meeks's, 'The Image of the Androgyne: Some Uses of a Symbol in Earliest Christianity', *HR* 13 (1974), pp. 165-208. He convincingly identifies the verse as a baptismal formula and suggests the androgyne myth behind it.

13. Examples of this interpretation include Krister Stendahl, *The Bible and the Role of Women: A Case Study in Hermeneutics* (Philadelphia: Fortress Press, 1966); and (more carefully nuanced) Dennis R. MacDonald, *There Is No Male and Female: The Fate of a Dominical Saying in Paul and Gnosticism* (HDR, 20; Philadelphia: Fortress Press, 1987), and Schüssler Fiorenza, *In Memory of Her,* pp. 205-36. Most commentaries reflect it: see, e.g., Sam K. Williams, *Galatians* (ANTC; Nashville: Abingdon Press, 1997), pp. 106-107; Richard N. Longenecker, *Galatians* (WBC, 41; Dallas: Word Books, 1990), pp. 156-57; see also the earlier version of this essay.

14. See especially Lone Fatum, 'Image of God and Glory of Man: Women in the Pauline Congregations', in Kari Elisabeth Børresen (ed.), *Image of God and Gender Models in Judaeo-Christian Tradition* (Oslo: Solum Forlag, 1991), pp. 56-137; *idem*, 'Women, Symbolic Universe and Structures of Silence', *ST* 43.1 (1989), pp. 61-80; Dale B. Martin, *The Corinthian Body* (New Haven: Yale University Press, 1995), esp. pp. 199, 229-49; Moxnes, 'Social Integration'; and John S. Kloppenborg, 'Egalitarianism in the Myth

clause of the formula alludes to the creation account: according to Gen. 1.27, out of Adam, God created 'male and female', that is, sexual differentiation. The formula announces that in Christ this sexual differentiation has been reversed ('there is no "male and female"') and the original unity has been restored. But, it is now plausibly claimed, that original unity was not regarded as asexual or bisexual, but as masculine.[15] Thus the elimination of sexual differentiation would not promote a doctrine of social equality of women and men. It would mean that the feminine was swallowed up by the masculine, the weaker by the stronger. This eschatological vision would be realized among Christians, not by promoting an egalitarian community, but by renouncing sexual activity.[16] Yet, celibacy, though not a sign of gender equality, could provide women a basis for increased autonomy and power.[17]

and Rhetoric of Pauline Churches', in Elizabeth A. Castelli and Hal Taussig (eds.), *Reimagining Christian Origins: A Colloquium Honoring Burton L. Mack* (Valley Forge, PA: Trinity Press International, 1996), pp. 247-63.

15.   There is not complete agreement on this. Phyllis Trible, e.g., argues that *ha-adam* (Adam) should not be understood as a single androgynous creature but as two creatures, one male and one female (*God and the Rhetoric of Sexuality* [OBT, 2; Philadelphia: Fortress Press, 1978], pp. 15-21); and Daniel Boyarin insists that the androgyne archetype was pre- or un-gendered (*A Radical Jew: Paul and the Politics of Identity* [Berkeley: University of California Press, 1994], pp. 180-200).

16.   Implicit in this renunciation was the devaluation of women as women, for in becoming celibate, in controlling their female passions, they were on their way to becoming male. See, e.g., Martin, *Corinthian Body*, *passim*; Fatum, 'Image of God', pp. 81-88.

17.   See Elizabeth A. Castelli, 'Interpretations of Power in 1 Corinthians', in David Jobling and Stephen D. Moore (eds.), *Poststructuralism as Exegesis* (*Semeia*, 54; Atlanta: Scholars Press, 1991), pp. 197-222, esp. pp. 211-12. On the persistent links among celibacy, autonomy, and power, see Rosemary Radford Ruether, 'Mothers of the Church: Ascetic Women in the Late Patristic Age', in Rosemary Radford Ruether and Eleanor McLaughlin (eds.), *Women of Spirit: Female Leadership in the Jewish and Christian Traditions* (New York: Simon & Schuster, 1979), pp. 71-98; Constance F. Parvey, 'The Theology and Leadership of Women in the New Testament', in Rosemary R. Ruether (ed.), *Religion and Sexism: Images of Women in the Jewish and Christian Traditions* (New York: Simon & Schuster, 1974), pp. 117-49; Peter Brown, *The Body and Society: Men, Women and Sexual Renunciation in Early Christianity* (New York: Columbia University Press; London: Faber & Faber, 1988); Antoinette Clark Wire, 'The Social Functions of Women's Asceticism in the Roman East', in Karen L. King (ed.), *Images of the Feminine in Gnosticism* (Studies in Antiquity and Christianity; Philadelphia: Fortress Press, 1988), pp. 308-23; Elisabeth Schüssler Fiorenza, 'Response to "The Social Functions of Women's Asceticism in the Roman East" by Antoinette Clark Wire', in King (ed.), *Images of the Feminine in Gnosticism*, pp. 324-28; Elizabeth A. Clark, *Reading Renunciation: Asceticism and Scripture in Early Christianity* (Princeton, NJ: Princeton University Press, 1999); Ross Shepard Kraemer, *Her Share of the Blessings: Women's Religions among Pagans,*

The earliest evidence for this link between celibacy and the empowerment of Christian women comes from Paul's first letter to the Corinthians, and especially as that letter has been interpreted through Antoinette
Wire's historical reconstruction.[18] Wire draws from Paul's rhetoric a
compelling picture of women in Corinth empowered with God's spirit,
who understood themselves to have been recreated in God's image at
baptism and filled with holy wisdom. These women were praying and
prophesying in the churches, probably also working miracles and teaching, and thus acquiring status and authority in the Christian community.
Most of these women had withdrawn from sexual relations, many even
from marriage itself, which not only confirmed their consecration for
prayer and prophecy but also enhanced their autonomy.[19] Such a move
also, however, enhanced the possibility of offending the social and sexual
mores of the non-Christian world, even of offending some within the
church, for marriage was the norm, the expectation, indeed almost a
requirement for women in the Roman world.[20]

Because of female infanticide and high mortality rates associated with
childbirth, men outnumbered women, sometimes and in some places by
a high percentage.[21] The social and legal pressure to marry was great,
and celibacy — a permanent rejection of marriage and sexual relations —
was not a real option for most women in this world.[22] Brief periods of

---

Jews, and Christians in the Greco-Roman World (New York: Oxford University Press,
1992); Virginia Burrus, 'Word and Flesh: The Bodies and Sexuality of Ascetic Women
in Christian Antiquity', *JFSR* 10 (1994), pp. 27-51.

18. Wire, *Corinthian Women Prophets*.

19. As Wire notes, '[t]hose who withdraw from sexual relations are not under the
authority of another person in the same sense as before' (Wire, *Corinthian Women
Prophets*, p. 181). What life-support arrangements these women had can only be
guessed at (see, e.g., Wire, *Corinthian Women Prophets*, pp. 91-93).

20. Augustan legislation imposed penalties on women, including widows and
divorcees, between the ages of 20 and 50 who did not marry or remarry; see Hugo
Montgomery, 'Women and Status in the Greco-Roman World', *ST* 43 (1989), pp. 115-
24, esp. p. 118; Jane F. Gardner, *Women in Roman Law and Society* (London: Croom
Helm, 1986), pp. 50-56, 77-78; Susan Treggiari, *Roman Marriage: Iusti Coniuges from the
Time of Cicero to the Time of Ulpian* (Oxford: Clarendon Press, 1991), pp. 60-80; Sarah B.
Pomeroy, *Goddesses, Whores, Wives, and Slaves: Women in Classical Antiquity* (New York:
Schocken Books, 1975), pp. 149-204. The laws applied only to Roman citizens, but they
established cultural expectations for all women of freeborn or freed status throughout
the Empire.

21. Some studies suggest that the ratio reached as high as 135:100; see Treggiari,
Roman Marriage, p. 409, esp. n. 55; see also Wire, *Corinthian Women Prophets*, pp. 64,
181; Pomeroy, *Goddesses*, pp. 164-70.

22. See Turid Karlsen Seim, 'Ascetic Autonomy? New Perspectives on Single
Women in the Early Church', *ST* 43 (1989), pp. 125-40, esp. pp. 126-28.

continence for married women to prepare for cultic activities would have been tolerated, but, as Treggiari notes, 'lifelong celibate women are…practically unexampled'.[23] Cultural esteem of the *univira*,[24] the devoted wife who married only once, was strong, and it generated an ideal of lifelong monogamy that provided ideological support for celibate widowhood. But societal needs and cultural practice were against this ideal, and widows were expected to remarry. The pressure on divorced women to remarry was just as great and without the counterbalance of the *univira* ideal.[25] The result was that most women over the age of 18 or so would probably have been married.

The nature of the marriage relationship varied widely in the Roman Empire, and the social freedom available to the wife varied along with it.[26] By the first century, many Roman women were married *sine manu*, that is, without transfer of legal authority over the wife to her husband. These women remained under the authority of their fathers, for women were expected to be under the legal authority of a male relative. And whether legal authority was transferred at marriage or not, marriage remained in general practice essentially patriarchal, with power and authority concentrated in the hands of the husband. Wealthy divorced women and widows could acquire significant autonomy in many areas of the empire,[27] yet their numbers were small, and the ideal for women, encoded in the honor-shame culture of Mediterranean society, continued to be defined by the structure and presuppositions of the patriarchal household.[28] This is revealed with particular clarity by tombstone inscrip-

23.   Treggiari, *Roman Marriage*, p. 83.
24.   On *univirae*, see Jean-Baptiste Frey, 'La signification des termes MONANDROS et *univira*', *RSR* 20 (1930), pp. 48-60; Harry J. Leon, *The Jews of Ancient Rome* (Philadelphia: Jewish Publication Society of America, 1960), pp. 129-30; Marjorie Lightman and William Zeisel, 'Univira: An Example of Continuity and Change in Roman Society', *CH* 46 (1977), pp. 19-32. The debate over the meaning of this term is briefly summarized in David C. Verner, *The Household of God: The Social World of the Pastoral Epistles* (SBLDS, 71; Chico, CA: Scholars Press, 1983), pp. 62-63.
25.   Treggiari, *Roman Marriage*, pp. 232-37, 466-82.
26.   On marriage in the Roman Empire, see Treggiari, *Roman Marriage, passim*; James S. Jeffers, 'Jewish and Christian Families in First-Century Rome', in Karl P. Donfried and Peter Richardson (eds.), *Judaism and Christianity in First-Century Rome* (Grand Rapids: Eerdmans, 1998), pp. 128-50, esp. p. 134; Pomeroy, *Goddesses*, 149-63; Carolyn Osiek and David L. Balch, *Families in the New Testament World: Households and House Churches* (The Family, Religion, and Culture Series; Louisville, KY: Westminster/John Knox Press, 1997), pp. 54-64, esp. p. 62.
27.   Montgomery, 'Women and Status', beginning pp. 117-18.
28.   See Karen Jo Torjesen, 'In Praise of Noble Women: Gender and Honor in Ascetic Texts', in Wimbush (ed.), *Discursive Formations*, pp. 41-64.

tions and funeral orations of the period, such as the praise of Turia by her husband:

> Why recall your inestimable qualities, your modesty, deference, affability, your amiable disposition, your faithful attendance to the household duties, your enlightened religion, your unassuming elegance, the modest simplicity and refinement of your manners? Need I speak of your attachment to your kindred, your affection for your family — …you who share countless other virtues with Roman ladies most jealous of their fair name?[29]

The tendency across the centuries was toward a reduction in the power of the husband over the wife and increased social freedom for married women, but the older, more conservative ideal was very tenacious, especially in the eastern provinces.

In this world a young woman's decision not to marry would have been decidedly countercultural and alarming. A decision to remain unmarried after divorce or the death of a spouse would have generated mixed responses, with the cultural and legal pressure to remarry in tension with the lingering ideal of the *univira*. Paul himself, though advocating celibacy as the better way (1 Cor. 7.7, 8, 26, 38), placed firm limits on it within his churches.[30] Those who were married were to have full sexual relations with their spouse, except for brief periods devoted to prayer (7.1-5), and they were not to divorce, even if the spouse was an unbeliever (7.10-16). Only those unmarried or widowed at the time of their conversion (or widowed after conversion) could live celibate lives, and then only if they demonstrated by their lack of sexual passion that they had received the gift of celibacy from God (7.7-9, 25-38).[31]

Paul gives two explicit reasons for placing limits on the practice of celibacy: Not all have adequate mastery of their passions (7.2, 5, 9, 36-37)

29. *CIL* 6.1527, in Mary R. Lefkowitz and Maureen B. Fant (trans.), *Women in Greece and Rome* (Toronto: Samuel-Stevens, 1977), p. 104. See also Ludwig Friedländer, *Darstellungen aus der Sittengeschichte Roms* (4 vols.; Leipzig: Hirzel, 1922), I, pp. 313-14. The inscription is from Rome and has been dated to 9 or 10 BCE.

30. For various explanations of Paul's own reasons for preferring celibacy, see Martin, *Corinthian Body*, pp. 198-228; Wire, *Corinthian Women Prophets*, pp. 72-97; Boyarin, *Radical Jew*, pp. 158-79; all briefly summarized and analyzed by Elizabeth A. Castelli, 'Disciplines of Difference: Asceticism and History in Paul', in Leif E. Vaage and Vincent L. Wimbush (eds.), *Asceticism and the New Testament* (New York: Routledge, 1999), pp. 171-85.

31. Under the assumption that 1 Cor. 14.34-35 is authentic (see Wire, *Corinthian Women Prophets*, pp. 149-52, 229-32), some argue that Paul applied these restrictions to married women and accepted only celibate and unmarried women as prophets and as active partners in his mission field. See, e.g., Seim, 'Ascetic Autonomy?', p. 129; Fatum, 'Image of God', pp. 85-86 and esp. nn. 77, 101; Moxnes, 'Social Integration', p. 111.

and the urgency of the apocalyptic timetable did not commend radical social change (7.17-24). Some scholars have looked beneath the surface of Paul's explanations to identify other factors at work. Elizabeth Castelli, for example, sees behind Paul's rhetoric a strong resistance to the nature of the power claimed and exercised by the celibate women, and Peter Brown suggests that Paul was afraid to erode too much the lines and presuppositions of patriarchal control by which he exercised his own authority over the church.[32] In any case, the result was that from the outset a pattern of conflict was created between women who found personal and spiritual enhancement through celibacy and authorities who sought to restrict and control it.

The primary evidence for this pattern comes, of course, from Corinth. It seems reasonable to assume, though, that Paul's message and women's religious experience were consistent enough to foster celibacy in all of his churches, with concomitant gains for women in status and autonomy.[33] The prominence of two women in the church in Philippi lends support to this assumption,[34] and the enigmatic advice to the Thessalonians to 'control your body in holiness and honor' seems to point in the same direction.[35] Certainly the popularity of the apocryphal acts attests to the powerful attraction that ascetic Christianity held for women in the second century, and the *Acts of Thecla* locates this popularity precisely within the orbit of Pauline Christianity.[36] On the other hand, the emphasis on the obedience and submission of women that emerges in the

32. Castelli, 'Interpretations of Power', pp. 211-12; Brown, *Body and Society*, pp. 53-56.

33. Not all concur. Boyarin, e.g., sees sexual asceticism as a pervasive component of Paul's message (*Radical Jew*, pp. 158-79); P. Brown, however, thinks 'sexual renunciation played no part in Paul's message to other churches' (*Body and Society*, p. 53). For an analysis of these authors' hermeneutical assumptions, see Castelli, 'Disciplines of Difference'.

34. See Valerie Abrahamsen, 'Women at Philippi: The Pagan and Christian Evidence', *JFSR* 3.2 (1987), pp. 17-30; see also n. 8 above.

35. See Jouette M. Bassler, 'Σκεῦος: A Modest Proposal for Illuminating Paul's Use of Metaphor in 1 Thessalonians 4.4', in Michael L. White and O. Larry Yarbrough (eds.), *The Social World of the First Christians: Essays in Honor of Wayne A. Meeks* (Minneapolis: Fortress Press, 1995), pp. 53-66.

36. On celibacy in the apocryphal acts, see Dennis R. MacDonald, *The Legend and the Apostle: The Battle for Paul in Story and Canon* (Philadelphia: Westminster Press, 1983), *passim*; Virginia Burrus, *Chastity as Autonomy: Women in the Stories of the Apocryphal Acts* (Studies in Women and Religion, 23; Lewiston, NY: Edwin Mellen Press, 1987); Stevan L. Davies, *The Revolt of the Widows: The Social World of the Apocryphal Acts* (Carbondale, IL: Southern Illinois University Press, 1980); Ross S. Kraemer, 'The Conversion of Women to Ascetic Forms of Christianity', *Signs* 6.2 (1980), pp. 298-307.

household codes of Colossians and Ephesians may have been, at least in part, a conservative response to the empowerment of women through celibacy in the Pauline churches.[37] This trajectory continues in the Pastoral Letters, where it is most clearly revealed in the passage about the widows.

The Pastoral Letters and Celibate Women

External Pressure and an Internal Crisis

Before addressing 1 Tim. 5.3-16 and its references to widows, we should review some widely recognized aspects of the Pastoral Letters which will prove useful to our investigation. First, these letters are permeated with a strong concern for the opinion of contemporary society.[38] As a minority sect worshiping as God someone who had been condemned and executed by the Roman Empire, Christians had good reason for caution, and the cautious author of these letters reveals an anxiety about behavior that might be criticized. Bishops must be 'well thought of by outsiders' (1 Tim. 3.7). Young widows and wives are to show proper domesticity so 'that the word of God may not be discredited' (Tit. 2.5) and the outside critic may have 'no occasion to revile us' (1 Tim. 5.14). Young men are to have such integrity of speech and behavior that 'any opponent will be put to shame' (Tit. 2.8). And slaves are to be submissive and obedient to their masters 'so that the name of God and the teaching may not be blasphemed' by outsiders who would be offended by disre-

37. The New Testament household codes (Eph. 5.21–6.9; Col. 3.18–4.1; 1 Pet. 2.18–3.7), with their insistence on the obedience and submission of the subordinate members of the family, have long been regarded as deliberate accommodations to the cultural norms of the Greco-Roman world, undertaken to correct the egalitarian enthusiasm of these members (so, e.g., James E. Crouch, *The Origin and Intention of the Colossian Haustafel* [Göttingen: Vandenhoeck & Ruprecht, 1972]) or to defend against growing public concern over their behavior (so David L. Balch, *Let Wives Be Submissive: The Domestic Code in 1 Peter* [SBLMS, 26; Chico, CA: Scholars Press, 1981]). Margaret Y. MacDonald has suggested that sexual asceticism should be seriously considered as one of the issues these letters seek to redress ('Citizens of Heaven and Earth: Asceticism and Social Integration in Colossians and Ephesians', in Vaage and Wimbush [eds.], *Asceticism and the New Testament*, pp. 269-98).

38. Peter Lippert articulates a strong consensus when he states that the Pastoral Epistles are structured by this concern and thus have a predominantly defensive stance against a growing uproar in the surrounding society over Christian actions and attitudes (*Leben als Zeugnis: Die werbende Kraft christlicher Lebensführung nach dem Kirchenverständnis neuetestamentlicher Briefe* [SBM, 4; Stuttgart: Katholisches Bibelwerk, 1968]). See also Verner, *Household of God*, pp. 127-47, 180-86; D.R. MacDonald, *Legend and the Apostle*, pp. 78-79; Philip H. Towner, *1–2 Timothy and Titus* (Downers Grove, IL: InterVarsity Press, 1994), p. 30.

spectful behavior (1 Tim. 6.1; see also Tit. 2.10). In the author's view, the behavior of these groups was under public scrutiny and had the potential of creating problems for the church.

Second, the leadership of the church was being challenged by a rival group of teachers. The author of the Pastorals does not reveal much about these teachers, but through the screen of stereotypical accusations that characterize his polemics, the charge that they promote a celibate piety emerges with concrete vividness ('they forbid marriage and demand abstinence from foods', 1 Tim. 4.3).[39] The letters also indicate that the opponents arose from within the church (they have, e.g., 'deviated from' sincere faith, 1 Tim. 1.6-7; see also 6.10; 2 Tim. 2.17; Tit. 3.10-11), and though there were theological differences between the opposing groups, the most immediate issue was a social one: a battle for the leadership of the church.[40] To judge from the energy with which the author refutes them, these teachers were having significant success, and to judge from the emphasis that the author places on non-celibate roles for women (1 Tim. 2.15; 5.10, 14; Tit. 2.4-5), they were having particular success among women (2 Tim. 3.6-7).

---

39.   Robert J. Karris employs careful methodological procedures to extract the actual nature of these opponents from the author's stereotypical accusations. His conclusions are cautious: he cannot identify the opponents with any known Gnostic sect, though many commentaries do not hesitate to apply that label ('The Background and Significance of the Polemic of the Pastoral Epistles', *JBL* 92 [1973], pp. 549-64). On the difficulty of separating rhetoric from reality in the depiction of the opponents, see also Luke T. Johnson, 'II Timothy and the Polemic Against False Teachers: A Re-examination', *JRelS* 6 (1978), pp. 1-26.

40.   See, e.g., Lewis R. Donelson, *Pseudepigraphy and Ethical Argument in the Pastoral Epistles* (HUT, 22; Tübingen: Mohr–Siebeck, 1986), esp. pp. 116-27. Gordon D. Fee identifies the opponents as the church's own elders (*1 and 2 Timothy, Titus* [New International Biblical Commentary; Peabody, MA: Hendrickson, rev. edn, 1988], pp. 7-10), while MacDonald identifies them as celibate women church leaders, including the widows themselves (*Legend and the Apostle, passim*); MacDonald is followed by, among others, Linda Maloney, 'The Pastoral Epistles', in Elisabeth Schüssler Fiorenza (ed.), *Searching the Scriptures: A Feminist Commentary* (2 vols.; New York: Crossroad, 1994), II, pp. 361-80, and Ulrike Wagener, *Die Ordnung des 'Hauses Gottes': Der Ort von Frauen in der Ekklesiologie und Ethik der Pastoralbriefe* (WUNT, 2.65; Tübingen: Mohr–Siebeck, 1994). This intriguing suggestion deserves serious consideration, for women are often described in the letters in ways that associate them with the opposing teachers. Yet these teachers, when identified, are always men (1 Tim. 1.20; 2 Tim. 2.17-18; 3.6-9; see also Tit. 1.10). The connections the author creates between the activities of the women and those of these teachers serve his rhetorical goals by justifying the hierarchical structure he wishes to impose on the women. They function to discredit the women and do not necessarily require identification of the women as the teachers.

These two factors explain to some extent a third feature of these letters. As the first round of defense against the opposing teachers and as a first round of response to outside criticism, the author promotes the traditional hierarchy of the patriarchal family.[41] Thus we find a concern for the obedient submissiveness of slaves toward their masters (Tit. 2.9-10), of children toward their fathers (1 Tim. 3.4, cf. Tit. 1.6), and of women toward both their husbands (Tit. 2.5) and church leaders (1 Tim. 2.11). The women are admonished to be 'self-controlled, chaste, good managers of the household, kind, [and] submissive toward their husbands' (Tit. 2.5), to 'dress themselves modestly and decently', and to 'learn in silence with full submission', for 'she will be saved through childbearing, provided they continue in faith and love and holiness, with modesty' (1 Tim. 2.9-15).[42] As indicated above, the explicit motivation for this advice, which focuses on the traditional wifely virtues of submissive domesticity and childbearing, is the concern for the opinion of outsiders. Not far beneath the surface, however, lies an equally strong concern to render the women immune to the celibate piety proclaimed by the opposing teachers,[43] and probably the author's own aversion to women's leadership in the church.[44]

41. Lippert identifies this dual connection clearly (*Zeugnis, passim*); see also Verner, *Household of God*, pp. 80-86.

42. The most frequently encountered term in these lists is the noun σωφροσύνη (or the related adjective σώφρων), which designates one of the four cardinal virtues of Stoic philosophy. When applied to men it connotes soundness of judgment and self-control (see 1 Tim. 3.2, where the NRSV translates the same word as 'sensible' when it refers to bishops). When applied, as here, to women, it connotes the 'softer' virtue of modesty, that is, shyness, self-restraint, and a deferential attitude. It was often paired with chastity to connote sexual restraint, and together these terms defined the cultural ideal for women (see, e.g., Halvor Moxnes, 'Honor and Shame', *BTB* 23 [1993], pp. 167-76, esp. p. 171).

43. This link between the opponents' message and the various admonitions to and about women is widely recognized, though not all have developed the connection to the same extent. Thus, e.g., Joachim Jeremias, *Die Briefe an Timotheus und Titus* (NTD, 9; Göttingen: Vandenhoeck & Ruprecht, 1975) sees evidence of a polemic against the opponents in 1 Tim. 2.8-15 and (weakly) in 1 Tim. 5.3-16; while C. Spicq, *Saint Paul: Les épîtres pastorales* (EBib; Paris: Lecoffre, 1947), and Martin Dibelius and Hans Conzelmann, *The Pastoral Epistles* (Hermeneia; Philadelphia: Fortress Press, 1972), mention it in connection with 1 Tim. 2.8-15 and Tit. 2.3-5. Charles K. Barrett, *The Pastoral Epistles in the New English Bible* (New Clarendon Bible; Oxford: Clarendon Press, 1963), and J.N.D. Kelly, *A Commentary on the Pastoral Epistles* (BNTC; London: A. & C. Black, 1963), on the other hand, only mention the opponents in connection with 1 Tim. 2.8-15. Recently this connection has been more vigorously developed and defended; see, e.g., D.R. MacDonald, *Legend and the Apostle*; Maloney, 'Pastoral Epistles'; L.A. Brown, 'Asceticism and Ideology'.

44. This argument is developed with particular vigor and cogency by Wagener, *Die Ordnung, passim*.

When the author turns his attention to the widows, a group that has preserved the legacy of the celibacy cautiously promoted by Paul and at least a measure of the attendant autonomy and power, his reactionary concerns surface with particular intensity. Though written from an unsympathetic perspective, the author's rhetoric reveals something of the lives of the women known as widows. It reveals a great deal more, however, about the author's attempt to disperse the group of women and to defuse their power.

The Widows: Inside the Celibate Circle

Before we can ask about the situation of the widows, we need to address the question of the unity of this passage. Do all the references to widows concern the same group, so that the 'real' widows (αἱ ὄντως χῆραι) are also the ones 'enrolled' (RSV) or 'put on the list' (NRSV)? Or is the author addressing two groups and two sets of issues? Scholars are divided on this point.

There is a strong impression of unity, for the entire passage focuses on widows and the term χήρα ('widow') appears throughout (vv. 3 [twice], 4, 5, 9, 11, 16 [twice]). An *inclusio* cements the impression of unity, with v. 16 repeating in inverted order the ideas introduced in vv. 3-4, using the same phrases and grammatical constructions.

Verses 3-4	*Verse 16*
Χήρας τίμα τὰς ὄντως χήρας.	Εἴ τις πιστὴ ἔχει χήρας,
Εἰ δέ τις χήρα τέκνα...ἔχει,	ἐπαρκείτω αὐταῖς...
μανθανέτωσαν...ἀμοιβὰς	ἵνα [ἡ ἐκκλησία] ταῖς ὄντως χήραις
ἀποδιδόναι τοῖς προγόνοις.	ἐπαρκέσῃ.
Honor widows who are real widows.	If any faithful woman has widows
If any widow has children...	let her assist them...
let them learn...to make some	so that the church can assist the real
repayment to their parents	widows.

The opening exhortation to honor (τιμᾶν) widows denotes first the public recognition so important in Roman culture.[45] But it also implies financial support, as the following passage makes abundantly clear with the explanation that 'double honor' is due to elders because 'the laborer deserves to be paid' (5.17-18). Thus the reference to the church assisting real widows in v. 16b corresponds to the admonition to honor them in v. 3. Likewise, both v. 4 and v. 16a qualify the extent of the financial

45. On honor-shame cultures, see Moxnes, 'Honor and Shame'. These issues abound in the Pastoral Letters (see, e.g., 1 Tim. 1.17; 3.7, 13; 4.12; 6.1; 2 Tim. 1.8, 12, 16; 2.15; 4.8; Tit. 2.15).

obligations of the church with conditional sentences, and while the protasis (if-clause) in v. 4 considers the case of widows with children,[46] v. 16a considers the nearly opposite situation, a Christian woman with widows to support.[47] In both verses the conclusion is the same: the number of women eligible for support is reduced.[48]

In spite of this formal evidence supporting the unity of the text, the criteria put forward in it seem so contradictory that many find it difficult to maintain that vv. 3-8, 16 and vv. 9-15 refer to the same group, that is, that the true widows (v. 3) are identical to listed or enrolled (καταλέγειν) ones (v. 9).[49] Verses 3-8 and 16, for example, emphasize the present solitude and piety of the real widow, who is to receive assistance (honor) from the church. Verses 9-15, however, present standards of age (not less than 60 years), marital relations (wife of one husband), and behavior (well attested for good deeds, having brought up children, washed the feet of the saints, and helped the afflicted) for the widows who are to be enrolled[50]—qualities that parallel in almost every regard the qualifications for bishop (3.1-7; see also Tit. 1.5-9). The orientation of vv. 3-8 and 16 is thus very different from that of vv. 9-15. The first set of verses identifies solitude, and perhaps attendant material need, as the basis for

---

46. The wording of v. 4 is ambiguous in the Greek. It could be taken to mean that the widow is to do her duty to her family, and not the other way around. Most translations and commentaries follow the second line of interpretation given above, but there are strong reasons for preferring the first. For a more complete discussion, see G. Stählin, 'χήρα', *TDNT*, IX, pp. 440-65 (esp. 453-54); Wagener, *Die Ordnung*, pp. 149-54; Jouette M. Bassler, *1 Timothy, 2 Timothy, Titus* (ANTC; Nashville: Abingdon Press, 1996), pp. 94-96.

47. The NRSV translates v. 16 in a way that makes the connection with v. 4 seem even closer than it is: 'if any believing woman has *relatives who are really* widows...' The italicized words are not found in the Greek text, and the actual situation the author has in mind is that of relatively prosperous Christian women, probably themselves widows, supporting other widows, possibly in their homes. Acts 9.36-42 may reflect a similar situation; see Bonnie Bowman Thurston, *The Widows: A Women's Ministry in the Early Church* (Minneapolis: Fortress Press, 1989), pp. 31-35.

48. Wagener argues that v. 16 is a later interpolation that introduces for the first time the issue of a financial burden on the church (*Die Ordnung*, pp. 223-27). There is, however, no textual support for rejecting the authenticity of the verse, which creates an impressive *inclusio* for the passage.

49. Thus, e.g., Gerhard Delling, *Paulus Stellung zu Frau und Ehe* (BWANT, 4.5; Stuttgart: W. Kohlhammer, 1937), p. 138; Lippert, *Zeugnis*, p. 38; Spicq, *Epîtres*, p. xlviii; Fee, *1 and 2 Timothy* (NIBC), pp. 100-106, reject the unity of the passage.

50. The word 'enroll' is not used elsewhere in these letters or in the rest of the New Testament, but it appears frequently in other documents almost as a technical term for registration, e.g., onto a ship or into the cavalry.

financial support.[51] The second set presents what seem to be qualifications for membership in an official group within the church. Taken separately they make sense: financial assistance for those left utterly alone; enrollment in an official group for those qualified by age and experience. But they are not presented separately. The instructions for the former are wrapped around those for the latter, pulling the two sets of instructions into an unambiguous but uneasy whole. In fact, the text looks like a hybrid, formed by inserting a passage of one provenance and purpose into a passage of another and uniting the disparate components within an *inclusio* of 'real widows'. If this suspicion is correct, the questions remain why the author has combined these two passages, and to what effect?[52]

Many of the difficulties that the text poses stem from the fact that the author is not initiating a new benevolence, which would have involved a more careful explication of terms and conditions, but is seeking to limit an existing one.[53] Indeed, this goal unites the contents of the two otherwise disparate halves of the passage, since both seek to exclude various categories of women and to reduce the circle of widows supported by the church to an absolute minimum.[54] It would seem that the circle of

51.   It is not clear that solitude necessarily implies material need. Wagener makes a good case for the existence of an earlier widows' rule underlying this text, which equated solitude with spiritual devotion (*Die Ordnung*, pp. 135-43, 165-69). The ambiguous wording of vv. 4 and 8 leaves unclear whether the author of this text regards the widows as the recipients or providers of family support, and thus whether he has added the nuance of need to the concept of solitude. Verse 16 seems to tilt the meaning of the ambiguous verses in that direction.

52.   For additional support for the hypothesis that the author has deliberately formed the material in this passage into a unified whole, see Johannes Müller-Bardorff, 'Zur Exegese von 1. Timotheus 5,3-16', in *Gott und die Götter: Festgabe für Erich Fascher zum 60. Geburtstag* (Berlin: Evangelische Verlagsanstalt, 1958), pp. 113-33. Wagener has approached the task of explaining the disparate material by attempting to separate traditional material from redaction rather than postulating the uniting of originally discrete components (*Die Ordnung, passim*, esp. pp. 227-33). Her analysis warrants careful attention, for certainly the author has redacted the material, whether it is from one source or two. The questions about the purpose and effect of the author's work remain, however, the same.

53.   Müller-Bardorff makes this point most vigorously ('1. Timotheus 5,3-16', pp. 113-33); see also Hans-Werner Bartsch, *Die Anfänge Urchristlicher Rechtsbildungen. Studien zu den Pastoralbriefen* (TF, 34; Hamburg: Evangelischer Verlag, 1965), p. 134; D.R. MacDonald, *Legend and the Apostle*, pp. 73-77. On the possible origin of this benevolence, see Thurston, *The Widows*, pp. 9-55; Müller-Bardorff, pp. 126-31.

54.   It is not at all clear whether one should speak of an 'office' in the technical sense or merely of a 'circle' of widows. I have followed the latter convention, though without debating the issue. The answer rests to a large extent on how one construes

church-supported widows had grown too large, or that the church's practice of unrestricted support for widows had become problematic for the author of this letter. In either case, an explanation is needed. Why had the number of church-supported widows increased? Or, why had the widows' group lost the author's support? The answers to these two questions converge on a single hypothesis.

Had the number of women who had lost their spouses suddenly increased beyond the ability of the church to support them? Two factors make this unlikely. First, though we do not know what level of assistance was provided to the widows, the church addressed in these letters seems to have been relatively prosperous.[55] Women are instructed not to wear gold, pearls, and expensive clothes (1 Tim. 2.9) — gratuitous advice if it were not a possibility for at least some of them. Some men were wealthy enough to own slaves (1 Tim. 6.1-2), and twice the author directs instructions to the rich (1 Tim. 6.9-10, 17-19). The clear impression is that the church did not lack resources to provide assistance to widows. Second, while the mortality rate was high (by modern standards) throughout the Roman Empire, there is no reason to suspect that it had suddenly

the duties of the widows. It seems clear that the widows received financial assistance, but it is not so clear that they performed specific duties in return. Barrett, *Pastoral Epistles*, p. 76; Delling, *Stellung*, p. 135; Dibelius and Conzelmann, *Pastoral Epistles*, p. 75; and Kelly, *Pastoral Epistles*, p. 118, claim that the widows had duties that centered on making house calls (1 Tim. 5.13), but this activity is vigorously opposed in this letter and thus hardly can constitute the proper duty of a widow. Norbert Brox, *Die Pastoralbriefe* (RNT, 7.2; Regensburg: Pustet, 4th edn, 1969), p. 189; Jeremias (*Die Briefe*, p. 37; Johannes Leipoldt, *Die Frau in der antiken Welt und im Urchristentum* (Leipzig: Koehler & Amelang, 1954), p. 203; Müller-Bardorff, '1. Timotheus 5,3-16', pp. 123-25, Francine Cardman, 'Women, Ministry, and Church Order in Early Christianity', in Kraemer and D'Angelo (eds.), *Women and Christian Origins*, pp. 300-329, esp. p. 304; and Wagener, *Die Ordnung*, pp. 132-49, among others, see v. 5 as the key to the task of the widows, which is thus defined as prayer. Yet this interpretation seems to be based more on the comments of the later *Didascalia Apostolorum* (chs. 14–15) than on this verse, which points to a prerequisite attitude rather than to a duty. Georg G. Blum regards Tit. 2.4-5 as a delineation of the widows' duties ('Das Amt der Frau im Neuen Testament', *NovT* 7 [1964–65], pp. 142-61, esp. p. 159), though widows are not mentioned there. Stählin is probably correct in assuming that the question of tasks receives no express answer in this passage ('χήρα', p. 457), a conclusion that others support; e.g., Roger Gryson, *The Ministry of Women in the Early Church* (Collegeville, MN: Liturgical Press, 1976), p. 10; Verner, *Household of God*, pp. 164-65; Margaret Y. MacDonald, 'Rereading Paul: Early Interpreters of Paul on Women and Gender', in Kraemer and D'Angelo (eds.), *Women and Christian Origins*, pp. 236-53 (esp. 247-48).

55. So, too, Verner, *Household of God*, pp. 174-75, 180-81; see also Reggie M. Kidd, *Wealth and Beneficence in the Pastoral Epistles* (SBLDS, 122; Atlanta: Scholars Press, 1990).

soared to produce an unusual number of bereaved women.[56] The explanation of an increase in numbers could lie, however, in a broader definition of the word translated 'widow' (χήρα).

The root meaning of χήρα is 'empty' or 'forsaken', and it was sometimes applied not strictly to bereaved women, but more generally to
women living without husbands.[57] Thus an increase in 'widows' could
derive, for example, from a high divorce rate, possibly between recently
converted women and their unconverted husbands. The phenomenon
was widespread enough in Corinth to merit a significant amount of
Paul's attention, and though his advice was for the couple to remain
married, it is important to note that he did not insist on it (1 Cor. 7.10-24).
Furthermore, we do not know how rigorously his advice was followed.[58]
Yet 'widow' need not even indicate an earlier marriage. The comment in
1 Tim 5.12 ('they [younger widows] incur condemnation for having
violated their first pledge') points to a pledge or vow (πίστις) of chastity
required of all members of the group, and the requirement that young
widows marry (γαμεῖν, vv. 11, 14) does not have any qualifiers like
'again' (πάλιν; cf. 1 Cor. 7.5) or 'a second time' (τὸ δεύτερον; cf. Tit. 3.10)
to indicate that the author actually had *re*marriage in mind. It appears
that the widows' circle had evolved to the point that sexual abstinence,
not bereavement, was the determinative feature.[59] Virgins, probably also

56. Local conditions are, of course, impossible to determine given the uncertainty
about the authorship, date, and provenance of these letters. The only available evidence is the content, which reveals no life-threatening crisis.

57. Contemporary examples can be found in Stählin, 'χήρα', pp. 440-65; see also
Wagener, *Die Ordnung*, pp. 127-35. The use of the Latin *vidua* in this way is even more
common.

58. A recurring motif in the second- and third-century acts is the conversion of a
woman, usually high-born, her rejection of her unconverted husband or fiancé, and
subsequent persecution by this spurned man (see, e.g., Paul J. Achtemeier, 'Jesus and
the Disciples as Miracle Workers in the Apocryphal New Testament', in Elisabeth
Schüssler Fiorenza [ed.], *Aspects of Religious Propaganda in Judaism and Early Christianity* [Notre Dame, IN: University of Notre Dame Press, 1976], pp. 149-86, esp. pp. 162-
63; Kraemer, 'Conversion of Women', *passim*; Burrus, *Chastity as Autonomy*, pp. 31-60).
The opponents of Christianity made this conversion pattern the basis of accusations
against the new religion (Celsus *apud* Origin, *C. Cels.* 3.55; Porphyry *apud* Augustine,
Civitate Deo 19.23).

59. At approximately the same time, Ignatius sent greetings to 'the virgins who are
called widows' (τὰς παρθένους τὰς λεγομένας χήρας, *Smyrn.* 13.1). Ignatius's letter to
Polycarp hints at the presence of a similar group in Philadelphia, and indicates further
that their promotion of celibacy was becoming problematic for these church leaders
(Ign., *Pol.* 4.1, 5.1-2). For discussion, see MacDonald, *Legend and the Apostle*, p. 74. It is
likely that the term 'widow' (rather than 'virgin') was used for the group because of its
origins in a traditional benevolence.

converted and divorced women, had joined the widows' circle. But what had attracted them?

It is possible, of course, that voluntary association with the group was motivated by the esteem and remuneration that members received. Yet this takes no account of the celibacy that the widows embraced. Müller-Bardorff is on firm ground in locating the attraction of women to the widows' circle precisely in the sexual abstinence that it required. He explores the radical eschatology that gave initial support to the ideal of celibate devotion to God (1 Cor. 7.25-40), and the body–soul dualism that, in his view, later sustained it.[60] These are, however, gender-neutral considerations. Müller-Bardorff does not address the fact that celibacy emerges as an issue in a group restricted to women. The implications *for women* of a life of sexual renunciation must also be taken into account.

The life demanded of the widows was one of celibacy, but celibacy, at least among women in Pauline churches, was linked with a sense of spirit-given power and autonomy. It is plausible to assume that the widows' circle was an attractive option for women because the celibacy it required continued to ground an empowering spirituality and autonomy.[61] Linked together by a vow of celibacy, protected by that vow against the pressure to marry which was intensifying in the church, provided official recognition, sanction, and support by the church, the widows were granted remarkable autonomy. Freed from hierarchical dominance of either husband or father,[62] freed from the dangers of childbearing and the demands of child rearing, freed even from pressing economic concerns, the widows were free of the domestic constraints on other women. But what were they freed to do?

Here we must distinguish between what the author of this letter accuses the widows of doing and what they actually were doing. As with other groups of which he disapproves, the author assails widows with stereo-typed invective. 'The widow who lives for pleasure (σπαταλᾶν; literally, "to live in excess comfort or luxury") is dead even while she lives' (v. 6). This charge of living for pleasure reflects the widespread stereotype of the indulgent, idle woman.[63] It cannot be taken to reveal anything about

60. Müller-Bardorff, '1. Timotheus 5,3-16', pp. 126-31.

61. See also Cardman, 'Women', pp. 302-305, and especially Wagener, *Die Ordnung*, pp. 132-43, 165-69, 229-31.

62. The author's insistence that family members should provide for their relatives (v. 8) points to a situation in which the women in the widows' circle were not being supported — and therefore not controlled — by male relatives.

63. The stereotype was used, e.g., by Horace to mock women who studied philosophy (*Epode* 8.15-16), and it was presumed by Musonius Rufus when he assured his readers that philosophy would *not* make women live heedlessly or intemperately

the actual lives of these women, except to suggest that they were not conforming to society's (and the author's) domestic expectations, and perhaps that they had no pressing financial need.[64]

Later the author is more specific: 'They [the widows] learn to be idle, gadding about from house to house; and they are not merely idle, but also gossips and busybodies, saying what they should not say' (v. 13). The charge of idleness reflects again the fact that these women are not caught up in domestic activities (see v. 14; Tit. 2.4-5). The charges of 'gadding about', gossiping, and meddling use cultural stereotype to condemn their active lives outside the confines of the patriarchal household.[65] The charge that they were 'saying what they should not say' (λαλοῦσαι τὰ μὴ δέοντα) is not the charge of garrulousness that was part of the cultural stereotype of women,[66] but an objection to the content of what they were saying.[67] It also indicates the autonomy of their actions, for here was speech — the imparting of information — that did not conform to approved guidelines. It is similar to the charge in Tit. 1.11 that certain insubordinate (NRSV: 'rebellious') opponents were 'teaching what it is not right to teach' (διδάσκοντες ἃ μὴ δεῖ) and recalls the warnings to Timothy to follow sound teaching (e.g. 1 Tim. 1.10; 4.6; 6.3; cf. Tit. 1.9; 2.1) and not 'old wives tales' (γραώδεις μύθοι, 1 Tim. 4.7). The widows, one can surmise, were circulating freely in the community, speaking without direct authorization of male church leaders, on topics these leaders did not (or, from the author's perspective, should not) approve. Quite apart from their numbers, this situation alarmed the author.[68]

Beyond that, the lifestyle of the widows seems to have produced a

---

(*Orations* 3; Cora E. Lutz [trans.], *Musonius Rufus* [New Haven: Yale University Press, 1947], pp. 43-44).

64. Wagener, *Die Ordnung*, pp. 155-56.

65. Juvenal, e.g., condemns women who rush 'boldly about the entire city' (*Satires* 6.398-99) and Musonius Rufus acknowledges widespread concern 'that women who associate with philosophers are bound to be arrogant...abandoning their own household...when they should be sitting at home spinning' (*Or.* 3); see also Plutarch, *Advice to Bride and Groom* 9, 30, 32; Philo, *Spec. Leg.* 3.169-74.

66. See Juvenal, *Satires* 6.398-412; Plutarch, *Advice to Bride and Groom* 32; *How to Profit by One's Enemies* 8.

67. The author does not reveal what they were saying. With good cause, Wagener surmises that the content of their speech corresponded in some way to their counter-cultural practices (*Die Ordnung*, pp. 206-11, 221-23).

68. So, too, Maloney, 'Pastoral Epistles', p. 370; MacDonald, *Legend and the Apostle*, *passim*. Drawing on information from the third-century *Didascalia Apostolorum*, Müller-Bardorff suggests that the widows were engaged in charismatic prophecy ('1. Timotheus 5,3-16', p. 125). The difference may be more semantic than substantive, for prophecy and teaching were overlapping activities (1 Cor. 14.6, 19, 31).

reaction in the wider society, which objected to their free and apparently idle behavior. Or, the author is concerned that their lifestyle *might* produce a negative reaction, for he instructs the younger widows to marry and engage in domestic pursuits 'so as to give the adversary no occasion to revile us' (v. 14b).[69] Finally, the circle of widows provided a natural avenue of defection to the opposing teachers, who also required a commitment to celibacy. Indeed, the reference in v. 15 to some widows who 'have already turned away to follow Satan', indicates that this was no idle fear.[70] Some had already chosen that path.

The Author's Response: Circumscribing the Circle
The instructions about widows address the situation in two ways. First, the author attempts to reduce the number of women in this group by recalling the church to a rigid concept of real widows who were entirely without other resources or responsibilities. Thus widows with children or grandchildren are excluded (v. 4). Widows who are being supported by 'faithful women' are also excluded (v. 16). And church members who do not provide for family members, including widows, are soundly castigated as having 'denied the faith' and being 'worse than an unbeliever' (v. 8).[71] Beyond this, however, the inclusion of the criteria listed in vv. 9-10 has the impact, and probably also the intent, of molding the much-reduced widows' circle into a group that affirms contemporary social norms. A brief survey of some other Greco-Roman cults clarifies this point.

69. Ὁ ἀντικείμενος (NRSV: 'the adversary'; literally, 'the one opposing') probably refers to an outsider, who was a real or potential objector to indiscreet behavior (cf. ὁ ἐξ ἐναντίας, 'the opponent', in Tit. 2.8). Brox, *Pastoralbriefe*, p. 197, Dibelius and Conzelmann, *Pastoral Epistles*, p. 76, Spicq, *Epîtres*, p. 173, Jürgen Roloff, *Der erste Brief an Timotheus* (EKKNT, 15; Zürich: Benziger Verlag; Neukirchen–Vluyn: Neukirchener Verlag, 1988), p. 299, and most emphatically Lippert, *Zeugnis*, p. 44, follow this interpretation. Lorenz Oberlinner sees an allusion to Satan in this phrase (*Die Pastoralbriefe: Kommentar zum Ersten Timotheusbrief* [3 vols.; HTKNT, 11.2; Freiburg: Herder, 1994], II, p. 242); see also Wagener, *Die Ordnung*, pp. 212-15.

70. 'Turning away to follow Satan', though somewhat ambiguous (thus, Dibelius and Conzelmann, *Pastoral Epistles*, p. 76), probably refers to joining the opposing teachers. The other uses of ἐκτρέπεσθαι ('turn away', see 1 Tim. 1.6; 6.20; 2 Tim. 4.4) occur in the context of references to this group (so, too, Bartsch, *Anfänge*, p. 134) and the use of τινες ('some') here corresponds to the author's style of combating his opponents (see, e.g., 1 Tim. 1.3, 6, 19; also Müller-Bardorff, '1. Timotheus 5,3-16', p. 132).

71. The antecedent of the indefinite pronoun ('whoever') is ambiguous. It could refer to a widow who is not fulfilling her responsibilities toward her family; see Wagener, *Die Ordnung*, pp. 149-54.

There were a number of religious cults in the ancient world that were restricted to women or appealed strongly to them.[72] Among the factors that contributed to the popularity and longevity of these cults, two are particularly significant. First, for the women who participated in them, whose lives were restricted in so many ways, the cults offered an outlet for religious emotion and an opportunity for enhancing social bonds with other women. Second, for the men whose permission was necessary in order for the women to participate but whose commitment was to perpetuating the values and structure of patriarchal society, the cults did not threaten the social order. In fact, the cults directly or indirectly affirmed that social order. Three examples illustrate this important phenomenon.

At one extreme, the Fortuna cults were explicit and direct in their affirmation.[73] Most of these cults were restricted to women (specifically women of good social standing) and the goddess served as patroness to these women as they moved through their various familial roles. The cultic rites exalted and reinforced the domestic virtues appropriate to each role: childbearing, marital fidelity, familial bonds, and domestic harmony.

The Isis cult was more complex.[74] Originally, it seems, Isis was an independent goddess, the mother of all the kings of Egypt, a powerful creatrix linked sometimes with heaven and sometimes with the fertile Nile delta. Eventually she was linked with Osiris, the god of vegetation and death, and her relationship with him evolved into that of faithful wife and mother. It is in this guise — as the model spouse, the divine patron of family life, the teacher of domestic arts — that her cult spread throughout the Greco-Roman world, attracting the devotion of both women and men. Isis was, however, often perceived by the Roman authorities as threatening, apparently because many of her devotees were from lower classes, and probably also because many women of all classes were attracted to her cult. Her devotees were also held to periods of strict sexual abstinence, which was viewed with some suspicion and hostility

---

72. For a fuller discussion of the following summary, see Pomeroy, *Goddesses*, pp. 205-26; Kraemer, *Her Share of the Blessings*, pp. 36-79; Deborah F. Sawyer, *Women and Religion in the First Christian Centuries* (Religion in the First Christian Centuries, 1; London: Routledge, 1996), pp. 59-72; and Lynn R. LiDonnici, 'Women's Religions and Religious Lives in the Greco-Roman City', in Kraemer and D'Angelo (eds.), *Women and Christian Origins*, pp. 80-102.

73. On the Fortuna cults, see Pomeroy, *Goddesses*, pp. 206-10; Kraemer, *Her Share of the Blessings*, pp. 55-61.

74. On the Isis cult, see Pomeroy, *Goddesses*, pp. 217-26; Kraemer, *Her Share of the Blessings*, pp. 71-79; Sawyer, *Women and Religion*, pp. 66-68; Sharon Kelly Heyob, *The Cult of Isis among Women in the Greco-Roman World* (Leiden: E.J. Brill, 1975).

by outsiders; yet, her basically domesticated nature seems to have made her generally acceptable, even useful in promoting the feminine ideal.

At the other extreme the sexual and moral excesses of the Dionysiac cult were remarkably well tolerated by the conservative Greek and Roman societies.[75] Though the nature of the cult changed over the centuries, it was often restricted to women. During the cultic rites, participating women left their homes, abandoned their children, loosed their hair, dressed in animal skins and crowns of leaves, and ran and danced in ecstatic frenzy. Cultural toleration of this behavior has been attributed to the fact that it was regarded as the temporary product of religious possession and involved a deliberate and recognizable role reversal. That is, the women engulfed by Dionysiac madness enacted the reverse of the submissive, domestic, nurturing role expected of them, but since this reverse behavior was recognized as the product of religious insanity, the sanity and appropriateness of the traditional behavior was simultaneously upheld.

These examples of various ways in which religious cults, even those with countercultural impulses, were made to reinforce basic cultural values provide a key to understanding the criteria for inclusion on the list of officially 'honored' and financially supported widows in 1 Tim. 5. The situation in the Pastoral Letters falls between the extremes of the Fortuna cults (direct reinforcement of social values) and the cult of Dionysus (reverse affirmation of social values). The vow of celibacy — the basic but potentially dangerous and objectionable feature of the widows' circle — was retained, but the other criteria that are introduced effectively defuse the danger and meet potential objections. An age limit was established (not less than 60 years old) that would dramatically reduce the number of widows on the list.[76] Moreover, the age limit restricted the vow of celibacy to those women who were expected to have already abandoned sexual intercourse.[77] These celibate elderly women would not have threatened cultural values and social expectations. They would have reinforced them.

---

75. On the cult of Dionysus, see Sawyer, *Women and Religion*, pp. 61-66; Kraemer, *Her Share of the Blessings*, pp. 36-49; and especially *idem*, 'Ecstasy and Possession: The Attraction of Women to the Cult of Dionysus', *HTR* 72 (1979), pp. 55-80.

76. According to P. Brown, the average life expectancy in the Roman Empire in the second century was less than 25 years, and fewer than 4 out of every 100 females born lived beyond the age of 50 (*Body and Society*, p. 6). These calculations are, however, disputed. Furthermore, consideration of the high infant mortality rate gives a girl who reached the age of 10 a significant probability of surviving until 50 or 60 (see Treggiari, *Roman Marriage*, pp. 398-403).

77. Brown, *Body and Society*, p. 68.

Participation in the widows' circle would have permitted freedom from a patriarchal household and the control of a spouse or other male family member. Yet this was replaced by the supervision of male church leaders, who controlled access to the group; and the criteria for access included prior participation in the domestic behavior from which the widows would be exempt. They were to be wife of one husband (NRSV: 'married only once'), a criterion that reflected the cultural esteem for *univirae* but also—importantly—required them to have been married. With this requirement, then, virgins were excluded. Enrolled widows were also to have brought up children. The phrase does not specify that the children were the widow's own, and many understand the requirement to mean that she must have cared for orphans.[78] Yet coming as it does right after the requirement of prior marriage, a reference to raising her own children is likely and certainly not excluded by the wording.[79] Beyond these domestic virtues, the women were to have performed acts of Christian piety, but even these acts were basically home-centered. Each was to be known for her deeds of hospitality toward visiting Christians, presumably by welcoming them into her home (see Phlm. 27; 2 Jn 10).[80] She was also to have 'washed the saints' feet', a humble gesture of welcome to one's home, with implicit overtones of subordination.[81]

If there is a consistent rationale to these criteria, it is probably to be found in the author's desire to reform and control a group that nurtured autonomy, to reduce the membership of a group that fostered the celibacy favored by his opponents, and to eliminate the offense of a group whose active, celibate lives challenged cultural expectations. The widows would retain their vow of celibacy, but for women at the age of 60 or above, that would be unremarkable. The author would also accept into the celibate widows' circle only those who, in their earlier years, had

---

78. So, e.g., Dibelius and Conzelmann, *Pastoral Epistles*, p. 75; Anthony T. Hanson, *The Pastoral Epistles* (NCBC; Grand Rapids: Eerdmans, 1982), p. 98; Roloff, *Erste Brief*, p. 295; Oberlinner, *Pastoralbriefe*, II, p. 234.

79. See, e.g., Müller-Bardorff, '1. Timotheus 5, 3-16', p. 121, esp. n. 16; Wagener, *Die Ordnung*, pp. 178-86.

80. The verb used here (ξενοδοχεῖν) seems to specify the actual performance of hospitable acts: providing meals or a room for visiting Christians. By contrast, the analogous requirement for bishops uses an adjective instead of a verb (φιλόξενος, 1 Tim. 3.2; Tit. 1.8), one that suggests a hospitable spirit more than hospitable actions (see Brown, 'Asceticism and Ideology', pp. 83-84).

81. We cannot assume that the gesture practiced in this church was charged with the meaning given to it through Jesus' act in the Gospel of John. It is, at any rate, only explicitly required of widows. See also Wagener, *Die Ordnung*, pp. 187-99.

participated in patriarchal households and exemplified domestic virtues. The church would 'honor' elderly matrons known for their piety as mistresses of Christian households, and in doing so it would honor the value system of Greco-Roman society. Beyond this, the requirement that younger widows marry and bear children (v. 14) encouraged *them* to conform to society's expectations. This is also, however, a distinctly anti-celibate requirement probably intended to counter the opposing teachers' message of sexual abstinence.

We have covered as much of the social history of this community as this passage allows us to grasp. The text reveals that there were celibate women in this community—probably in significant numbers—who showed more autonomy and had more active roles than the author of this letter was willing to grant. If the author prevailed, it is possible to propose a trajectory of subsequent events. Since the opposing teachers, with their message of sexual renunciation, offered support for the celibate women akin to that of the widows' circle, it seems probable that the rate of defections to this group would increase as the church enacted these draconian measures. It is unlikely that women who entered the widows' circle to realize their autonomy and power 'in Christ' would have been content with the subordinate lifestyle thrust upon them.

Would the 'unlisted' widows—those excluded from official recognition and support by the author's criteria and yet unwilling to marry and relinquish their celibate autonomy—have found a viable option in the private widows' houses mentioned in v. 16 ('If any faithful woman has widows, let her support them')? This terse comment suggests a situation in which a relatively wealthy Christian woman, probably herself a widow, supported other widows in her home. Under these circumstances, their commitment to celibacy could be preserved, with its attendant benefits for the women. Yet any power and autonomy *these* widows derived from their celibacy would not be 'honored' or legitimized by membership in an official circle. And it is possible that the designation of the patroness of these widows as a 'faithful woman' (πιστή; NRSV: 'believing woman') points to a presupposition that she, like everything else designated 'faithful' in these letters, conforms to the sound teaching promoted by this author.[82] It would thus be a 'safe house', but safe from the perspective of the church leadership.

82. See, e.g., 1 Tim. 1.12, 15; 4.3, 9; 2 Tim. 2.2, 11; Tit. 1.9; 3.8. Wagener also raises this as a possibility but rejects it in favor of dismissing the entire verse as an interpolation (*Die Ordnung*, pp. 223-27).

Conclusions

This analysis of the logic and purpose of 1 Tim. 5.3-16 has uncovered an apparently calculated attempt to decimate and neutralize a group that nurtured women's spirituality and empowerment in the early post-Pauline church. It is not clear whether the author was primarily motivated by concern over public opinion, the threat of opposing teachers, or his own distrust of women's empowerment. Probably all three factors were at work. It is also not clear that he was entirely successful, at least for the short term. The deuterocanonical acts attest to widespread esteem and support for autonomous, celibate women and their distinctive spiritual gifts and power well into the third century.

The church orders (also produced during this period) send a mixed message. They continue to limit and restrict the widows' order and thus foster the message and goals of the Pastoral Letters. Yet the very persistence of the concern to control the widows suggests that the church hierarchy continued to feel threatened by their (latent or active?) spiritual power.[83] Of course, the author was successful in the long term. The Pastoral Letters were accepted into the canon and their pronouncements on widows in particular, and women in general, attained the normative status of inspired authority. Fortunately, the author left enough cracks in the letters' rhetorical façade that we can get glimpses of the early struggle and expose his words for what they are—a calculus of suppression.

---

83. See, e.g., Carolyn Osiek, 'The Widow as Altar: The Rise and Fall of a Symbol', *Second Century* 3 (1983), pp. 159-69.

'GOOD CITIZENSHIP' IN THE HOUSEHOLD OF GOD:
WOMEN'S POSITION IN THE PASTORALS RECONSIDERED
IN THE LIGHT OF ROMAN RULE

Lilian Portefaix

Introduction

The three New Testament writings, under the name of Pastorals, cannot be said to belong to its most exciting components. They were originally considered as the work of Paul,[1] but since the beginning of the nineteenth century Paul's authorship has been questioned;[2] nowadays, most scholars agree that the letters were written at a later period in the name of the Apostle and addressed to his co-workers Timothy and Titus who are said to have been left in Ephesus (1 Tim. 1.3) and Crete (Tit. 1.5) respectively.[3] The pseudo-Pauline theory makes the origin and the date of the Pastorals problematic. Bearing in mind the existing consonance of their contents, they ought to be taken as a whole; however, in spite of their separate destinations it seems reasonable to locate the author of the three letters to the western part of Asia Minor. References to Ephesus and the province of Asia (1 Tim. 1.3; 2 Tim. 1.15, 18; 4.12), and quotations in the letters of Polycarp, Bishop of Smyrna, point to this part of the Aegean. In addition, western Asia Minor was an important center of early Christian literature where possibly the Pauline letters were collected.[4] Regarding the date of the letters, the pseudo-Pauline theory suggests the reign of Trajan (98–117 CE) since the Pastorals have the character of church tracts; they reflect the adaptation of Christians to a new era in this world when the eschatological expectations were fading.[5] Furthermore, the fact that Ignatius's letters to the churches in Asia Minor, dated to about 110 CE, reflect similar cir-

---

1.   C.K. Barrett, *The Pastoral Epistles in the New English Bible* (New Clarendon Bible; Oxford: Clarendon Press, 1963), p. 2.

2.   Barrett, *Pastoral Epistles*, pp. 4-19; H. Conzelmann, *The Pastoral Epistles* (Hermeneia; Philadelphia: Fortress Press, 4th edn, 1984), pp. 1-5.

3.   Barrett, *Pastoral Epistles*, p. 18.

4.   Barrett, *Pastoral Epistles*, p. 19.

5.   D.J. Bosch, *Transforming Mission* (Maryknoll, NY: Orbis Books, 1991), p. 191.

cumstances, strengthens the possibility of assigning the author of the Pastorals to this area and also to the same period of time.[6]

Nowadays, the Pastorals have been brought to the fore by feminist scholars who raise opposition to the guiding idea of female life to be found in the household code in 1 Tim. 2.9-15;[7] these statements, confining women to childbearing and housework, are often considered as an argument against women ministers in the Church.[8] This seeming expression of misogyny on the part of the author is usually explained with reference to internal conditions within the early church and is most often seen as a protest of orthodox Christians against some Gnosticizing sects which used to treat women as equal to men in their communities.[9] In my view the letters must also be seen in the wider context of Roman history and society if we want to reach a more correct understanding of these statements. The attack against the heretical teachers, which is said to have incited the letters (1 Tim. 1.3-4), cannot be considered in isolation from the family politics of the Roman government inaugurated by Augustus; particularly the teaching against marriage ought to be discussed against this background. Since this sociopolitical aspect has been neglected up until now, as far as I know, I intend to fill this gap in the investigation of the Pastorals by demonstrating their apologetic function against the Roman state. In exploring my subject I take my starting point in the pseudo-Pauline theory. Moreover, I treat the three letters as a whole in spite of their diverse destinations and I claim that it is reasonable to assume that heretical teaching caused problems in the orthodox congregations all over the Aegean. First I discuss the political climate in the Empire principally drawn from literature of the age, and its consequences for Christians of both sexes in view of the non-Christian environment; in this respect I pay no attention to the Jewish influence since that side has been thoroughly investigated. Subsequently I concentrate on the moral climate (similarly using literary sources) as a background for the ethical teaching on Christian women which is found in the letters. In particular the steps taken by Augustus to regenerate the family life of ancient times and the consequences on various levels for Christian women will be brought into close focus.

---

6.   Barrett, *Pastoral Epistles*, p. 18. P. Vielhauer, *Geschichte der urchristlichen Literatur* (Berlin: W. de Gruyter, 3rd edn, 1981), p. 237. P. Feine, J. Behm and W.G. Kümmel, *Einleitung in das Neue Testament* (Heidelberg: Quelle & Meyer, 14th edn, 1965), p. 280.

7.   E. Schüssler Fiorenza, *In Memory of Her: A Feminist Theological Reconstruction of Christian Origins* (New York: Crossroad, 1983), pp. 288-91.

8.   Schüssler Fiorenza, *In Memory of Her*, p. 53.

9.   Barrett, *Pastoral Epistles*, p. 13.

The Political Climate

The political climate of the period did not favor the Christians. It was characterized by fear of rebellion on various levels, and particularly in Asia Minor the imperial cult had gained strength since the reign of Domitian (81–96 CE); in Ephesus, the capital of Asia, the province dedicated a temple to the Flavian family.[10] Even the reign of Trajan (98–117 CE), a man known for his justice and mildness, constituted a threat against Christian communities. As is evident from the correspondence between the emperor and the younger Pliny, who was a governor of Bithynia c. 111–113 CE, Trajan was alarmed that all kinds of associations might be latent movements of rebellion; the following advice to Pliny not to organize even a fire-brigade testifies to the fear of the emperor: 'If people assemble for a common purpose, whatever name we give them and for whatever reason, they soon turn into a political club.'[11] Furthermore, according to Pliny, Trajan even raised objections against forming benefit societies.[12] Also, it is well known that secret agents used to explore people's attitudes towards the emperors. The Stoic philosopher Epictetus (c. 50–120 CE) reports:

> In this fashion the rash are ensnared by the soldiers in Rome. A soldier, dressed like a civilian, sits down by your side and begins to speak ill of Caesar, and then you, too, just as though you had received from him some guarantee of good faith in the fact that he began the abuse, tell likewise everything you think, and the next thing is—you are led off to prison in chains.[13]

Although this activity is said to be located to Rome there is reason to assume that the same business was also going on in other parts of the Empire. Finally, the fear of slave rebellions was latent in the Roman Empire. In a letter to one of his friends Pliny, after reporting of a landed proprietor who was cruelly murdered by his slaves, makes the following commentary:

> There you see the dangers, outrages and insults to which we are exposed. No master can feel safe because he is kind and considerate; for it is their brutality, not their reasoning capacity, which leads slaves to murder masters.[14]

---

10. S.J. Friesen, *Twice Neokoros: Ephesus, Asia and the Cult of the Flavian Imperial Family* (Leiden: E.J. Brill, 1993).
11. Pliny, *Epistles* 10.34 (trans. B. Radice; LCL, 59).
12. Pliny, *Epistles* 10.92 and 93.
13. Epictetus, *Gnomologium Epicteteum* 4.13.5 (trans. W.A. Oldfather; LCL, 218).
14. Pliny, *Epistles* 3.14.5 (trans. B. Radice; LCL, 55).

The historian Tacitus (c. 55–120 CE) tries to find some reasons for such brutal behavior:

> To our ancestors the temper of their slaves was always suspect, even when they were born on the same farm or under the same roof, and acquired an affection for their masters forthwith. But now that we have in our households foreigners with customs different from our own, with alien religions or none at all, you will not restrain such a motley rabble except by fear.[15]

In our context it may be worth noting that adherence to foreign religions (including Christianity) is considered to cause treacherous behavior among slaves.

Christians and the Roman Authorities

From the sources we have a picture of the Roman government during the reign of Trajan as attentively infiltrating all kinds of societies and rebellions. In this respect 2 Timothy points to the dangerous situations for the Christians since it is said to have been written during Paul's imprisonment in Rome (2 Tim. 1.16-17). The danger of persecution was brought to mind particularly in Asia Minor by Ignatius's letters. These he addressed to the churches in the area as he journeyed from Antioch to Rome where he was martyred.[16] Against this background it is easy to understand the strong concern with the opinion of contemporary society shown by the author of the Pastorals, and also his reaction in response to the Gnosticizing heretics who were spreading a message that would easily cast suspicion upon his audience; because of the existing informer system mentioned above he could be sure that the contents of the letters would reach the ears of the Roman authorities — all the more since Christianity was regarded as a revolutionary sect (Acts 17.5-7). Such ideas of equality, as expressed in Gal. 3.28, could easily have strengthened the concept of Christianity in that direction.[17] In this situation the author of the Pastorals had to face two problems. First of all, the heretical teachers had to be repudiated in order to save the communities from disintegration. Secondly, the Roman authorities had to be convinced of the Christians' civic loyalty with a view to avoiding persecution, and we find references to the imperial cult and to the slave problem as will be evident in the following. As regards the imperial cult, the text provides evidence that Christians used to transform their sacrifices to prayers for

---

15. Tacitus, *Annals* 16.42-45 (trans. J. Jackson; LCL, 249).

16. Vielhauer, *Geschichte der urchristlichen Literatur*, pp. 544-45.

17. H.D. Betz, *Galatians: A Commentary on Paul's Letter to the Churches in Galatia* (Philadelphia: Fortress Press, 1979), p. 192.

the welfare of the emperor instead of making offerings before his image;[18] the author urges 'that supplications, prayers, intercessions, and thanksgivings be made for all men, for kings and all who are in high positions, that we may lead a quiet and peaceable life, godly and respectful in every way' (1 Tim. 2.1-2; cf. Tit. 3.1).

Furthermore, with the suspicion that Christianity was a revolutionary sect in mind, it was important for the author to convince the authorities that Christian leaders were no revolutionaries. It has been noticed that the catalogue of virtues demanded of the office-bearers (bishops, deacons, and elders) in the church (1 Tim. 3.1-7; 8-12; Tit. 1.5-9) corresponds to the fixed pattern of traditional qualities appropriate to a military commander (the office in itself embodying the virtue of reliability) which are listed in the *Strategikos* by the tactician Onosander. In the first paragraph of this writing dated to the first century CE we read as follows:

> I believe, then, that we must choose a general, not because of noble birth as priests are chosen, nor because of wealth as the superintendents of the gymnasia, but because he is temperate, self-restrained, vigilant, frugal, hardened to labor, alert, free from avarice, neither too young nor too old, indeed a father of children if possible, a ready speaker, and a man with a good reputation.[19]

The catalogue of virtues attributable to an army leader embodies the Roman ideal of a paterfamilias who keeps a tight hand over his family; this ideal is prescribed for bishops and deacons (1 Tim. 3.4-5, 12; cf. Tit. 1.9) who, besides their own families, are set to govern the household of God. Turning to the slave problem, the necessity of maintaining the peace of the church made it urgent that Christian slaves of both sexes — particularly those belonging to the leaders of the church[20] — adapted themselves to the social pattern of the Empire. Slaves owned by non-Christian masters are told to pay honor to them 'so that the name of God and the teaching may not be defamed', and those belonging to Christian masters must be submissive and serve them — even if master and slave are brethren in Christ (1 Tim. 6.1-2; cf. Tit. 2.9-10). Presumably the 'one-in-Christ' formula (Gal. 3.28), concealing social and political implications, had tended to place master and slave on an equal footing outside the community and had attracted the attention of non-Christians.[21]

---

18. S.R.F. Price, *Rituals and Power: The Roman Imperial Cult in Asia Minor* (Cambridge: Cambridge University Press, 1984), pp. 210-15.

19. Onosander's text is reproduced in Conzelmann, *Pastoral Epistles*, Appendix 3; see also pp. 50-51 and p. 158 n. 21.

20. Cf. Barrett, *Pastoral Epistles*, p. 82.

21. Betz, *Galatians*, p. 192.

The Moral Climate

In dealing with the moral condition of the Empire, we know from literature of the time that in the Augustan era there was a general decline of religion and morality in Roman society; the birth rate decreased and radical changes took place in family life that affected the position of the paterfamilias.[22] One of Augustus's political goals was to restore public morality, and his program of social and moral regeneration is reflected in contemporary literature which contrasted the present generation with the 'good old days'. The Roman poet Juvenal (at the end of the first and beginning of the second century CE) gives in one of his satires the following report:

> In days of old, the wives of Latium were kept chaste by their humble fortunes. It was toil and brief slumbers that kept vice from polluting their modest homes... We are now suffering the calamities of long peace. Luxury, more deadly than any foe, has laid her hand upon us, and avenges a conquered world... There is nothing that a woman will not permit herself to do, nothing that she deems shameful, when she encircles her neck with green emeralds and fastens huge pearls to her elongated ears[23]... So important is the business of beautification; so numerous are the tiers and the storeys piled one upon another on her head![24]... Meantime she pays no attention to her husband; she never speaks of what she costs him.[25]

In addition, these 'modern' women are said to be busybodies, running about the town and discussing the news with everyone in the street:

> This same woman knows what is going on all over the world...she picks up the latest rumors at the city gates, and invents some herself...how cities are tottering and lands subsiding, she tells to everyone she meets at every street crossing.[26]

Also, in an essay under name of *Advice to Bride and Groom*, written by Plutarch (c. 46–120 CE), we find a similar statement on women's proneness to luxury in dress and adornment:

> It is not gold or precious stones or scarlet that makes her such [i.e. a woman adorned], but whatever betokens dignity, good behavior, and modesty...

---

22. L. Portefaix, *Sisters Rejoice: Paul's Letter to the Philippians and Luke–Acts as Received by Philippian Women* (Stockholm: Almquist & Wiksell, 1988), pp. 15-19.
23. Juvenal, *Satires* 6.457-459 (trans. G.G. Ramsay; LCL, 91).
24. Juvenal, *Satires* 6.501-13.
25. Juvenal, *Satires* 6.508-509.
26. Juvenal, *Satires* 6.402-12.

and most women, if you take from them gold-embroidered shoes, bracelets, anklets, purple, and pearls, stay indoors.[27]

In passing we notice that both writers parallel women's inclination for luxury with indifference to their husbands. In the same writing Plutarch further characterizes the behavior of the ideal wife towards men in the picture of a tortoise, carrying her house on her back and communicating with other males only through her husband:

> Pheidias made the Aphrodite of the Eleans with one foot on a tortoise, to typify for womankind keeping at home and keeping silence. For a woman ought to do her talking either to her husband or through her husband, and she should not feel aggrieved if, like the flute-player, she makes a more impressive sound through a tongue not her own.[28]

However, the ideal of a Roman wife was not merely a figure of fiction. In one of Pliny's letters we find a description of the deceased wife of one of his friends which encapsulates the ideal Roman wife of ancient times:

> Our friend Macrinus has had a terrible blow; he has lost his wife, one who would have been exemplary even in former times, after they had lived together for 39 years without a quarrel or misunderstanding. She always treated her husband with the greatest respect, while deserving the highest regard herself, and she seemed to have assembled in herself the virtues of every stage of life in the highest degree.[29]

In the funeral eulogy for Turia, preserved on a large tombstone and written by her husband whom she saved from proscription in 42 BCE, we get another picture of a good wife:

> Why recall your inestimable qualities, your modesty, deference, affability, your amiable disposition, your faithful attendance to household duties, your enlightened religion, your unassuming elegance, the modest simplicity and refinement of your manners? Need I speak of your attachment to your kindred, your affection for your family — when you respected my mother as you did your own parents and cared for her tomb as you did for that of your own mother and father...[30]

Besides listing the usual virtues distinguishing an honorable wife this text adds to our knowledge that women were expected also to care for their relatives. Summing up in passing, from these quotations we get a picture of the Roman ideal wife as a woman who marries only once, is

---

27. Plutarch, *Moralia* 141E (trans. F.C. Babbitt; LCL, 222).
28. Plutarch, *Moralia* 142D.
29. Pliny, *Epistles* 8.5.
30. *CIL* 6.1527 (in M.R. Lefkowitz and M. Fant [trans.], *Women in Greece and Rome* [Toronto: Samuel Stevens, 1977], p. 107).

chaste, submissive towards her husband, unpretentious in dress, and who shows care and attention to her relatives.

However, Augustus's program of social and moral regeneration was not confined to a nostalgic ideal to be found only in literature. In order to restore public morality and to encourage marriage and family life as well as to further the population growth, he enacted marriage laws,[31] on one side making adultery a criminal offence, and on the other penalizing celibacy, granting privileges to married people, and rewarding childbearing. The age at which the laws required childbearing was for men between 25 and 60, and for women between 20 and 50. Women were exempted from marriage two years after the death of a husband, and a year and six months after a divorce. Unmarried people were not allowed to inherit from their next of kin, and couples without children had to give up half their legacy to other heirs or to the state. Freeborn women, on the other hand, who had three children and freedwomen who had four (after manumission) obtained permission to act in their own right without having a male tutor. The result of the laws, affecting Roman citizens and rich members of the population only, was widespread evasion and opposition.

In Tacitus's *Annals* we find a critical passage on the subject:

> A motion was then introduced to qualify the terms of the *Lex Papia Poppaea* (9 CE). This law, complementary to the *Julian Rogations* (18 BCE), had been past by Augustus in his later years, in order to sharpen the penalties of celibacy and to increase the resources of the exchequer. It failed, however, to make marriage and the family popular—childlessness remained the vogue. On the other hand, there was an ever-increasing multitude of persons liable to prosecution, since every household was threatened with subversion by the arts of the informers; and where the country once suffered from its vices, it was now in peril from its laws.[32]

According to this text the efficacy of the laws referring to the Roman aristocracy seems to have been limited in spite of the operating informer system. The Augustan marriage laws were, nevertheless, retained down to the time of Justinian and were included in his codification.[33]

---

31. K. Burns and O. Gradenivitz (eds.), *Fontes Iuris Romani Antiqui* (Tübingen, 7th edn, 1909), pp. 112, 115-16. English translation in N. Lewis and M. Reinhold, *Roman Civilization* (2 vols.; New York: Harper & Row, 1955), II, pp. 48-52.

32. Tacitus, *Annals* 3.25 (trans. J. Jackson; LCL, 249).

33. Lewis and Reinhold, *Roman Civilization*, II, p. 47.

Christian Women and the Roman Family Ideal

Seen in the light of the Augustan ambition to revive the spirit of family life of the Republican era, it is evident that the author of the Pastorals is acting in the same conservative spirit in suggesting this ideal to the minds of the women he addresses. The idea of the ideal Roman wife, pictured in the above-quoted texts, is visible in the qualifications required for women deacons (or possibly deacons' wives[34]) who ought to be 'serious, no slanderers, but temperate, faithful in all things' (1 Tim. 3.11; cf. Tit. 2.3) as well as in the guidelines for women's conduct inside the church. In this passage the author, like other, non-Christian writers, couples their ostentatious appearance with their behavior towards men:

> I desire...that women should adorn themselves modestly and sensibly in seemly apparel, not with braided hair or gold or pearls or costly attire, but by good deeds, as befits women who profess religion. Let a woman learn in silence with all submissiveness. I permit no woman to teach or to have authority over men; she is to keep silent (1 Tim. 2.8-12; cf. Tit. 2.4-5).

Christian women are told not to show off by wearing expensive clothes and headdresses, but instead they should be recognized by means of their virtues and their good deeds. Furthermore, they are told neither to expose their learning nor to teach nor to hold power over men; from a feminist point of view it is worth noting that Christian women actually are expected to learn. All these demands correspond to the virtues of the ideal wife described in the non-Christian sources quoted above. Christian women are further told to marry and to bear children; they are even said to gain redemption through childbearing (1 Tim. 2.15). This demand, also imposed on young widows (1 Tim. 5.14-15), shows the ambition of the author to demonstrate Christians as obeying the Augustan marriage laws and also fulfilling the demand of bringing up their children. The women mentioned in this section seem to have been wealthy, and, consequently, would have suffered heavy financial losses if they did not fulfil the requirements of the laws.

However, the marriage laws, in combination with Christian ethics, indirectly affected poor women of the community. From the letters it is clear that the church had taken on too heavy a burden of caring for women who had been left to support themselves, and the author is seeking to limit an existing benevolence by reducing the number of women supported by the church.[35] These women are constantly called 'widows'

---

34. Cf. Barrett, *Pastoral Epistles*, pp. 61-62.
35. J. Müller-Bardoff, 'Zur Exegese von 1. Timotheus 5,3-16', in *Gott und Götter:*

but in accordance with our knowledge about woman's position in pagan society[36] we may discern various categories among this group. Moreover, 'widow' (χήρα) has a more general meaning: a woman living without a husband, and not previously married.[37] First of all, widows could have been deserted by their pagan families, and as a consequence deprived of their means of support; this was true also for Christian women divorced by pagan husbands (cf. 1 Cor. 7.15). Secondly, women caught in adultery or prostitution found that converting to Christianity presented difficulties when it came to making a living, as freeborn men were according to the marriage laws not allowed to marry these women. It is easy to imagine that the 'weak women, burdened with sins' listening to the heretical teachers (2 Tim. 3.6-7) belonged to these categories; adherence to a group hostile to marriage would make them in their own eyes equal to their married sisters. Thirdly, girls belonging to Christian families who could not afford a dowry would be left to the charity of the community; such poor parents might also have been believers in the teaching of the heretics.

As well as supporting these groups of needy women the community was burdened by families who left their female relatives to the charge of the church instead of caring for them themselves (1 Tim. 5.16); in this respect these Christian wives deviated from the true ideal of a Roman wife, who was expected to care for the members of the family (1 Tim. 5.8). Apparently in order to check this misuse the author carefully points to the qualifications required for a widow to be enrolled among those who were supported by the church. Such a 'real' widow had to be at least 60 years old (1 Tim. 5.9) and be left all alone (1 Tim. 5.5); in this respect it is worth noting that poor single women between 50 and 60 lacking relatives must have been thrown upon the resources of the church. From a Roman point of view the following demands came up to those of the Roman ideal of a good wife: to have been married only once (1 Tim. 5.9), to have brought up children (1 Tim. 5.10), and to have fulfilled the duties toward the members of her own family (1 Tim. 5.16). Finally, a group of young widows (possibly including also unmarried girls) caused disciplinary problems; their behavior was running the risk of attracting the attention of the authorities. They are characterized in the following way: 'they learn to be idlers, gadding about from house to

Festgabe für Erich Fascher zum 60. Geburtstag (Berlin: Evangelische Verlagsanstalt, 1958), pp. 113-33.

36. Portefaix, *Sisters Rejoice*, pp. 23-32.

37. G. Stählin, 'χήρα', *TDNT*, IX, pp. 440-65. Cf. Ignatius, *Epistulae Polycarpe de Smyrne* 13.1: 'virgins called widows'.

house, and not only idlers but gossips and busybodies, saying what they should not' (1 Tim. 5.13; cf. Tit. 2.3).

Unfortunately, we are not told about the substance of their gossip. However, if these women (answering to pastoral house calls[38]) were spreading the slander of the day, most often including scandals of the imperial court, or were propagating heretical ideas of celibacy, their activity might have been a danger to the church; their behavior could easily attract the attention of Roman informers who might report the Christians as being critical towards the emperor or indifferent to the marriage laws. The author, seemingly well aware of the situation, goes on: 'So I would have younger widows marry, bear children, rule their households, and give the enemy no occasion to revile us' (1 Tim. 5.14). In commanding these women to marry and bear children, even if they belonged to groups outside the jurisdiction of the Augustan laws, he was sure to persuade the Roman authorities that Christians were compliant to the requirements of the Roman authorities and were eager to be integrated into Roman society.

Summary

From the Pastoral letters, seen in the context of Roman rule, we learn that in a period of danger to the church, aggravated by the activity of Gnosticizing heretical teachers, not only women but also slaves and leaders of the church on various levels were encouraged to adapt themselves to the social pattern of Roman society in order to escape persecution. In order to appease the Roman authorities the leaders were told to take on the virtues expected of military commanders and to fulfil the duties of a paterfamilias in order to enjoy public confidence in the eyes of non-Christians. Slaves, for their part, had to adapt to the existing social structure by being submissive to non-Christian as well as to Christian masters — even if, in the perspective of Christianity, the two categories were equal to each other. Finally, Christian women were directed to take on the virtues of the ideal of a Roman woman—congruent with Christian ethics — which implied marriage, submissiveness, and care for relatives. Consequently, we can state that the demands, confining women to housework and child-bearing, which are to be found in the Pastorals, cannot reasonably be said to have their origin in the misogynous ideas of the author. Unfortunately, however, his admonitions, originally addressed to a few communities in the eastern part of the Aegean during the reign of Trajan, have in course of time been considered valid for all Christian

---

38. Conzelmann, *Pastoral Epistles*, p. 75.

women of all periods, causing oppression inside and outside the church from late antiquity up to the present time. Instead they should be read and appreciated as an attempt at contextualization in a situation when evolving Christian communities had to adjust themselves to conditions dictated for them by an oppressive regime.

1 TIMOTHY 5.3-16 AND THE LEADERSHIP OF WOMEN IN THE EARLY CHURCH*

Bonnie Thurston

In her excellent chapter on the Pastoral Epistles in *Searching the Scriptures*, Linda Maloney observes about these letters that 'nowhere else do we find so much concentrated attention devoted to women's roles in early Christian Communities'.[1] Indeed, in few other places in the New Testament do we find so much material on early church order. 'The Pastorals are concerned with regulating the conduct of the congregation, specifying the qualifications and duties for congregational leaders…and the duties for congregational members…'[2] The writer of 1 Timothy is particularly interested in 'offices', especially those of bishop, deacon, widow, and elder. Although until recently it has not been interpreted as such, it is my contention that the material on widows in 1 Tim. 5.3-16 is to be read as we do the material on the office of bishop (3.1-7), deacon (3.8-13), and elder (5.17-19). The text seeks to limit a particular leadership ministry for women in the church.

An enormous body of work exists on the questions of authorship, date, and the purpose of the Pastoral Epistles.[3] I work on the assumption that they are pseudonymous works produced in and for churches in Asia Minor. They date from the beginning of the second century, probably

---

* Portions of this essay appeared previously in ch. 3 of my book, *The Widows: A Women's Ministry in the Early Church* (Minneapolis: Fortress Press, 1989), now out of print.

1. Linda Maloney, 'The Pastoral Epistles', in Elisabeth Schüssler Fiorenza (ed.), *Searching the Scriptures: A Feminist Commentary* (2 vols.; New York: Crossroad, 1994), II, pp. 361-80 (361).

2. Joanna Dewey, '1 Timothy', in C. Newsom and S. Ringe (eds.), *The Women's Bible Commentary* (Louisville, KY: Westminster/John Knox Press, 1992), pp. 353-58 (353).

3. For surveys of these issues see M. Dibelius and H. Conzelmann, *The Pastoral Epistles* (Hermenia; Philadelphia: Fortress Press, 1972); A.T. Hanson, *The Pastoral Epistles* (NCBC; Grand Rapids: Eerdmans, 1982); and J.D. Quinn, 'Epistles to Timothy', *ABD*, IV, pp. 560-71.

between 100 and 105 CE, and depict the church as it moves from primitive simplicity to a more institutional form. This allows for Polycarp's knowledge of the Pastorals, but places them before Ignatius of Antioch's letters which reveal a persecution not evident in our documents.[4] I agree with Margaret MacDonald that 'in many respects the community life and worldview reflected in these works are closer to such early Christian writings as the letters of Ignatius of Antioch or 1 Clement than they are to Paul's undisputed letters'.[5] In them we see the 'author's need to adapt Paul's language and thought to an entirely new historical context'.[6] That context included internal church problems (inner-ecclesial dissent) and external difficulties, both socio-economic pressures and political oppression by Rome.[7] We find these issues in the Pastoral Epistles in their concern for church order, false teaching, and social acceptability.

The concern with church order is reflected in the writer's discussion of offices of ministry. In the authentic Pauline correspondence, ministry is usually charismatic, but the writer of the Pastoral Epistles presents ministry from the disciplinary angle of *Gemeindeordnung*. The church has reached a turning point in understanding of ministry; *Amt* has become *Beruf*.[8] As Cardman writes in her essay 'Women, Ministry, and Church Order in Early Christianity', 'The Pastorals tend to transmute charisma into duties'.[9] In the groundbreaking study *In Memory of Her*, Schüssler Fiorenza suggests that the shift in the second century was not from charismatic to institutional leadership but from charismatic and communal authority to authority vested in local officers. The basic functional distinction is between the local and the translocal.[10] In either scenario, leaders of the second-century church had become aware of threats to the church from within (among which seemed to be the activity of Christian women). To prevent divisiveness and heresy, they felt the need to

---

4.   See Hans von Campenhausen, *Polykarp von Smyrna und die Pastoralbriefe* (Heidelburg: Carl Winter Universitätsverlag, 1951). He suggests that Polycarp is the author of the Pastorals.

5.   Margaret Y. MacDonald, 'Rereading Paul: Early Interpreters of Paul on Women and Gender', in Ross S. Kraemer and Mary Rose D'Angelo (eds.), *Women and Christian Origins* (New York: Oxford University Press, 1999), pp. 236-53 (246).

6.   J.C. Beker, *Heirs of Paul* (Minneapolis: Fortress Press, 1991), p. 43.

7.   Beker, *Heirs of Paul*, p. 44.

8.   See André Lemaire, 'The Ministries in the New Testament: Recent Research', *BTB* 3.2 (1973), pp. 133-66 (138).

9.   Francine Cardman, 'Women, Ministry, and Church Order in Early Christianity', in Kraemer and D'Angelo (eds.), *Women and Christian Origins*, pp. 300-29 (304).

10.   Elisabeth Schüssler Fiorenza, *In Memory of Her: A Feminist Reconstruction of Christian Origins* (New York: Crossroad, 1983), ch. 3, pp. 68-96.

organize into recognized channels the freedom that Paul had allowed in the exercise of ministry.[11]

The precise nature of the false teaching that the Pastoral writer attacks has given rise to a great deal of speculation. The present consensus seems to be that it was some form of Gnosticism to which women were especially attracted.[12] The problem of Gnosticism was not, of course, sex specific. Both men and women were in danger of wandering into 'vain discussion' (1 Tim. 1.6), 'godless and silly myths' (1 Tim. 4.7), 'stupid controversies, genealogies, dissensions' (Tit. 3.9). But asceticism held particular appeal for women in the eastern provinces of the Empire. Well-to-do women embraced an ascetic way of life that featured chastity and the severing of family ties. Because they felt their traditional roles were inadequate or socially marginal, women looked to ascetic forms of religion for standards of worth more consonant with what they felt were their circumstances.[13] Certainly 'heterodox' sects of the later second century featured prominent women as the Gnostic gospels attest. The Nicolaitans and Naassenses received their doctrines from women, and the Gnostics paid special heed to prophetesses. St Jerome says that Marcion sent a woman ahead of him to prepare people for his 'errors'. Women were also prominent in Montanism.[14]

11.   The letters of Ignatius of Antioch (d. 115) also address these problems. Before him the monarchical episcopacy is not clearly attested; after his time it became universal. See W.R. Schoedel, *A Commentary on the Letters of Ignatius of Antioch* (Hermenia; Philadelphia: Fortress Press, 1985). I find nothing in the authentic Pauline material that forbids women's leadership in the church (see my *Women in the New Testament* [New York: Crossroad, 1998]). With many Pauline scholars, I have concluded that 1 Cor. 14.33b-35 is an interpolation. And see Bruce Metzger, *A Textual Commentary on the New Testament* (New York: United Bible Society, 1994).

12.   To my knowledge the first sustained discussion of the false teachers occurs in W. Lütgert, *Die Irrlehrer der Pastoralbriefe* (Guttersloh: C. Bertelsmann, 1909). It has been treated by Linda Maloney in an unpublished manuscript, *Die Stellung der Frau in der Kirche nach der Auffassung der Pastoralbriefe*, 1984. And see Elaine Pagels, *The Gnostic Gospels* (New York: Random House, 1979) and Robert McL. Wilson, *Gnosis and the New Testament* (Oxford: Oxford University Press, 1968).

13.   See Elizabeth A. Clark, 'Ascetic Renunciation and Feminine Advancement: A Paradox of Late Ancient Christianity', *ATR* 63.3 (1981), pp. 140-57; Ross S. Kraemer, 'The Conversion of Women to Ascetic Forms of Christianity', *Signs* 6.2 (1980), pp. 298-307; and R. Gryson, *The Ministry of Women in the Early Church* (Collegeville, MN: Liturgical Press, 1976).

14.   Good general articles with bibliographies on Gnostic sects are to be found in E. Ferguson (ed.), *Encyclopedia of Early Christianity* (New York: Garland, 1990). Probably the best introductions to the subject are Pagels's *Gnostic Gospels* and Pheme Perkins's *Gnosticism and the New Testament* (Minneapolis: Fortress Press, 1993). Primary docu-

Robert J. Karris has pointed out that in an attempt to cause aversion for the false teachers, the Pastoral writer borrowed the conventional rhetorical patterns found in popular philosophy. The false teachers are called deceivers, quibblers, full of vice, unable to practice what they preach, and quick to prey on women.[15] By 'calling names', the author hopes to cause aversion toward his opponents' and sympathy for his own point of view.

> Thus we have in the Pastorals the paradoxical situation that false teachers are fiercely attacked, but we are left without any very clear picture of their doctrine; and the true teaching is to be carefully guarded, though we are never told precisely what it is.[16]

The writer of 1 Timothy commends sound teaching (1.10; cf. Tit. 1.9) without reproducing it for the reader.

The polemic against false teachers and their appeal to women is linked by the church's preoccupation with social acceptability. The author of the Pastorals is anxious for the church to appear well to those outside it (see 1 Tim. 2.1-2; 5.14; 6.1-2; Tit. 2.1-10). The Christian community's transcendence of normal social patterns, evidenced by Paul's principle given in Gal. 3.28, threatened *patria potestas* (*pater familias*) and thus the whole Roman social order. The writer of the Pastorals wants to curb that tendency and orient the Christian community toward the dominant cultural patterns of the Empire. As Maloney has pointed out, he has chosen the household (οἶκος) as the governing image of the letter. 'The pattern of the church is to be that of the patriarchal household, with God as head, Christ as son and heir, *episkopoi* and other elders as stewards, and the remaining members as obedient...'[17]

In *The Household of God*, David C. Verner shows that, just as the household was the basic unit of the church, the church became a social unit modeled on the household. He describes in detail the household in the Hellenistic-Roman world (and his descriptions have recently been corroborated by Carolyn Osiek and David Balch in their masterful study, *Families in the New Testament World: Households and House Churches*) and concludes that 'social tensions related to the household in this period appear to have centered around the changing position of women in

---

ments are found in James M. Robinson (ed.), *The Nag Hammadi Library* (San Francisco: Harper & Row, 1978).

15. Robert J. Karris, 'The Background and Significance of the Polemic of the Pastoral Epistles', *JBL* 92 (1973), pp. 549-64.

16. Hanson, *Pastoral Epistles*, p. 26.

17. Maloney, 'Pastoral Epistles', p. 376.

society'.[18] The patriarchal household was associated on a symbolic level with the preservation of a stable society. People whose behavior defied 'household convention' were viewed not just as social oddities, but as politically subversive. As noted, the Pastoral Epistles show a strong concern for the opinion of outsiders. To preserve its standing, the church began to conform to social norms, particularly in regard to the behavior of women (see 1 Tim. 2; 5.24; Tit. 2). And, predictably, as the church limited their freedom, women moved toward communities where they believed Christianity's original spirit of equality was preserved.

In her work on 1 Tim. 5.3-16 Jouette Bassler depicts exactly this pattern. Women turned to celibacy to find freedom from the inequalities imposed by marriage. Celibacy was required of the widows, but they were thereby freed from patriarchal household norms.

> The widows of the Pastoral Epistles were like the vestal virgins, under special restrictions, but again like the vestals, these restrictions were not those binding ordinary women. Indeed, widows were remarkably free of these ordinary restraints.[19]

Bassler suggests that as the church adapted more to society's norms, the numbers in the widows' circle increased as women sought greater freedom. (Somewhat later St Jerome remarked in a letter, 'they know by experience what a husband's rule is like, and they prefer their liberty as widows' [*Epistle* 22.16].) The increasing number of widows was met by the Pastoral writer with injunctions drawn from society's patriarchal norms: criteria for enrollment were introduced 'that affirmed the very behavior from which the widows themselves were exempt—domesticity, marital fidelity, childbearing, etc'.[20] The goal was to reduce the group by selecting widows with the domestic virtues expected by contemporary society, but the result was an exacerbation of the heresy problem as women sought out groups that presented equality.

These issues—church order, false teaching/heresy, and social acceptability—must be kept in mind as we read 1 Tim. 5.3-16. The passage is

18.   David C. Verner, *The Household of God: The Social World of the Pastoral Epistles* (Chico, CA: Scholars Press, 1983), p. 64. See also Carolyn Osiek and David Balch, *Families in the New Testament World: Households and House Churches* (The Family, Religion, and Culture Series; Louisville, KY: Westminster/John Knox Press, 1997).

19.   Jouette M. Bassler, 'The Widow's Tale: A Fresh Look at 1 Timothy 5.3-16', *JBL* 103 (1984), pp. 23-41 (36). For more information on parallels between the Christian widows and the vestal virgins, see Ross S. Kraemer, *Her Share of the Blessings: Women's Religions among Pagans, Jews, and Christians in the Greco-Roman World* (New York: Oxford University Press, 1992) and Pauline S. Pantel (ed.), *A History of Women: From Ancient Goddesses to Christian Saints* (Cambridge, MA: Belknap Press, 1992).

20.   Bassler, 'Widow's Tale', p. 38.

typical of the Pastoral writer in the amount of space given to prescribing norms for women's action and in its hints that the leadership of women in the Christian community raises his anxiety level.[21] Bassler correctly notes that many

> of the difficulties presented by the text stem from the fact that the author is not initiating a new benevolence, which would have involved a more careful explanation of terms and conditions, but is seeking to limit an existing one.[22]

In the words of Maloney, 'Here we find a constellation of persons who may well have represented the best-organized opposition to the "Pastor's" ideals, and one which he was therefore most concerned to put "in its place".'[23] In the passage we meet two categories of widows, the enrolled and those who were, by reason of family connection or age, ineligible to be enrolled. I assume (along with Danielou, Döllinger, Frend, Stählin, and Schweizer) that the widows are a special group with assigned duties or functions in the Christian community.[24] Along with Sand, I take the position that 1 Tim. 5.3-16 speaks to 'true' or enrolled widows (5.3, 5-7, 9-10), widows (usually older) who are not enrolled (5.4, 8, 16), and younger widows (5.11-15).[25] The division is made primarily on the basis of need, not age.

It is the 'true' widows who formed the order, and I shall discuss them in detail shortly. Verses 4, 8, and 16 discuss widows who are not enrolled because they have another means of support. While they might be able and qualified to do the work of the order, they are excluded because of the financial strain they would place on the church. This point is repeated three times in the passage (5.4, 8, 16). Acts provides an example of this unenrolled widow in the person of Tabitha (9.36-43). Inscriptional evidence attests another, one Rigine, 'mother, widow, who remained a widow sixty years and never burdened the Church; an *univira* who lived eighty years, five months, twenty-six days'.[26]

---

21. See Maloney, 'Pastoral Epistles', pp. 377-78.

22. Bassler, 'Widow's Tale', p. 34.

23. Maloney, 'Pastoral Epistles', p. 371.

24. J. Danielou and H. Marrou, *The First Six Hundred Years* (New York: McGraw–Hill, 1964), p. 118; J. Döllinger, *The First Age of Christianity and the Church* (London: Gibbings, 1906), p. 312; W.H.C. Frend, *The Rise of Christianity* (Philadelphia: Fortress Press, 1984), p. 411; G. Stählin, 'χήρα', *TDNT*, IX, pp. 440-65 (453); E. Schweizer, *Church Order in the New Testament* (London: SCM Press, 1961), p. 86.

25. A. Sand, 'Witwenstand und Amterstructuren in den urchristlichen Gemeinden', *BibLeb* 12 (1971), pp. 186-97 (193). Stählin notes three groups: widows in the family unit, younger widowed women, and true widows (Stählin, 'χήρα', pp. 453-56).

26. Quoted in M. Lightman and W. Zeisel, 'Univira: An Example of Continuity

Stählin believes wealthy widows took charge of house churches.[27] Tabitha in Acts 9 took responsibility for less fortunate widows. If we use the general definition of χήρα as a woman living without a husband[28] and make the standard assumption that women mentioned alone had no husbands, then there are several widows with house churches in the New Testament, among them Mary mother of John Mark (Acts 12.12), Lydia (Acts 16.11-15),[29] and Nympha (Col. 4.15). Archaeological evidence from Judaism suggests that the religious leadership of women was sometimes connected with their financial support of their community. Bernadette Brooten's work has drawn the connection between financial support and leadership terminology used in connection with women. She cites Theopempta of Myndos, called ἀρχισυνάγωγος ('leader of the synagogue') with no mention of a husband. The Roman tombstone of Vetruia Paucla says she was *mater* of two synagogues.[30] Tabitha and Lydia would represent similar patronage by Christian widows, although they could not have been 'real widows' or 'enrolled' since need was one of the prerequisites for enrollment. (And see Phoebe in Rom. 16.1-2 whom Paul calls benefactress, literally a 'helper of many', προστάτις πολλῶν.) As Joanna Dewey notes, family support of such older widows not only saved the church money, it returned such women to the control of the household.[31] That is, they were literally returned to the household to live in its patriarchal structure.

The young widows of 5.11-15 bring into focus the problem of the attitude of the larger society toward the church ('Give the enemy no occasion to revile us', 5.14) and of false teachers (5.13, 16). In ancient

and Change in Roman Society', *CH* 46 (1977), pp. 19-32 (27). The Latin inscription reads:

> RIGINE VENEMERENTI FILIA SUA FECIT
> VENE, RIGINE MATRI VIDUAE QUE SEDIT
> VIDUA ANNOS LX ET ECLESA
> NUMQUA GRAVAVIT, UNIBYRA QUE
> VIXIT ANNOS LXXX; MESIS V DIES XXVI

27. Stählin, 'χήρα', p. 457.

28. Stählin, 'χήρα', p. 440.

29. These and other texts on widows are treated in Robert M. Price's quirky but interesting study *The Widow Traditions in Luke–Acts: A Feminist-Critical Scrutiny* (SBLDS, 155; Atlanta: Scholars Press, 1997).

30. D. Irvin, 'The Ministry of Women in the Early Church: The Archaeological Evidence', *Duke Divinity School Review* 45 (1980), pp. 76-80. And see Bernadette Brooten, *Women Leaders in the Ancient Synagogue: Inscriptional Evidence and Background Issues* (BJS, 36; Chico, CA: Scholars Press, 1982).

31. Dewey, '1 Timothy', p. 357.

polemic no charges against a group were more effective than those against the character of its women. Antiquity generally had high praise for young, chaste widows.[32] Here and in Tit. 2.4-5 the writer stresses traditional, domestic virtues that would be acceptable and praiseworthy in order that 'the word of God may not be discredited' (2.5b). 'Younger women are to follow the societal and legal requirements of women of their age so that the Christian reputation will be preserved.'[33] In spite of Paul's advice in 1 Corinthians 7 that 'she is happier if she remains as she is', here remarriage is encouraged. (This is further evidence that Paul did not write the Pastorals.) Note that this second marriage would disqualify a woman from later enrollment in the order since 'real widows' can have been married only once.

Furthermore, the writer seems concerned that younger widows allowed freedom of movement might encourage the spread of false teaching. Prohibition against marriage was apparently a prominent feature of the false teachers (see 1 Tim. 4.3). It calls to mind the sexual asceticism of the Apocryphal Acts, especially the *Acts of Paul and Thecla*. Dennis MacDonald argues that the Pastorals were written to refute oral stories that Paul had commissioned women to teach. To limit the number of widows was to limit the number of tale-bearers who carried a message that would upset the household order.[34] Young widows were problematic. They were drawn to 'false teaching' that offered emancipation from the household and leadership in the church.

Having looked briefly at some of the issues connected with the unenrolled (both older and younger) widows, we turn now to the enrolled widows who made up the order. What evidence is there in the passage for an 'order' of widows? Key points in favor of an order include the context in 1 Timothy, the terms τίμα and καταλεγέσθω, and the suggestion of a vow or pledge taken upon admittance. That the widows appear in a roster of church officials including bishop, deacon, and elder suggests that they, too, are church officials.[35] Almost as much space is devoted to them as to the bishop.

While the term 'real widows' (ὄντως χήρας) suggests a special category, 'honor' (τίμα) is also suggestive. Its general meaning is 'honor', 'respect', or 'value', but it can also mean 'pay' or 'compensation'. In later

---

32. See, e.g., Josephus, *Ant.* 18.66.

33. Schüssler Fiorenza, *In Memory of Her*, p. 312.

34. Dennis R. MacDonald, 'Virgins, Widows, and Paul in Second Century Asia Minor' (SBLSP; Missoula, MT: Scholars Press, 1979), pp. 169-84.

35. See Verner, *Household of God*, p. 163.

church orders, τιμᾶν is a technical term for payment.[36] Sirach, written about 180 BCE and translated into Greek about 132 BCE, uses τίμα in the sense of pay in 38.1: 'Honor (τίμα) the physician with the honor (τιμαῖς) due him.' The term was used in this technical sense in the religious literature that preceded and followed the Pastorals. Additionally Dibelius and Conzelmann point out that in parallel literature καταλεγεῖν ('to enroll') is a technical term for the registration of levied troops.[37] Stählin says the term means to be adopted into a fellowship by election and notes that the requirements for selection immediately follow the use of the term.[38]

Finally, although in the section on younger widows, the phrase 'the first faith' (τὴν πρώτην πίστιν, 5.12) refers to 'an initial oath of celibacy taken by widows on the occasion of their enrollment'.[39] C.K. Barrett describes it as 'an undertaking not to marry, but to engage herself wholly to the Church'.[40] Βούλομαι expresses more than resolution; the phrase is used regularly in legislative formulations and official decrees of the time.[41] The point is that if a widow had so pledged herself to Christ, a subsequent marriage would, technically, be infidelity to Him, tantamount to adultery.

While none of these elements alone provides conclusive proof of an order, taken together they are a classic case of the whole being more than the sum of the parts. Further, the text goes on to enumerate requirements for the order and to suggest tasks its members performed. Döllinger provides a useful summary of the qualifications of a 'real widow'. Such women 'had a special relation to the church. Their names were to be marked in a catalogue, and they were to have had a special ministry assigned to them.'[42] Requisite conditions for enrollment included that the widow be over 60 years of age and the wife of one husband, and that she have witnesses to her good works, skill with children, hospitality, and compassion. In short, the widow was to be chaste and devout and to

---

36. For the most complete discussion of the term, see Hans-Werner Bartsch, 'Die Witwenregel', in idem, *Die Anfänge urchristlicher Rechtsbildungen: Studien zu den Pastoralbriefen* (Hamburg: Evangelischer Verlag, 1965), pp. 117-20. And compare Verner, *Household of God*, pp. 162-63.

37. Dibelius and Conzelmann, *Pastoral Epistles*, p. 73. And see J. Ernst, 'Die Witwenregel des ersten Timotheusbriefs Hinweis auf die biblischen Ursprünge des weiblichen Ordenswesens?', *Theologie und Glaube* 59 (1969), pp. 343-445 (439).

38. Stählin, 'χήρα', p. 456.

39. Verner, *Household of God*, p. 164.

40. C.K. Barrett, *The Pastoral Epistles* (Oxford: Clarendon Press, 1963), p. 76.

41. Dibelius and Conzelmann, *Pastoral Epistles*, p. 75.

42. Döllinger, *First Age of Christianity*, p. 312.

have female accomplishments acceptable to middle- and upper-class Greco-Roman social norms. To be enrolled, the real widow must be alone (dependent upon God and the church and not other persons), must be continually faithful, and must be chaste (5.5-7). Verse 9 begins, 'enroll a widow', which suggests that qualifications will follow, and they do: age, marital status, and the general condition of having performed good deeds. Each requirement relates to one of the problems of the second-century church enumerated above.

The faithfulness and chastity mentioned in 5.5-6 reflect the preoccupation of the non-Christian world with continence. In Cynic–Stoic diatribes, continence is crucial to the ideal of the detached wise man. In Neoplatonism, asceticism reaches its highest point; the first perfection was to subdue the body. There is New Testament evidence for the lofty regard for virginity in the early church in Mt. 19.29; 1 Cor. 7.7-9, 32-34.[43] (This is in marked contrast to Judaism which, with the exception of sects like the Essenes and the Therapeutae, viewed fecundity as a special sign of God's favor.[44]) The command that widows be chaste and continent demonstrates the church's concern about society's opinion of it. Verse 6 may be a proverb in general use at the time, or it may reflect a fear that widowhood would lead to prostitution (as well it might if the woman had no other means of support). The command in 5.7 emphasizes that the church's conduct must be above reproach. As Barrett notes, 'all members of the church should be free of reproach, but it is particularly important that this should be true of those who hold public position within it, and draw their support from it'.[45]

Sixty is set as the age of enrollment probably in part because this was the age of the 'elderly' in ancient literature. Since it was the practice for men to marry much younger women, there were younger widows who, by Roman law, should remarry and, by Christian standards, would require guidance. A woman of 60 was assumed to have mature experience of life and to be at less sexual peril as she carried out the duties of the order, duties which could be accomplished without undue exertion. (Recall that the ethnographic fieldwork of Carol L. Meyers suggests that the average lifespan of a Palestinian woman in the biblical period was about 30 years.[46])

---

43.   And see R. Nugent, *Portrait of the Consecrated Woman in Greek Christian Literature of the First Four Centuries* (Washington: Catholic University Press, 1941).

44.   For an excellent study of this and related matters see Tal Ilan, *Jewish Women in Greco-Roman Palestine* (Peabody, MA: Hendrickson, 1996).

45.   Barrett, *Pastoral Epistles*, p. 75.

46.   Carol L. Meyers, *Discovering Eve: Ancient Israelite Women in Context* (New York: Oxford University Press, 1988).

That the widow is to have been the wife of one husband is, again, tied to social expectations of the time. A frequent theme in ancient literature is that of the flighty widow who moves from her dead husband through a series of relationships (see, e.g., the matron of Ephesus in Petronius's *Satyricon*). Such a woman was an object of scorn. In the Roman world *univira* was an epithet for a good wife, and from terms used to praise a once-married woman, *univira* and *monandros* came to connote praise of chastity for the love of God.[47] The parallel phrases μιᾶς γυναικὸς ἄνδρα and ἑνὸς ἀνδπὸς γυνή appear several times in the Pastorals as qualifications for office, in spite of the fact that the author encourages remarriage for young widows at 5.14 (see 1 Tim. 3.2, 12; 5.9; Tit. 1.6). Such once-married persons preserved the church's moral standing in the community.

Continence, age, and marital status as qualifications of real widows are followed by evidence of a life of active service. Verse 10 opens and closes with the phrase 'doing good'. The examples of good works ('brought up children', 'shown hospitality') are domestic activities expected of all females. Karen Torjesen has studied extensively the relationship between the Greco-Roman household and the early church and has explained that leadership roles in the church were based on parallel roles in the household.[48] The good deeds in 5.10 can be seen as those of household management; each qualified a woman for leadership in the church.

> So long as church leadership continued to model itself on the familiar role of household manager, there was no cultural barrier to women assuming leadership roles… Christians, familiar with the authority and leadership role of the female head of household, would have perceived women's leadership within the church as…natural.[49]

If the widow's office were associated with proper female duties in the οἶκος, the larger society would not be affronted. Additionally, behind the 'good deeds' of v. 10 stands the understanding of leadership taught by Jesus who says in Jn 13.14, 'If I then, your Lord and Teacher, have

47.   J.B. Frey, 'La Signification des Termes MONANDROS et *univira* coups d'oeil sur La Famille Romaine aux Premiers siecles de Notre Ere', *RSR* 20 (1930), pp. 48-60.

48.   Karen Jo Torjesen, 'From the Private Sphere of the Hellenistic Household to the Public Sphere of the Imperial Church: Women's Roles in Transition' (paper delivered at Society of Biblical Literature Annual Meeting, Anaheim, CA, 24 November 1985). And see her book *When Women Were Priests: Women's Leadership in the Early Church and the Scandal of their Subordination in the Rise of Christianity* (San Francisco: HarperSanFrancisco, 1993), especially ch. 2, 'Household Management and Women's Authority'.

49.   Torjesen, *When Women Were Priests*, p. 82.

washed your feet, you also ought to wash one another's feet'. The 'real widows' will be to the church what the woman with the ointment in Mk 14.3-9 was to Jesus. Jesus taught that the primary characteristics of all Christian leaders are humility and willingness to serve. Some heard the message more clearly than others, and from being expected of all Christian leaders, humility and service became required of Christian women.

In addition to age, marital status, and lifestyle requirements, we can assume from v. 12 in the section on young widows that a vow or pledge (πίστιν) is expected of 'real widows'. Their willingness to take it is both the final qualification for the order and the means of enrollment in it. The verb καταλεγεῖν in v. 9 is a technical term for the enrollment process. This vow must have been intended to secure in practice the chaste life described in 5.5-6.

Having listed in detail qualifications for the office (which is crucial to the intent to limit it), the writer only suggests its special duties. His readers, of course, would have known what they were. Schweizer notes the widow is to have performed diaconal services before she is enrolled. 'That may lead one to suppose that she continues to perform such services; but…it is not demanded explicitly here.'[50] (Schweizer does not specify what such services were, and the New Testament itself gives no single list. Later church orders do list the work of deacons.) It should be noted that the absence of a 'duty roster' should not exclude an office since no duties were spelled out for deacons and the existence of that office has not been called into question. Several responsibilities of the widow are, however, implied.

The first duty of the widows is prayer and intercession (5.5). To 'pray continually' is enjoined of all Christians, but the widows of the church have before them the special example of Anna (Lk. 2.36-38), and the early church especially encouraged the elderly to engage in a life of contemplation. Several New Testament passages associate continence, fasting, and prayer (see Acts 13.2-3; 1 Cor. 7.5). These activities are especially appropriate for the elderly first because the normal physical deterioration of aging precludes more active service. Anyone regardless of physical condition can pray. Second, if need is a requirement for the order, destitution makes the widows more likely to devote themselves to prayer since they have no means for acts of benevolence. Presumably the hunger of the elderly poor is thereby transformed into religious fasting! From a practical standpoint, freedom from domestic responsibility gives the widow more time for public and private devotion.

---

50. Schweizer, *Church Order in the New Testament*, p. 86.

The strongest reason for assigning the duty of prayer to the widows is not practical but theological. Jesus concludes the parable of the unjust judge, 'And will not God vindicate his elect, who cry to him day and night?' (Lk. 18.7). Hope in God is prerequisite to persistent prayer. And the widow has no one else upon whom to depend. According to Sir. 35.14 and 17 God's ears are especially attuned to hear persons totally dependent upon God. God's preference is for them. The church's prayers are thus at the top of the list of the widow's tasks because, since she is totally dependent upon God, God will be most likely to hear prayers from her lips.[51]

The second duty of the 'real widows' is suggested by the fact that the younger widows are scolded for 'gadding about from house to house' (v. 13). Dibelius and Conzelmann assume this going about was in the context of house calls.[52] The widows were paying what we might call 'pastoral home visits', perhaps connected with the teaching function mentioned in Tit. 2.3-5. Teaching does not appear in 1 Tim. 5.3-16 (unless we extract it from 'bringing up children', v. 10). However, there is other evidence for the likelihood that widows had a teaching function.

Titus 2 deals with the teaching of sound doctrine. It addresses the older men, the older women, the young women, the young men, and slaves. Schweizer notes that in the 'sociological group of the older church members…those who perform a special ministry are referred to more and more clearly as the "older men", just as among the women the "widows" appear as a special group'.[53] We can read 'older women' (πρεσβύτιδας) in Tit. 2.3 in this light. There is an almost exact correspondence between the qualities required of an older woman in Titus (that she be reverent, not slanderous or a slave to drink, and a teacher of 'what is good', Tit. 2.3) and those required of a woman deacon in 1 Tim. 3.11. Furthermore, the offices of deaconess and of widow occur very early in church documents and orders. In fact, the interchangeability of the terms has made tracing the history of either group difficult. And there is inscriptional evidence for a technical use of πρεσβύτις. 'An epitaph for Kale *pre(s)-b(ytis)* is reprinted…(Centuripae, Sicily; IV/V). Another with this title is probably referred to in one of the so-called Angels of Thera inscriptions: *Aggelos Epiktous presbytidos* (III–V).'[54] Lampe uses this text as evidence of

51. For more on this see my article, 'The Widows as the "Altar" of God' (SBLSP, 24; Missoula, MT: Scholars Press, 1985), pp. 279-89.

52. Dibelius and Conzelmann, *Pastoral Epistles*, p. 75.

53. Schweizer, *Church Order in the New Testament*, p. 186.

54. G.H.R. Horsley, *New Documents Illustrating Early Christianity* (North Rude, Australia: Macquarie University Press, 1981), p. 121.

an office bearer, as well as for the adjectival sense 'elderly woman'. It seems logical to conclude that these older female office holders might well be the widows whom the Pastoral writer addresses.

Titus's older women are to serve the church as teachers of the younger women, teachers of good (καλοδιδασκάλους). The good to be taught involves acceptable female behavior: sensibility, chastity, domesticity, kindness, submissiveness to husbands, 'that the word of God may not be discredited' (Tit. 2.4-5). If this is the substance of the widow's message, it is even more crucial for her to have lived the life described in 1 Tim. 5.10.

Conclusion

A reading of 1 Tim. 5.3-16 must take into account the situation of the church at the beginning of the second century, particularly problems connected with church order, false teaching, and social acceptability. The widows are listed in a roster of church officials. Of those officials (bishop, deacon, deaconess, widow, elder) only the widows are limited with regard to support, finances, and sexual continence. As Maloney notes, 'the author of these letters had an agenda, and that agenda did not include fostering the advancement of women'.[55]

It seems clear from 1 Tim. 5.3-16 that an office for older women not only existed in the early church, but it was large and active enough to require regulation and limitation. This text 'aims to ensure that only women who are truly widows who are alone receive support'.[56] To be enrolled in the order a woman must have no other means of support, be at least 60 years of age, and be the wife of one husband. She must have attested good deeds of domesticity, hospitality, humility, and compassion. It is probable that she took a vow of enrollment by which she pledged lifelong fidelity to Christ and his church. Since in the text the Pastoral writer is limiting an existing order, he gives little information about its duties as he assumes his readers know what they are. Since we do not, we must speculate. The widows were apparently called to live lives of contemplation and prayer. They probably taught younger women, and they may have made pastoral house calls and been in charge of house churches.

The problem group in the passage is young widows. They bring into focus the problem of false teaching (v. 13) and of the attitude of the larger society toward the church (v. 14). Charges brought against Christian women were particularly damning to the church. By excluding

---

55. Maloney, 'Pastoral Epistles', p. 630.
56. MacDonald, 'Rereading Paul', p. 246.

younger widows from the order and insisting they remarry (which was the law until Constantine rescinded it), the Pastoral writer is urging young widows to 'follow the societal and legal requirements of women of their age so that the Christian reputation will be preserved'.[57] We know from parallel sources that one of the prominent features of the false teaching (at least false from the Pastoral writer's perspective!) of the period was sexual asceticism (see 1 Tim. 4.1-5).[58] The young widows were problematic to the church in part because they found asceticism appealing and because enrollment in the widows' order would offer them a certain degree of emancipation. In the order, celibacy was required, but women were thereby freed from normal restrictions and received some form of compensation. They 'got out of the house' as it were. That is, they left the patriarchal household and its controls.

As the church adapted to society's norms, applicants for the widows' order increased (we know this from the extensive limits placed on them in church orders of the second through fifth centuries). Women sought a degree of freedom, a freedom that, as I have argued elsewhere, characterized earliest Christianity.[59] The growing size of the order was met by injunctions and limitations drawn from society's norms, and the criteria for enrollment affirmed the very behavior from which the widows, by virtue of enrollment, were exempt: domesticity, marital fidelity, child-rearing. With 20/20 hindsight we can now see two paradoxes in this situation. First, when the church structured itself on the household model, women had more positions of authority, but domestic life with its attendant responsibilities (see, e.g., 1 Tim. 5.14) for children and elderly relatives and for household management (which might have included food production, preservation and preparation, spinning and weaving, making clothing, oversight of slaves, and even a family business) severely limited women's sphere of activity. Second, some women seeking to escape the limitations of the Greco-Roman household sought out the widows' order only to discover that domesticity was required for entrance to the order.

By the time the Pastoral Epistles were written, the order of widows was large and vigorous. It attracted women, some of whom apparently abused their position. At least this is what the Pastoral writer would have us think with his references to intemperance, 'gadding about', and gossip (e.g. 1 Tim. 5.13; 2 Tim. 3.6-7; Tit. 2.3-5). The requirements for enrollment set out in our text were strict enough to limit the number of

---

57. Schüssler Fiorenza, *In Memory of Her*, p. 312.
58. Clark, 'Ascetic Renunciation'. And see Kraemer, *Her Share of the Blessings*.
59. See my *Women in the New Testament* (New York: Crossroad, 1998).

enrolled widows, which thus relieved the financially burdened church, prevented embarrassment caused when the younger widows broke their pledge by remarrying or trespassing society's norms, and limited the number of older women 'telling tales'.[60] The Pastoral writer's goal was reduction of the group by selecting those widows who most needed support and those with the domestic virtues of which society approved. However when we read more widely in early second-century church history we find that the result seems to have been an exacerbation of the heresy problem. Women excluded from the widows' order sought out teachers and groups which presented them with greater equality, if not with greater doctrinal orthodoxy. 'Despite attempts to limit their influence, the widows remained a difficult group to control, which prompted renewed efforts to restrain them in the third and fourth centuries.'[61]

60.   D.R. MacDonald, 'Virgins, Widows and Paul in Second Century Asia Minor', p. 177.
61.   Cardman, 'Women, Ministry, and Church Order', p. 305. See my *The Widows*, especially chapters 4, 5, 6.

BIBLIOGRAPHY

Abrahamsen, V., 'Women at Philippi: The Pagan and Christian Evidence', *JFSR* 3.2 (1987), pp. 17-30.

Achtemeier, P.J., 'Jesus and the Disciples as Miracle Workers in the Apocryphal New Testament', in E. Schüssler Fiorenza (ed.), *Aspects of Religious Propaganda in Judaism and Early Christianity* (Notre Dame, IN: University of Notre Dame Press, 1976), pp. 149-86.

Ackermann, D.M., 'Being Woman, Being Human', in Ackermann, Draper and Mashinini (eds.), *Women Hold Up Half the Sky*, pp. 93-105.

—'Defining Our Humanity: Thoughts on a Feminist Anthropology', *JTSA* 79 (1992), pp. 13-23.

—'Faith and Feminism: Women Doing Theology', in J. De Gruchy and C. Villa-Vicencio (eds.), *Doing Theology in Context: South African Perspectives* (Maryknoll, NY: Orbis Books, 1994), pp. 197-211.

Ackermann, D.M., J.A. Draper and E. Mashinini (eds.), *Women Hold Up Half the Sky: Women in the Church in Southern Africa* (Pietermaritzburg: Cluster, 1991).

Adams, C.J., and Marie Fortune, *Violence Against Women and Children: A Christian Theological Sourcebook* (New York: Continuum, 1995).

Arbuckle, G.A., *Grieving for Change: A Spirituality for Refounding Gospel Communities* (London: Geoffrey Chapman, 1991).

Archer, G.L., 'Does 1 Timothy 2.12 Forbid the Ordination of Women?', in *Encyclopedia of Bible Difficulties* (Grand Rapids: Zondervan, 1982), pp. 411-15.

Aune, D., *Prophecy in Early Christianity and the Ancient Mediterranean World* (Grand Rapids: Eerdmans, 1983).

Balch, D.L., *Let Wives Be Submissive: The Domestic Code in 1 Peter* (SBLMS, 26; Chico, CA: Scholars Press, 1981).

Barber, E.W., *Women's Work: The First 20,000 Years* (New York: W.W. Norton, 1994).

Barrett, C.K., *The Pastoral Epistles in the New English Bible* (New Clarendon Bible; Oxford: Clarendon Press, 1963).

—'Things Sacrificed to Idols', *NTS* 11 (1964–65), pp. 138-41.

Barth, M., *Ephesians* (AB, 34-34A; 2 vols.; Garden City, NY: Doubleday, 1974).

Bartsch, H.-W., *Die Anfänge Urchristlicher Rechtsbildungen: Studien zu den Pastoralbriefen* (TF, 34; Hamburg: Evangelischer Verlag, 1965).

—'Die Witwenregel', in idem, *Die Anfänge Urchristlicher Rechtsbildungen*, pp. 117-20.

Bassler, J.M., 'Σκεῦος: A Modest Proposal for Illuminating Paul's Use of Metaphor in 1 Thessalonians 4:4', in M.L. White and O.L. Yarbrough (eds.), *The Social World of the First Christians: Essays in Honor of Wayne A. Meeks* (Minneapolis: Fortress Press, 1995), pp. 53-66.

—*1 Timothy, 2 Timothy, Titus* (ANTC; Nashville: Abingdon Press, 1996).

—'The Widows' Tale: A Fresh Look at 1 Timothy 5.3-16', *JBL* 103 (1984), pp. 23-41.

Beavis, M.A., '2 Thessalonians', in Schüssler Fiorenza (ed.), *Searching the Scriptures*, II, pp. 263-72.

Beker, J.C., *Heirs of Paul* (Minneapolis: Fortress Press, 1991).

Benko, S., 'Pagan Criticism of Christianity During the First Two Centuries A.D.', *ANRW*, 23.2, pp. 1055-1118.

Berger, K., and C. Colpe (eds.), *Religionsgeschichtliches Textbuch zum Neuen Testament* (NTD, 1; Göttingen: Vandenhoeck & Ruprecht, 1987).

Betz, H.D., *Galatians: A Commentary on Paul's Letter to the Churches in Galatia* (Philadelphia: Fortress Press, 1979).

Bitzer, L.F., 'The Rhetorical Situation', *Philosophy and Rhetoric* 1 (1968), pp. 1-14.

Bloesch, D.G., *Is the Bible Sexist? Beyond Feminism and Patriarchalism* (Westchester: Crossway, 1982).

Blum, G.G., 'Das Amt der Frau im Neuen Testament', *NovT* 7 (1964–65), pp. 142-61.

Boatwright, M.T., 'Plancia Magna of Perge: Women's Roles and Status in Roman Asia Minor', in S.B. Pomeroy (ed.), *Women's History and Ancient History* (Chapel Hill: University of North Carolina Press, 1991), pp. 249-72.

Booth, C., *Female Ministry; or, Woman's Right to Preach the Gospel* (London, 1859; repr. New York: Salvation Army Supplies Printing and Publishing Department, 1975).

Bosch, D.J., *Transforming Mission* (Maryknoll, NY: Orbis Books, 1991).

Botha, P.J.J., 'Folklore, Social Values and Life as a Woman in Early Christianity', *South African Journal for Folklore Studies* 3 (1992), pp. 1-14.

Boyarin, D., *A Radical Jew: Paul and the Politics of Identity* (Berkeley: University of California Press, 1994).

Brooten, B., 'Junia…Outstanding among the Apostles (Rom. 16.7)', in Swidler and Swidler (eds.), *Women Priests*, pp. 141-44.

—*Women Leaders in the Ancient Synagogue: Inscriptional Evidence and Background Issues* (BJS, 36; Chico, CA: Scholars Press, 1982).

Brown, A.L., 'Exegesis of 1 Corinthians xiv, 34, 35; and 1 Timothy ii, 11, 12', *Oberlin Quarterly Reviews* 3 (1849), pp. 358-73.

Brown, L.A., 'Asceticism and Ideology: The Language of Power in the Pastoral Epistles', in Wimbush (ed.), *Discursive Formations*, pp. 77-94.

Brown, P., *The Body and Society: Men, Women and Sexual Renunciation in Early Christianity* (New York: Columbia University Press; London: Faber & Faber, 1988).

—'Late Antiquity', in P. Veyne (ed.), *A History of Private Life: From Pagan Rome to Byzantium* (Cambridge, MA: Belknap Press/Harvard University Press, 1987), pp. 235-311.

Brox, N., *Die Pastoralbriefe* (RNT, 7.2; Regensburg: Pustet, 4th edn, 1969).

Bruce, F.F., *The Epistle to the Galatians: A Commentary on the Greek Text* (NIGTC; Grand Rapids: Eerdmans, 1982).

—'Women in the Church: A Biblical Survey', *Christian Brethren Review* 33 (1982), pp. 7-14.

Bultmann, R., *Theology of the New Testament* (2 vols.; New York: Charles Scribner's Sons, 1951).

Burns, K., and O. Gradenivitz, *Fontes Iuris Romani Antiqui* (Tübingen, 7th edn, 1909).

Burrus, V., *Chastity as Autonomy: Women in the Stories of the Apocryphal Acts* (Studies in Women and Religion, 23; Lewiston, NY: Edwin Mellen Press, 1987).

—'Word and Flesh: The Bodies and Sexuality of Ascetic Women in Christian Antiquity', *JFSR* 10 (1994), pp. 27-51.

Bushnell, K.C., *God's Word to Women: One Hundred Bible Studies on Woman's Place in the Divine Economy* (place and date uncertain; repr.; North Collins, NY: Ray B. Munson, c. 1975).

Campenhausen, H. von, *Polykarp von Smyrna und die Pastoralbriefe* (Heidelburg: Carl Winter Universitatsverlag, 1951).

Cardman, F., 'Women, Ministry, and Church Order in Early Christianity', in Kraemer and D'Angelo (eds.), *Women and Christian Origins*, pp. 300-29.

Castelli, E.A., 'Disciplines of Difference: Asceticism and History in Paul', in Vaage and Wimbush (eds.), *Asceticism and the New Testament*, pp. 171-85.

—'Interpretations of Power in 1 Corinthians', in D. Jobling and S.D. Moore (eds.), *Poststructuralism as Exegesis* (Semeia, 54; Atlanta: Scholars Press, 1991), pp. 197-222.

—'Paul on Women and Gender', in Kraemer and D'Angelo (eds.), *Women and Christian Origins*, pp. 221-35.

Clark, E.A., 'Ascetic Renunciation and Feminine Advancement: A Paradox of Late Ancient Christianity', *ATR* 63.3 (1981), pp. 140-57.

—*Reading Renunciation: Asceticism and Scripture in Early Christianity* (Princeton, NJ: Princeton University Press, 1999).

Clark, G., *Women in the Ancient World* (New Surveys in the Classics, 21; Oxford: Oxford University Press, 1989).

Clark, S.B., *Man and Woman in Christ: An Examination of the Roles of Men and Women in Light of Scripture and the Social Sciences* (Ann Arbor: Servant Books, 1980).

Cloete, G.D., and D.J. Smit, 'Preaching from the Lectionary: Eph 1.20-23', *JTSA* 63 (1988), pp. 59-67.

Cohen, D., 'Seclusions, Separation, and the Status of Women in Classical Athens', *Greece and Rome* 36 (1989), pp. 3-5.

Connolly, R.H. (ed.), *The Didascalia Apostolorum* (Oxford: Clarendon Press, 1929).

Conzelmann, H., *The Pastoral Epistles* (Hermeneia; Philadelphia: Fortress Press, 4th edn, 1984).

Cooey, P.M., 'Kenosis', in Russell and Clarkson (eds.), *Dictionary of Feminist Theologies*, p. 163.

Crook, R.H., *An Introduction to Christian Ethics* (Upper Saddle River, NJ: Prentice–Hall, 3rd edn, 1999).

Crouch, J.E., *The Origin and Intention of the Colossian Haustafel* (Göttingen: Vandenhoeck & Ruprecht, 1972).

D'Angelo, M.R., 'Colossians', in Schüssler Fiorenza (ed.), *Searching the Scriptures*, II, pp. 313-24.

—'Women Partners in the New Testament', *JFSR* 6 (1990), pp. 65-86.

Danielou, J., and H. Marrou, *The First Six Hundred Years* (New York: McGraw–Hill, 1964).

Davies, S.L., *The Revolt of the Widows: The Social World of the Apocryphal Acts* (Carbondale, IL: Southern Illinois University Press, 1980).

Davis, J.J., 'Ordination of Women Reconsidered: Discussion of 1 Timothy 2.8-15', *Presbyterian Communique* 12.6 (1979), pp. 1, 8-11, 15; repr. in R. Hestenes (ed.), *Women and Men in Ministry* (Pasadena, CA: Fuller Theological Seminary, 1980), pp. 37-40.

Dayton, D., *Luther Lee: Five Sermons and a Tract* (Chicago: Holrad House, 1975).

Deferrari, R.J. (ed.), *The Fathers of the Church* (New York: Fathers of the Church, 1959).

Delling, G., *Paulus Stellung zu Frau und Ehe* (BWANT, 4.5; Stuttgart: W. Kohlhammer, 1937).

Dentan, R.C., 'Head', *IDB*, II, p. 541.

—'Heart', *IDB*, II, p. 549.

Dewey, J., '1 Timothy', in Newsom and Ringe (eds.), *The Women's Bible Commentary*, pp. 353-58.

Dibelius, M., and H. Conzelmann, *The Pastoral Epistles* (Hermenia; Philadelphia: Fortress Press, 1972).

Döllinger, J., *The First Age of Christianity and the Church* (London: Gibbings, 1906).

Donelson, L.R., *Pseudepigraphy and Ethical Argument in the Pastoral Epistles* (HUT, 22; Tübingen: Mohr–Siebeck, 1986).

Douglas, M., *Natural Symbols* (London: Barry & Rockliff, 1970).

—*Purity and Danger* (London: Routledge & Kegan Paul, 1966).

Draper, J.A., 'Oppressive and Subversive Moral Instruction in the New Testament', in Ackermann, Draper and Mashinini (eds.), *Women Hold Up Half the Sky*, pp. 37-54.

Dubisch, J., 'Culture Enters through the Kitchen: Women, Food, and Social Boundaries in Rural Greece', in *idem, Gender and Power in Rural Greece* (Princeton, NJ: Princeton University Press, 1986), pp. 195-214.

Du Boulay, J., *Portrait of a Greek Mountain Village* (Oxford: Clarendon Press, 1974).

Du Toit, A.B., 'Alienation and Re-identification as Pragmatic Strategies in Galatians', *Neot* 26.2 (1992), pp. 279-95.

Engel, M.P., *Revisioning the Past: Prospects in Historical Theology* (ed. M.P. Engel and W.E. Wyman, Jr; Minneapolis: Fortress Press, 1992).

Ernst, J., 'Die Witwenregel des ersten Timotheusbriefs Hinweis auf die biblischen Ursprunge des weiblichen Ordenswesens?', *Theologie und Glaube* 59 (1969), pp. 343-445.

Evans, A., 'Common Ground in the Culture Wars?', *Oregon Quarterly* 77 (1998), p. 13.

Evans, M.J., *Woman in the Bible* (Downers Grove, IL: InterVarsity Press, 1984).

Falwell, J., *Listen, America!* (Garden City, NY: Doubleday, 1980).

Fatum, L., 'Image of God and Glory of Man: Women in the Pauline Congregations', in K.E. Børresen (ed.), *Image of God and Gender Models in Judaeo-Christian Tradition* (Oslo: Solum Forlag, 1991), pp. 56-137.

—'Women, Symbolic Universe and Structures of Silence', *ST* 43.1 (1989), pp. 61-80.

Fee, G.D., *1 and 2 Timothy, Titus* (Good News Commentary; San Francisco: Harper & Row, 1984).

—*1 and 2 Timothy, Titus* (New International Biblical Commentary; Peabody, MA: Hendrickson, rev. edn, 1988).

Feine, P., J. Behm, and W.G. Kümmel, *Einleitung in das Neue Testament* (Heidelberg: Quelle & Meyer, 14th edn, 1965).

Felder, C.H. (ed.), *Stony the Road We Trod: African American Biblical Interpretation* (Minneapolis: Fortress Press, 1991).

Fell, M., *Women's Speaking Justified, Proved and Allowed by the Scriptures* (London, 1666; repr. Amherst: Mosher Book and Tract Committee, New England Yearly Meeting of Friends, 1980).

Ferguson, E. (ed.), *Encyclopedia of Early Christianity* (New York: Garland, 1990).

Foh, S.T., *Women and the Word of God: A Response to Biblical Feminism* (Grand Rapids: Baker Book House, 1980).

Ford, J.M., 'A Note on Proto-Montanism in the Pastoral Epistles', *NTS* 17 (1970–71), pp. 338-46.

Fortune, M., *Keeping the Faith: Questions and Answers for the Abused Woman* (San Francisco: Harper & Row, 1987).

Fox, R.L., *Pagans and Christians* (Harmondsworth: Penguin Books, 1986).

Frend, W.H.C., *The Rise of Christianity* (Philadelphia: Fortress Press, 1984).

Frey, J.-B., 'La Signification des Termes MONANDROS et *univira* coups d'oeil sur La Famille Romaine aux Premiers siecles de Notre Ere', *RSR* 20 (1930), pp. 48-60.

Friedländer, L., *Darstellungen aus der Sittengeschichte Roms* (4 vols.; Leipzig: Hirzel, 1922).

Friesen, S.J., *Twice Neokoros: Ephesus, Asia and the Cult of the Flavian Imperial Family* (Leiden: E.J. Brill, 1993).

Fulkerson, M.M., 'Contesting Feminist Canons: Discourse and the Problem of Sexist Texts', *JFSR* 7 (1991), pp. 55-73.

Gardner, J.F., *Women in Roman Law and Society* (London: Croom Helm, 1986).

Gasque, W.W., 'The Role of Women in the Church, in Society, and in the Home', *Crux* 19.3 (1983), pp. 3-9.

Gillespie, T.W., 'Prophecy and Tongues: The Concept of Christian Prophecy in Pauline Theology' (PhD dissertation, Claremont Graduate School, 1971).

Gold, V.R., *The New Testament and Psalms: An Inclusive Version* (New York: Oxford University Press, 1995).

Gordon, A.J., 'The Ministry of Woman', *Missionary Review of the World* 7 (1894), pp. 910-21; repr. in [Fuller] *Theology, News and Notes* 21.2 (1975), pp. 5-9; repr. *Gordon College Alumnus* 8.1 (1978), pp. 3-4, 8-9; repr. *Equity* 1.1 (1980), pp. 26-31.

Grant, R.M., *Greek Apologists of the Second Century* (Philadelphia: Westminster Press, 1988).

Gryson, R., *The Ministry of Women in the Early Church* (Collegeville, MN: Liturgical Press, 1976).

Gundry, P., *Woman Be Free!* (Grand Rapids: Zondervan, 1977).

Hallett, J.P., *Fathers and Daughters in Roman Society* (Princeton, NJ: Princeton University Press, 1984).

Hanson, A.T., *The Pastoral Epistles* (NCBC; Grand Rapids: Eerdmans, 1982).

Hardesty, N.A., *Women Called to Witness: Evangelical Feminism in the 19th Century* (Nashville: Abingdon Press, 1984).

Harrison, B.W., *Making the Connections: Essays in Feminist Social Ethics* (Boston: Beacon Press, 1985).

Hartin, P.J., 'Ethics and the New Testament: How Do We Get from There to Here?', in Mouton and Lategan (eds.), *The Relevance of Theology for the 1990s*, pp. 511-25.

Hays, R.B., *Echoes of Scripture in the Letters of Paul* (New Haven: Yale University Press, 1989).

—'Scripture-Shaped Community: The Problem of Method in New Testament Ethics', *Int* 44 (1990), pp. 42-55.

Hendrix, H., 'On the Form and Ethos of Ephesians', *USQR* 42 (1988), pp. 3-15.

Hennecke, E., *New Testament Apocrypha* (2 vols.; Philadelphia: Westminster Press, 1963–65).

Hestenes, R. (ed.), *Women and Men in Ministry* (Pasadena, CA: Fuller Theological Seminary, 1980).

Heyob, S.K., *The Cult of Isis among Women in the Greco-Roman World* (Leiden: E.J. Brill, 1975).

Hill, D., *New Testament Prophecy* (New Foundations Theological Library; Atlanta: John Knox Press, 1981).

Hock, R.F., *The Social Context of Paul's Ministry: Apostleship and Tentmaking* (Philadelphia: Fortress Press, 1980).

Hommes, N.J., 'Let Women Be Silent in the Church: A Message Concerning the Worship Service and the Decorum to Be Observed by Women', *Calvin Theological Journal* 4 (1969), pp. 5-22.

Hoover, K.W., 'Creative Tension in 1 Timothy 2.11-15', *Brethren Life and Thought* 22 (1977), pp. 163-66.

Horsley, G.H.R., *New Documents Illustrating Early Christianity* (North Rude: Macquarie University Press, 1981).

Horsley, R.A. (ed.), *Paul and Politics: Ekklesia, Israel, Imperium, Interpretation* (Festschrift Krister Stendahl; Harrisburg, PA: Trinity Press International, 2000).

Howe, E.M., *Women and Church Leadership* (Grand Rapids: Zondervan, 1982).

Hultgren, A.J., and R. Aus, *I–II Timothy, Titus, II Thessalonians* (Minneapolis: Augsburg, 1984).

Hurley, J.B., *Man and Woman in Biblical Perspective* (Grand Rapids: Zondervan, 1981).

Ilan, T., *Jewish Women in Greco-Roman Palestine* (Peabody, MA: Hendrickson, 1996).

Irvin, D., 'The Ministry of Women in the Early Church: The Archaeological Evidence', *Duke Divinity School Review* 45 (1980), pp. 76-80.

Jeffers, J.S., 'Jewish and Christian Families in First-Century Rome', in K.P. Donfried and P. Richardson (eds.), *Judaism and Christianity in First-Century Rome* (Grand Rapids: Eerdmans, 1998), pp. 128-50.

Jenkins, C., 'Origen on 1 Corinthians', *JTS* 10 (1908–1909), pp. 41-42.

Jeremias, J., *Die Briefe an Timotheus und Titus* (NTD, 9; Göttingen: Vandenhoeck & Ruprecht, 1975).

Jewett, P.K., *Man as Male and Female: A Study in Sexual Relationships from a Theological Point of View* (Grand Rapids: Eerdmans, 1975).

Johnson, E.A., *She Who Is: The Mystery of God in Feminist Theological Discourse* (New York: Crossroad, 1992).

Johnson, E.E., 'Ephesians', in C.A. Newsom and S.H. Ringe (eds.), *The Women's Bible Commentary* (Louisville, KY: Westminster John Knox, expanded edn, 1998), pp. 428-32.

—'2 Thessalonians', in Newsom and Ringe (eds.), *The Women's Bible Commentary*, pp. 351-52.

Johnson, L.T., *1 Timothy, 2 Timothy, Titus* (Atlanta: John Knox Press, 1987).

—'II Timothy and the Polemic Against False Teachers: A Re-examination', *JRelS* 6 (1978), pp. 1-26.

—*The Writings of the New Testament: An Interpretation* (Minneapolis: Fortress Press, rev. edn, 1999).

Johnston, R.K., 'The Role of Women in the Church and Family: The Issues of Biblical Hermeneutics', in *idem, Evangelicals at an Impasse: Biblical Authority in Practice* (Atlanta: John Knox Press, 1979), pp. 48-76.

Judge, E.A., 'St. Paul and Classical Society', *JAC* 15 (1972), pp. 19-36.

Karris, R.J., 'The Background and Significance of the Polemic of the Pastoral Epistles', *JBL* 92 (1973), pp. 549-64.

Kelly, J.N.D., *A Commentary on the Pastoral Epistles* (BNTC; London: A. & C. Black, 1963).

Kidd, R.M., *Wealth and Beneficence in the Pastoral Epistles* (SBLDS, 122; Atlanta: Scholars Press, 1990).

King, K.L. (ed.), *Images of the Feminine in Gnosticism* (Studies in Antiquity and Christianity; Philadelphia: Fortress Press, 1988).

Kirby, J.C., *Ephesians: Baptism and Pentecost. An Inquiry into the Structure and Purpose of the Epistle to the Ephesians* (London: SPCK, 1968).

Kittredge, C.B., *Community and Authority: The Rhetoric of Obedience in the Pauline Tradition* (HTS; Harrisburg, PA: Trinity Press International, 1998).

—'Corinthian Women Prophets and Paul's Argumentation in 1 Corinthians', in R.A. Horsley (ed.), *Paul and Politics*, pp. 103-109.

Kloppenborg, J.S., 'Egalitarianism in the Myth and Rhetoric of Pauline Churches', in E.A. Castelli and H. Taussig (eds.), *Reimagining Christian Origins: A Colloquium Honoring Burton L. Mack* (Valley Forge, PA: Trinity Press International, 1996), pp. 247-63.

Knight, G.W., III, 'ΑΥΘΕΝ ΤΕΩ in Reference to Women in 1 Timothy 2.12', *NTS* 30 (1984), pp. 143-57.

—*Commentary on the Pastoral Epistles* (NIGTC; Grand Rapids: Eerdmans, 1992).

—*The New Testament Teaching on the Role Relationship of Men and Women* (Grand Rapids: Baker Book House, 1977).

Kraemer, R.S., 'The Conversion of Women to Ascetic Forms of Christianity', *Signs* 6.2 (1980), pp. 298-307.

—'Ecstasy and Possession: The Attraction of Women to the Cult of Dionysus', *HTR* 72 (1979), pp. 55-80.

—*Her Share of the Blessings: Women's Religions among Pagans, Jews, and Christians in the Greco-Roman World* (New York: Oxford University Press, 1992).

Kraemer, R.S. (ed.), *Maenads, Martyrs, Matrons, Monastics: A Sourcebook on Women's Religions in the Greco-Roman World* (Philadelphia: Fortress Press, 1988).

Kraemer, R.S., and M.R. D'Angelo (eds.), *Women and Christian Origins* (New York: Oxford University Press, 1999).

Kroeger, C.C., 'Ancient Heresies and a Strange Greek Verb', *Reformed Journal* 29.3 (1979), pp. 12-15; repr. in Hestenes (ed.), *Women and Men in Ministry*, pp. 14-18.

Kroeger, R., and C.C. Kroeger, 'May Women Teach? Heresy in the Pastoral Epistles', *Reformed Journal* 30.10 (1980), pp. 14-18.

Kuhns, D.R., *Women in the Church* (Focal Pamphlets, 28; Scottdale, PA: Herald Press, 1978).

Langley, M., *Equal Woman: A Christian Feminist Perspective* (Basingstoke: Marshall, Morgan & Scott, 1983).

LaPorte, J., *The Role of Women in Early Christianity* (Studies in Women and Religion, 7; Lewiston, NY: Edwin Mellen Press, 1982).

Lategan, B.C., 'Aspects of a Contextual Hermeneutics for South Africa', in Mouton and Lategan (eds.), *The Relevance of Theology for the 1990s*, pp. 17-30.

—'Hermeneutics', *ABD*, III, pp. 149-54.

—'Imagination and Transformation: Ricoeur and the Role of Imagination', *Scriptura* 58 (1996), pp. 213-32.

—'Introduction: Coming to Grips with the Reader', *Semeia* 48 (1989), pp. 3-17.

—'Reference: Reception, Redescription and Reality', in B.C. Lategan and W.S. Vorster, *Text and Reality: Aspects of Reference in Biblical Texts* (Philadelphia: Fortress Press, 1985), pp. 67-93.

—'Revisiting Text and Reality', *Neot* 28.3 (1994), pp. 121-35.

—'Textual Space as Rhetorical Device', in S.E. Porter and T.H. Olbricht (eds.), *Rhetoric and the New Testament: Essays from the 1992 Heidelberg Conference* (Sheffield: JSOT Press, 1993), pp. 397-408.

Lee, L., *Woman's Right to Preach the Gospel* (Syracuse, NY: self-published, 1853).

Lefkowitz, M.R., and M.B. Fant (trans.), *Women in Greece and Rome* (Toronto: Samuel-Stevens, 1977).

Leipoldt, J., *Die Frau in der antiken Welt und im Urchristentum* (Leipzig: Koehler & Amelang, 1954).

Lemaire, A., 'The Ministries in the New Testament: Recent Research', *BTB* 3.2 (1973), pp. 133-66.

Leon, H.J., *The Jews of Ancient Rome* (Philadelphia: Jewish Publication Society of America, 1960).

Lewis, N., and M. Reinhold, *Roman Civilization* (2 vols.; New York: Harper & Row, 1955).

LiDonnici, L.R., 'Women's Religions and Religious Lives in the Greco-Roman City', in Kraemer and D'Angelo (eds.), *Women and Christian Origins*, pp. 80-102.

Lightman, M., and W. Zeisel, 'Univira: An Example of Continuity and Change in Roman Society', *CH* 46 (1977), pp. 19-32.

Lincoln, A.T., *Ephesians* (WBC, 42; Dallas: Word Books, 1990).

Lippert, P., *Leben als Zeugnis: Die werbende Kraft christlicher Lebensführung nach dem Kirchenverständnis neuetestamentlicher Briefe* (SBM, 4; Stuttgart: Katholisches Bibel-werk, 1968).

Longenecker, R.N., *Galatians* (WBC, 41; Dallas: Word Books, 1990).

Louw, J.P., and Eugene A. Nida (eds.), *Greek–English Lexicon of the New Testament* (Cape Town: Bible Society of South Africa, 1989).

Lütgert, W., *Die Irrlehrer der Pastoralbriefe* (Guttersloh: C. Bertelsmann, 1909).

Lutz, C.E. (trans.), *Musonius Rufus* (New Haven: Yale University Press, 1947).

MacDonald, D.R., *The Legend and the Apostle: The Battle for Paul in Story and Canon* (Philadelphia: Westminster Press, 1983).

— *There Is No Male and Female: The Fate of a Dominical Saying in Paul and Gnosticism* (HDR, 20; Philadelphia: Fortress Press, 1987).

— 'Virgins, Widows, and Paul in Second Century Asia Minor' (SBLSP; Missoula, MT: Scholars Press, 1979), pp. 169-84.

MacDonald, M.Y., 'Citizens of Heaven and Earth: Asceticism and Social Integration in Colossians and Ephesians', in Vaage and Wimbush (eds.), *Asceticism and the New Testament*, pp. 269-98.

— *The Pauline Churches* (Cambridge: Cambridge University Press, 1988).

— 'Reading Real Women Through the Undisputed Letters of Paul', in Kraemer and D'Angelo (eds.), *Women and Christian Origins*, pp. 199-220.

— 'Rereading Paul: Early Interpreters of Paul on Women and Gender', in Kraemer and D'Angelo (eds.), *Women and Christian Origins*, pp. 236-53.

Malina, B.J., *The New Testament World: Insights from Cultural Anthropology* (Louisville, KY: Westminster/John Knox Press, 1993).

Maloney, L., 'The Pastoral Epistles', in Schüssler Fiorenza (ed.), *Searching the Scriptures*, II, pp. 361-80.

— *Die Stellung der Frau in der Kirche nach der Auffassung der Pastoralbriefe* (unpublished manuscript, 1984).

Marshall, A. (trans.), *The Greek–English New Testament* (Washington, DC: Christianity Today, 1975).

Martin, C., 'The *Haustafeln* (Household Codes) in African American Biblical Interpretation: "Free Slaves" and "Subordinate Women" ', in Felder (ed.), *Stony the Road We Trod*, pp. 206-31.

Martin, D.B., *The Corinthian Body* (New Haven: Yale University Press, 1995).

Massey, L., *Women in the New Testament: An Analysis of Scripture in the Light of New Testament Era Culture* (Jefferson, NC: McFarland & Co., 1989).

McFague, S., *Metaphorical Theology: Models of God in Religious Language* (Philadelphia: Fortress Press, 1982).

Meeks, W.A., *The First Urban Christians: The Social World of the Apostle Paul* (New Haven: Yale University Press, 1983).

—'The Image of the Androgyne: Some Uses of a Symbol in Earliest Christianity', *HR* 13 (1974), pp. 165-208.

—*The New Testament World: Insights from Cultural Anthropology* (Louisville, KY: Westminster Press, rev. edn, 1993).

—*The Origins of Christian Morality: The First Two Centuries* (New Haven: Yale University Press, 1993).

Metzger, B., *A Textual Commentary on the New Testament* (New York: United Bible Society, 1994).

Meyers, C.L., *Discovering Eve: Ancient Israelite Women in Context* (New York: Oxford University Press, 1988).

Meyers, C.L. (ed.), *Women in Scripture* (New York: Houghton Mifflin, 2000).

Mickelsen, A., *Women, Authority, and the Bible* (Downers Grove, IL: InterVarsity Press, 1986).

Mickelsen, A., and B. Mickelsen, 'May Women Teach Men?', *Standard* 74.4 (1984), pp. 34, 36-37.

Mollenkott, V.R., 'Interpreting Difficult Scriptures', *Daughters of Sarah* 5.2 (1979), pp. 16-17; repr. in *Daughters of Sarah* 7.5 (1981), pp. 13-16.

—*Women, Men, and the Bible* (New York: Crossroad, rev. edn, 1988).

Montgomery, H., 'Women and Status in the Greco-Roman World', *ST* 43 (1989), pp. 115-24.

Moo, D.J., '1 Timothy 2.11-15: Meaning and Significance', *Trinity Journal* 1 (1980), pp. 62-83.

—'The Interpretation of 1 Timothy 2.11-15: A Rejoinder', *Trinity Journal* 2 (1981), pp. 198-222.

Morris, L., 'The Ministry of Women', in R. Hestenes and L. Curley (eds.), *Women and the Ministries of the Church* (Pasadena, CA: Fuller Theological Seminary, 1979), pp. 14-25.

Mouton, E., *Reading a New Testament Document Ethically* (Atlanta: Society of Biblical Literature; Leiden: E.J. Brill, 2002).

—'Reading Ephesians Ethically: Criteria Towards a Renewed Identity Awareness?', *Neot* 28.2 (1994), pp. 359-77.

—'Remembering Forward and Hoping Backward? Some Thoughts on Women in the Dutch Reformed Church', *Scriptura* 76 (2001), pp. 77-86.

—'The (Trans)formative Potential of the Bible as Resource for Christian Ethos and Ethics', *Scriptura* 62 (1997), pp. 245-57.

—'The Transformative Potential of Ephesians in a Situation of Transition', *Semeia* 78 (1997), pp. 121-43.

—'Die Verhaal van Afrikaanse Christenvroue: Uitnodiging tot Morele Vorming', *Scriptura* 63 (1997), pp. 475-90.

Mouton, J., and B.C. Lategan (eds.), *The Relevance of Theology for the 1990s* (Pretoria: Human Sciences Research Council, 1994).

Moxnes, H., 'Honor and Shame', *BTB* 23 (1993), pp. 167-76.

— 'Social Integration and the Problem of Gender in St. Paul's Letters', *ST* 43 (1989), pp. 99-113.

Müller-Bardorff, J., 'Zur Exegese von 1. Timotheus 5,3-16', in *Gott und die Götter: Festgabe für Erich Fascher zum 60. Geburtstag* (Berlin: Evangelische Verlagsanstalt, 1958), pp. 113-33.

Murphy-O'Connor, J., '2 Timothy Contrasted with 1 Timothy and Titus', *RB* 98 (1991), pp. 403-18.

Newsom, C.A., and S.H. Ringe (eds.), *Women's Bible Commentary* (Louisville, KY: Westminster/John Knox Press, 1992; expanded edn, 1998).

Newton, M., *The Concept of Purity at Qumran and in the Letters of Paul* (Cambridge: Cambridge University Press, 1985).

Niebuhr, H.R., *The Meaning of Revelation* (New York: Macmillan, 1941).

Nugent, R., *Portrait of the Consecrated Woman in Greek Christian Literature of the First Four Centuries* (Washington: Catholic University Press, 1941).

Oberlinner, L., *Die Pastoralbriefe: Kommentar zum Ersten Timotheusbrief* (3 vols.; HTKNT, 11.2; Freiburg: Herder, 1994).

Olyan, S.M., 'Honor, Shame, and Covenant Relations in Ancient Israel and Its Environment', *JBL* 115 (1996), pp. 201-18.

Osburn, C.D., 'ΑΥΘΕΝΤΕΩ (1 Timothy 2.12)', *Restoration Quarterly* 25 (1982), pp. 1-12.

Osiek, C., 'The Widow as Altar: The Rise and Fall of a Symbol', *Second Century* 3 (1983), pp. 159-69.

Osiek, C., and D.L. Balch, *Families in the New Testament World: Households and House Churches* (The Family, Religion, and Culture Series; Louisville, KY: Westminster/John Knox Press, 1997).

Pagels, E., *The Gnostic Gospels* (New York: Random House, 1979).

Palmer, P., *Promise of the Father; or A Neglected Specialty of the Last Days* (Boston: Henry V. Degen, 1859; repr. Salem, OH: Schmul, 1981).

Panning, A.J., 'ΑΥΘΕΝΤΕΙΝ—a Word Study', *Wisconsin Lutheran Quarterly* 78 (1981), pp. 185-91.

Pantel, P.S. (ed.), *A History of Women: From Ancient Goddesses to Christian Saints* (Cambridge, MA: Belknap Press, 1992).

Pape, D.R., *In Search of God's Ideal Woman: A Personal Examination of the New Testament* (Downers Grove, IL: InterVarsity Press, 1976).

Parvey, C.F., 'The Theology and Leadership of Women in the New Testament', in R.R. Ruether (ed.), *Religion and Sexism: Images of Women in the Jewish and Christian Traditions* (New York: Simon & Schuster, 1974), pp. 117-49.

Payne, P.B., 'Libertarian Women in Ephesus: A Response to Douglas J. Moo's article, "1 Timothy 2.11-15: Meaning and Significance"', *Trinity Journal* 2 (1981), pp. 169-97.

Penn-Lewis, J., *The 'Magna Charta of Woman' according to the Scriptures* (Bournemouth: Overcomer Book Room, 1919; repr. Minneapolis: Bethany Fellowship, 1975).

Perdue, L.G., 'The Social Character of Paraenesis and Paraenetic Literature', *Semeia* 50 (1990), pp. 5-39.

Peristany, J.G. (ed.), *Honour and Shame: The Values of Mediterranean Society* (London: Weidenfeld and Nicolson, 1965).

Perkins, P., *Gnosticism and the New Testament* (Minneapolis: Fortress Press, 1993).

Pitt-Rivers, J., 'Honour and Social Status', in Peristany (ed.), *Honour and Shame*, pp. 19-77.

Pomeroy, S.B., *Goddesses, Whores, Wives and Slaves: Women in Classical Antiquity* (New York: Schocken Books, 1975).

—'The Relationship of the Married Woman to Her Blood Relatives in Rome', *Ancient Society* 7 (1976), pp. 215-27.

Pope-Lance, D.J., and J.C. Engelsman, *Domestic Violence: A Guide for Clergy* (Trenton, NJ: New Jersey Department of Community Affairs, 1987).

Portefaix, L., *Sisters Rejoice: Paul's Letter to the Philippians and Luke–Acts as Received by First-Century Philippian Women* (Stockholm: Almqvist & Wiksell, 1988).

Powers, B.W., 'Women in the Church: The Application of 1 Timothy 2.8-15', *Interchange* 17 (1975), pp. 55-59.

Price, R.M., *The Widow Traditions in Luke–Acts: A Feminist-Critical Scrutiny* (SBLDS, 155; Atlanta: Scholar's Press, 1997).

Price, S.R.F., *Rituals and Power: The Roman Imperial Cult in Asia Minor* (Cambridge: Cambridge University Press, 1984).

Quinn, J.D., 'Epistles to Timothy', *ABD*, IV, pp. 560-71.

—*The Letter to Titus* (AB, 35; New York: Doubleday, 1990).

Ricoeur, P., 'Biblical Hermenetics', *Semeia* 4 (1975), pp. 29-148.

—*Essays on Biblical Interpretation* (ed. L.S. Mudge; Philadelphia: Fortress Press, 1980).

—*Interpretation Theory: Discourse and the Surplus of Meaning* (Fort Worth: Texas Christian University Press, 1976).

—*The Rule of Metaphor: Multi-Disciplinary Studies of the Creation of Meaning in Language* (trans. R. Czerny, K. McLaughlin and J. Costello; Toronto: University of Toronto Press, 1977).

Roberts, A., and J. Donaldson (eds.), *Ante-Nicene Fathers* (10 vols.; Peabody, MA: Hendrickson, 1994).

Roberts, J.H., *The Letter to the Ephesians* (Cape Town: Lux Verbi, 1991).

Roberts, M.D., 'Woman Shall Be Saved: A Closer Look at 1 Timothy 2.15', *TSF Bulletin* 5.2 (1981), pp. 4-7.

Robinson, J.M., (ed.), *The Nag Hammadi Library* (San Francisco: Harper & Row, 1978).

Roloff, J., *Der erste Brief an Timotheus* (EKKNT, 15; Zürich: Benziger Verlag; Neukirchen–Vluyn: Neukirchener Verlag, 1988).

Ruether, R.R., 'Mothers of the Church: Ascetic Women in the Late Patristic Age', in R.R. Ruether and E. McLaughlin (eds.), *Women of Spirit: Female Leadership in the Jewish and Christian Traditions* (New York: Simon & Schuster, 1979), pp. 71-98.

—*New Woman, New Earth: Sexist Ideologies and Women's Liberation* (New York: Seabury, 1993 [1975]).

Russell, L.M., and J.S. Clarkson (eds.), *Dictionary of Feminist Theologies* (Louisville, KY: Westminster/John Knox Press, 1996).

Sampley, P.J., 'Scripture and Tradition in the Community as Seen in Ephesians 4:25ff'., *ST* 26 (1972), pp. 101-109.

Sand, A., 'Witwenstand und Ämterstructuren in den urchristlichen Gemeinden', *BibLeb* 12 (1971), pp. 186-97.

Sawyer, D.F., *Women and Religion in the First Christian Centuries* (Religion in the First Christian Centuries, 1; London: Routledge, 1996).

Scanzoni, L.D., and N. Hardesty, *All We're Meant to Be* (Waco, TX: Word Books, 1974).

Schnackenburg, R., *The Epistle to the Ephesians* (trans. H. Heron; Edinburgh: T. & T. Clark, 1991).

Schoedel, W.R., *A Commentary on the Letters of Ignatius of Antioch* (Hermenia; Philadelphia: Fortress Press, 1985).

Scholer, D.M., 'Exegesis: 1 Timothy 2.8-15', *Daughters of Sarah* 1 (1975), pp. 7-8; repr. in Hestenes (ed.), *Women and Men in Ministry*, p. 74.

—'Hermeneutical Gerrymandering: Hurley on Women and Authority', *TSF Bulletin* 6.5 (1983), pp. 11-13.

—'Paul's Women Co-Workers in the Ministry of the Church', *Daughters of Sarah* 6.4 (1980), pp. 3-6.

—'Unseasonable Thoughts on the State of Biblical Hermeneutics: Reflections of a New Testament Exegete', *American Baptist Quarterly* 2 (1983), pp. 134-41.

—'Women in Ministry, Session 1: Its Basis in Creation', *Covenant Companion* 72.22 (1983).

—'Women in Ministry, Session 3: Its Basis in the Early Church', *Covenant Companion* 73.1 (1984).

—'Women in Ministry, Session 4: Its Basis in Paul (Part 1)', *Covenant Companion* 73.1 (1984).

—'Women in Ministry, Session 5: Its Basis in Paul (Part 2)', *Covenant Companion* 73.2 (1984), pp. 12-13.

—'Women in Ministry, Session 6: 1 Corinthians 14.34, 35', *Covenant Companion* 73.2 (1984), pp. 13-14.

—'Women in Ministry, Session 7: 1 Timothy 2.8-15', *Covenant Companion* 73.2 (1984), pp. 14-15.

—'Women in Ministry, Session 8: Summary—Consistency and Balance', *Covenant Companion* 73 (1984), p. 15.

—'Women's Adornment: Some Historical and Hermeneutical Observations on the New Testament Passages', *Daughters of Sarah* 6.1 (1980), pp. 3-6.

Schottroff, L., *Der Glaubende und die feindlich Welt: Beobachtungen zum gnostischen Dualismus und seiner Bedeutung für Paulus und das Johannesevangelium* (Neu-kirchen–Vluyn: Neukirchener Verlag, 1970).

—'Die Schreckensherrschaft der Sünde und die Befreiung durch Christus nach dem Römerbrief des Paulus', *EvT* 39 (1979), pp. 497-510.

Schottroff, L., and M.-T. Wacker (eds.), *Kompendium Feministische Bibelauslegung* (Güters-loh: Gütersloher Verlaghaus, 1998).

Schüssler Fiorenza, E., 'The Apostleship of Women in Early Christianity', in Swidler and Swidler (eds.), *Women Priests*, pp. 135-40.

—*Bread Not Stone: The Challenge of Feminist Biblical Interpretation* (Boston: Beacon Press, 1992).

—*But She Said: Feminist Practices of Biblical Interpretation* (Boston: Beacon Press, 1992).

—'The Ethics of Biblical Interpretation', *JBL* 107 (1988), pp. 13-17.

—*In Memory of Her: A Feminist Theological Reconstruction of Christian Origins* (New York: Crossroad, 1983).

—'Paul and the Politics of Interpretation', in Horsley (ed.), *Paul and Politics*, pp. 40-57.

—'The "Quilting" of Women's History: Phoebe of Cenchreae', in P.M. Cooey, *et al.* (eds.), *Embodied Love: Sensuality and Relationship as Feminist Values* (San Francisco: Harper & Row, 1987), pp. 35-49.

—'Response to "The Social Functions of Women's Asceticism in the Roman East" by A.C. Wire', in King (ed.), *Images of the Feminine in Gnosticism*, pp. 324-28.

Schüssler Fiorenza, E., (ed.), *Searching the Scriptures: A Feminist Commentary* (2 vols.; New York: Crossroad, 1994).

—*Sharing Her Word: Feminist Biblical Interpretation in Context* (Boston: Beacon Press, 1998).

Schweizer, E., *Church Order in the New Testament* (London: SCM Press, 1961).

Scroggs, R., 'Paul and the Eschatological Woman', *JAAR* 40 (1972), pp. 283-303.

Seim, T.K., 'Ascetic Autonomy? New Perspectives on Single Women in the Early Church', *ST* 43 (1989), pp. 125-40.

Siddons, P., *Speaking Out for Women: A Biblical View* (Valley Forge, PA: Judson, 1980).

Sigountos, J.G., and M. Shank, 'Public Roles for Women in the Pauline Church: A Reappraisal of the Evidence', *JETS* 26 (1983), pp. 283-95.

Smit, D.J., 'Can We Still Be Reformed? Questions from a South African Perspective' (paper read at international conference on 'Reformed Theology: Identity and Ecumenicity', Heidelberg, Germany, 18–22 March 1999).

—'Morality and Individual Responsibility', *JTSA* 89 (1994), pp. 19-30.

Smith, C.R. (ed.), *The Inclusive New Testament* (Brentwood, MD: Priests for Equality, 1994).

Snodgrass, K., 'Paul and Women', *Covenant Quarterly* 34.4 (1976), pp. 3-19.

Spencer, A.D.B., 'Eve at Ephesus (Should Women Be Ordained as Pastors according to the First Letter to Timothy 2.11-15?)', *JETS* 17 (1974), pp. 215-22.

—'Paul, Our Friend and Champion', *Daughters of Sarah* 2.3 (1976), pp. 1-3.

Spicq, C., *Les épîtres pastorales* (2 vols.; EBib; Paris: Gabalda, 4th edn, 1969).

—*Saint Paul: Les épîtres pastorales* (EBib; Paris: Lecoffre, 1947).

Spretnak, C., 'The Christian Right's "Holy War" Against Feminism', in C. Spretnak (ed.), *The Politics of Women's Spirituality* (New York: Anchor Books, 1982), pp. 470-96.

Stählin, G., 'χήρα', *TDNT*, IX, pp. 440-65.

Standhartinger, A., *Studien zur Entstehungsgeschichte und Intention des Kolosserbriefs* (NovTSup, 94; Leiden: E.J. Brill, 1999).

Stanton, E.C., *The Woman's Bible* (Seattle: Coalition Task Force on Women and Religion, 1974).

Stendahl, K., *The Bible and the Role of Women: A Case Study in Hermeneutics* (Philadelphia: Fortress Press, 1966).

Stephens, S., *A New Testament View of Women* (Nashville: Broadman, 1980).

Surdyk, L.K., 'Making Connections: Integrating Christianity and Economics', *Journal of Biblical Integration in Business* (1995–96) (http://www.cedarville.edu/dept/ba/jbib/index2.htm).

Swartley, W.M., *Slavery, Sabbath, War, and Women: Case Histories in Biblical Interpretations* (Scottsdale, PA: Herald Press, 1983).

Swidler, L., *Women in Judaism: The Status of Women in Formative Judaism* (Metuchen, NJ: Scarecrow, 1976).

Swidler, L., and A. Swidler (eds.), *Women Priests: A Catholic Commentary on the Vatican Declaration* (New York: Paulist Press, 1977).

Taylor, M.K., *Remembering Esperanza: A Cultural-Political Theology for North American Praxis* (Maryknoll, NY: Orbis Books, 1990).

Tetlow, E.M., *Women and Ministry in the New Testament* (New York: Paulist Press, 1980).

Thatcher, A., ' "Crying Out for Discussion"—Premodern Marriage in Postmodern Times', *Theology and Sexuality* 8 (1998), pp. 73-95.

—*Marriage after Modernity: Christian Marriage in Postmodern Times* (New York: New York University Press, 1999).

Thiselton, A.C., *New Horizons in Hermeneutics: The Theory and Practice of Transforming Biblical Reading* (Grand Rapids: Zondervan, 1992).

Thistlethwaite, S.B., 'Every Two Minutes: Battered Women and Feminist Interpretation', in L. Russell (ed.), *Feminist Interpretations of the Bible* (Philadelphia: Westminster Press, 1985), pp. 96-107.

—'Violence Institutionalized', in Russell and Clarkson (eds.), *Dictionary of Feminist Theologies*, pp. 307-309.

Thurston, B.B., 'The Widow as the "Altar" of God' (SBLSP, 24; Missoula, MT: Scholars Press, 1985), pp. 279-89.

—*The Widows: A Women's Ministry in the Early Church* (Minneapolis: Fortress Press, 1989).

—*Women in the New Testament* (New York: Crossroad, 1998).

Torjesen, K.J., 'From the Private Sphere of the Hellenistic Household to the Public Sphere of the Imperial Church: Women's Roles in Transition' (paper delivered at Society of Biblical Literature Annual Meeting, Anaheim, CA, 24 November 1985).

—'In Praise of Noble Women: Gender and Honor in Ascetic Texts', in Wimbush (ed.), *Discursive Formations*, pp. 41-64.

—*When Women Were Priests: Women's Leadership in the Early Church and the Scandal of their Subordination in the Rise of Christianity* (San Francisco: HarperSanFrancisco, 1993).

Towner, P.H., *1–2 Timothy and Titus* (Downers Grove, IL: InterVarsity Press, 1994).

Treggiari, S., *Roman Marriage: Iusti Coniuges from the Time of Cicero to the Time of Ulpian* (Oxford: Clarendon Press, 1991).

Trible, P., *God and the Rhetoric of Sexuality* (OBT, 2; Philadelphia: Fortress Press, 1978).

—*Texts of Terror* (Philadelphia: Fortress Press, 1984).

Trompf, G.W., 'On Attitudes toward Woman in Paul and Paulist Literature: 1 Corinthians 11.3-16 and Its Context', *CBQ* 42 (1980), pp. 196-215.

Turner, V., *Dramas, Fields, and Metaphors: Symbolic Action in Human Society* (Ithaca, NY: Cornell University Press, 1974).

Vaage, L.E., and V.L. Wimbush (eds.), *Asceticism and the New Testament* (New York: Routledge, 1999).

Van Gennep, A., *The Rites of Passage* (trans. M.B. Vizedom and G.L. Caffee; London: Routledge & Kegan Paul, 1960).

Van Huyssteen, W., *The Realism of the Text: A Perspective on Biblical Authority* (Pretoria: University of South Africa, 1987).

Verhey, A., *The Great Reversal: Ethics and the New Testament* (Grand Rapids: Eerdmans, 1984).

Verner, D.C., *The Household of God: The Social World of the Pastoral Epistles* (SBLDS, 71; Chico, CA: Scholars Press, 1983).

Veyne, P., *Writing History: Essay on Epistemology* (trans. M. Moore-Rinvolucri; Middletown, CT: Wesleyan University Press, 1984).

Vielhauer, P., *Geschichte der urchristlichen Literatur* (Berlin: W. de Gruyter, 3rd edn, 1981).

Vorster, J.N., 'Toward an Interactional Model for the Analysis of Letters', *Neot* 24.1 (1990), pp. 107-30.

Vorster, W.S., 'The Reader in the Text: Narrative Material', *Semeia* 48 (1989), pp. 21-39.

Wagener, U., *Die Ordnung des 'Hauses Gottes': Der Ort von Frauen in der Ekklesiologie und Ethik der Pastoralbriefe* (WUNT, 2.65; Tübingen: J.C.B. Mohr [Paul Siebeck], 1994).

Walker, W.O., Jr, '1 Corinthians 11.2-16 and Paul's Views Regarding Women', *JBL* 94 (1975), pp. 94-110.

Wanamaker, C.A., *Commentary of 1 and 2 Thessalonians* (NIGTC; Grand Rapids: Eerdmans; Exeter: Paternoster Press, 1990).

Weber, M., *The Protestant Ethic and the Spirit of Capitalism* (New York: Charles Scribner's Sons, 1958).

Weems, R.J., *Battered Love: Marriage, Sex, and Violence in the Hebrew Prophets* (Minneapolis: Fortress Press, 1995).

—'Reading Her Way through the Struggle: African American Women and the Bible', in Felder (ed.), *Stony the Road We Trod*, pp. 57-77.

Wilckens, U., *Der Brief an die Römer* (EKKNT, 6; 3 vols.; Zürich: Benziger Verlag, 1978, 1980, 1982).

Williams, D., *The Apostle Paul and Women in the Church* (Van Nuys, CA: BIM Publishing Co., 1977).

Williams, S.K., *Galatians* (ANTC; Nashville: Abingdon Press, 1997).

Wilson, R.M., *Gnosis and the New Testament* (Oxford: Oxford University Press, 1968).

Wimbush, V.L. (ed.), *Discoursive Formations, Ascetic Piety and the Interpretation of Early Christian Literature* (Semeia, 57; Atlanta: Scholars Press, 1992).

Wire, A.C., *The Corinthian Women Prophets: A Reconstruction through Paul's Rhetoric* (Minneapolis: Fortress Press, 1990).

—'The Social Functions of Women's Asceticism in the Roman East', in King (ed.), *Images of the Feminine in Gnosticism*, pp. 308-23.

Yarbrough, O.L., *Not Like the Gentiles: Marriage Rules in the Letters of Paul* (Atlanta: Scholars Press, 1985).

INDEXES

INDEX OF REFERENCES

BIBLE

OTHER ANCIENT REFERENCES

INDEX OF AUTHORS

Related Feminist Titles from The Pilgrim Press

Introductions in Feminist Theology series

Introducing African Women's Theology
Mercy Amba Oduyoye

Mercy Amba Oduyoye describes the context and methodology of Christian theology by Africans in the past two decades, offering brief descriptions and sample treatments of theological issues such as creation, Christology, ecclesiology, and eschatology. The daily spiritual life of African Christian women is evident as the reader is led to the sources of African women's Christian theology. This book reflects how African culture and its multireligious context has influenced women's selection of theological issues.
ISBN 0-8298-1423-X
Paper, 136 pages
$17.00

Introducing Asian Feminist Theology
Kwok Pui-Lan

The book introduces the history, critical issues, and direction of feminist theology as a grass roots movement in Asia. Kwok Pui-Lan takes care to highlight the diversity of this broad movement, noting that not all women theologians in Asia embrace feminism. Amid a diverse range of sociopolitical, religiocultural, postcultural, and postcolonial contexts, this book lifts up the diversity of voices and ways of doing feminist theology while attending to women's experiences, how the Bible is interpreted, and the ways that Asian religious traditions are appropriated. It searches out a passionate, life-affirming spirituality through feminine images of God, new metaphors for Christ, and a reformulation of sin and redemption.
ISBN 0-8298-1399-3
Paper, 136 pages
$17.00

Introducing Body Theology
Lisa Isherwood and Elizabeth Stuart

Because Christianity asserts that God was incarnated in human form, one might expect that its theologies would be body affirming. Yet for women (and indeed also for gay men) the body has been the site for oppression. *Introducing Body Theology* offers a body-centered theology that discusses cosmology, ecology, ethics, immortality, and sexuality, in a concise introduction that proposes and encourages a positive theology of the body.
ISBN 0-8298-1375-6
Paper, 168 pages
$17.00

Introducing Feminist Images of God
Mary Grey

Mary Grey presents recent thinking reflecting early attempts to move beyond restrictive God language, opening up the possibilities of more inclusive ways of praying. The rich experiences of God, distinctive and diverse, are seen through the eyes of many different cultures and the women who struggle for justice. Using the figure of Sophia Wisdom as an example, Grey shows that there are many still-unplumbed images of God to discover.
ISBN 0-8298-1418-3
Paper, 136 pages
$17.00

Introducing Feminist Pastoral Care and Counseling
Nancy J. Gorsuch
Foreword by Peggy Way

Nancy Gorsuch identifies themes that are critical in pastoral care and ministry, including faithfulness to God, resistance to oppression, and interconnection with others, and explores the contributions of feminist theology and feminist psychotherapeutic theory in addressing these issues. With practical illustrations of how these contributions might influence pastoral care, counseling, and consultation, Gorsuch offers a pastoral care method that is revitalized by feminist theology and psychotherapeutic theory.
ISBN 0-8298-1440-X
Paper, 148 pages
$16.00

Introducing Feminist Perspectives on Pastoral Theology
Zoë Bennett Moore

Introducing Feminist Perspectives on Pastoral Theology is designed for concerned practitioners and also has specifically in mind the needs of students of pastoral theology. Beginning with the lived experience of violence in Church and society, this book moves through to the implications of this for our understanding of the human community and the divine, and it seeks to explore why the inclusion of women's experiences and of feminist perspectives is of vital importance to Christian pastoral practice and to a Christian understanding of God.
ISBN 0-8298-1549-X
Paper, 144 pages
$17.00

To order (Mon–Fri, 8:30am – 4:30pm, ET), call 1-800-537-3394, fax 216-736-2206, or visit our Web site at www.pilgrimpress.com. Prices do not include shipping and handling. Prices subject to change without notice.